A Cook's Garden

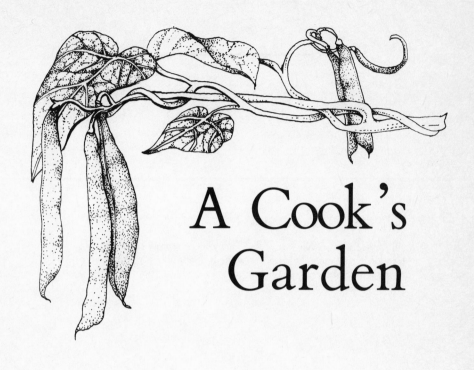

A Cook's Garden

Jan Mahnken

COUNTRYMAN PRESS
Woodstock, Vermont 05091

Library of Congress Cataloging in Publication Data

Mahnken, Jan.
  A Cook's Garden.
  Includes index.
  1. Vegetable gardening. 2. Herb gardening.
3. Cookery (Vegetables) I. Title.
SB321.M36 1985 635 85-397
ISBN 0–88150–036–4 (pbk.)

Designed and produced by Robinson Book Associates
Line drawings by Linda Cabassa
Composed by PostScript
Printed in the United States by Capital City Press

Contents

The Basics   1

Rhubarb's Up   12

The Early Garden   44

Summer's Here   63

Summer Delights   109

A Side Trip to Fruits and Berries   120

Full Moon Tonight   143

Records and Resolutions   176

Index   191

Recipe Index   196

For Mum and Dad

CHAPTER 1

The Basics

All you need is a kitchen and a garden. Once you've had the pleasure of eating garden-fresh produce, respectfully prepared, the array at the supermarket loses some of its appeal. You may not have time and space to grow all the vegetables and fruits you enjoy, but that's no great problem. You can always swap with friends and neighbors or supplement the harvest with locally grown products, since none of us can grow all the items he would like to eat. But we can't deny the boon that trucked-in produce has been, because we now demand fresh salad greens even when they're out of season in our area.

But the best eating comes from in-season fruits and vegetables, locally grown. And that's what this book is all about. I'm assuming that the first batch of peas you pick—that is, those that make it to the pot—will be prepared simply and quickly and savored all the more because they're innocent of any additives but a little butter and salt. A good half of the first green peas I pick don't get cooked at all. Son Tom stuffs as many pods in his pockets as will fit and grabs an extra handful to sustain him on the way to the barn to get his bike. Husband Bud casually snitches them from the bowl while I'm shelling them. Often, from both Tom and our older son, Bob, when he's home, I get a request for a bowl of raw peas for dinner, please.

You don't get that kind of quality from the supermarket. Can't. We're talking *fresh* peas.

After the first giddy enthusiasms wear off, though, it's time to get out the cookbooks or ask your neighbor about different ways of preparing produce from the garden. Perhaps you want to preserve some of the abundance for later. Before we get down to specifics, though, let's talk about the basics: the kitchen and the garden.

I'm pretty easy to get along with in the matter of kitchens. For the most part I'm willing to make do, to improvise. Only two things are important to me. I want a window, preferably one that looks out on something that's interesting at any time of the year, in any weather. The other requirement involves the geography of the kitchen. Either it ought to be big enough for people to hang around in or it ought to be on the open plan, communicating with other areas of the house. I spend a lot of time in the kitchen. I don't want to miss anything just because I'm checking the roast or replenishing the hors-d'oeuvres tray.

Sure, I've had lots of different kitchens, and I've examined the magazines that show you super-deluxe kitchens, models of glamour and efficiency. I even have a vision of my ideal kitchen. It would be an enormous cavern of a room with flagstone floor, fireplace with crane, wood cookstove as well as an electric range, beamed ceiling, yards of cabinets, multitudinous drawers, acres of counter space, chopping blocks. Blender, microwaves, mixers, processors, every appliance you can think of, and space to accommodate those yet to be invented. Bay window with cushioned window seats and shelves for innumerable plants. Huge oak table, rocker by the fireplace. You get the picture. I've never seen one anything like it, except in my imagination. I've worked in nine kitchens of my own since marriage and, now and then, in the kitchens of at least a dozen friends and relatives. Each had its own faults and virtues. (My mother disagrees, convinced that *her* kitchen was designed by someone who loathed anyone who cooks). Anyway, I like the one I have now, even though its only similarity to my dream kitchen is size.

What I have now has been variously described as (a) a double kitchen (that's what the realtor called it) and (b) a nightmare (my mother's version). Actually, what she said was, "Good Lord, Sis, how do you expect to get anything done in here?" That was her first reaction, later considerably embellished. Actually, it's typical of comments we get, when we get any.

Okay, it's weird. I like it. It's inefficient. It's peculiar. It's unhandy. It isn't anything like my mental image of The Kitchen of My Fondest Dreams and Desires. It suits me.

Any kitchen designer worth his salt would take one look at our arrangement and fall victim to an attack of apoplexy. Let me describe it to you. One part measures 13 feet by 13 feet. This room has in it the stove and the refrigerator, on the south side. Between them is the door to the mudroom, where the freezers, some cabinets for canned goods, and various cookbooks are located. A three-shelved teacart and a slate topped cabinet flank the stove and hold a variety of small appliances. A kitchen stepstool lives next to the refrigerator. As nearly as I can determine, its sole use is to stand on while cleaning the top of the refrigerator.

A large picture window, looking out across the driveway to the formal garden and the pasture beyond it, is centered in the east wall. Its usefulness is unquestioned since we can look at the horses, the birdfeeder, and anyone who comes into the driveway. And watch for the school bus. There's a radiator beneath the window, on which snow-wet mittens, caps, boots, and gloves steam in winter. To say nothing of an occasional cat. A pair of Boston ferns hangs there to catch the morning light—and the heads of the unwary. Our breakfast table is positioned beside this window. On the north wall is a bookcase devoted to more of the cookbook collection (still others reside in a case in the sitting room). Beside it is a doorway to the 3-foot-by-7-foot side entry hall; another door opens to the back stairs to an upper floor. An embarrassment of doors graces the kitchen.

On the west wall is the door to a 6-foot-by-9-foot pantry and the narrow opening (20 inches wide) to the rest of the kitchen, which is actually another room, 8 feet by 11 feet. To the right through this opening are counter and sinks. Above and below, cabinets and drawers. On the adjoining wall to the north is more counter, dishwasher, cabinets. And a door into the sitting room. (You can't escape the sitting room. But then, it's a pleasant place to be.) On the west is a large picture window overlooking lawn and flower beds. Beneath it is another radiator; beside it, shelves. The remaining wall, going back to the 20-inch opening, boasts more counter, cabinets and drawers below, shelves above. The pantry is furnished with shelves, a large cupboard, and the washer and dryer.

Sounds complicated? It is. Not designed with step saving in mind. In fact, scarcely designed at all. It's fifteen feet between the stove where potatoes are cooked and the sink in which they were first washed and peeled and then must be drained. A time-motion student would go berserk in short order. No wonder my mother is appalled.

Why, then, am I complacent about it? What do I find to like in such a monster? I spend a lot of time in the kichen, but it doesn't drive me frantic. I guess the answer is a matter of aesthetics and values.

To begin with, despite the articles I read on effective home engineering, I can't think of our home merely in terms of efficiency. It is neither a factory nor a business of any sort. If it were, there would be ample room for complaint about the kitchen. The main function of our home (as I see it) is to provide a haven, and it (including and perhaps especially the kitchen) does just that.

No other room in the house is the scene of so much and such varied activity as the kitchen, from early morning until late at night. First thing in the morning we put the dogs out and let the cats in. We need plenty of room to maneuver amid four cats demanding breakfast. Quiet descends for a while as the cats eat in the mudroom and we take care of barn chores. But soon the kitchen is humming again. I take on the job of short-order cook. Younger son, Tom, sets the table; older son, Bob, if he's home, pours coffee and stares uncomprehendingly into the depths of the refrigerator, still too much asleep to remember if he's after eggs or milk—or maybe a skillet. Traffic clogs the passageway—the dishes, linens, flatware are on one side of it, the table on the other. No matter, we manage. The dogs are underfoot. There's a cat on each windowsill, another at the door demanding to be let out, a fourth lowering from the stepstool.

Finally all the hungry mouths, including ours, are fed. The dishes have been carried from the table back to the other room to the sink and dishwasher. Days I'm home, I have the kitchen to myself now, except for the dogs and one cat (always the *same* cat, Small), who declines to go out. I pour some coffee and start the first load of laundry (now that's *very* handy, right there in the pantry). I go to the garden room connecting house and barn for a bushel of tomatoes and prepare to make juice. I dump them in one sink to wash, transfer them to the other, from which they'll be cut, and put in the kettle. I can never remember which sink to start with for greatest efficiency. (Can you believe efficiency in such a madhouse?) As soon as I start cutting, the dogs reappear. Something for us? I quarter tomatoes and take a batch (all of us trying to squeeze through that 20-inch passageway simultaneously) to their dishes, in the mudroom. The Boxer, Max, is appreciative (and how I miss our other, Dutch, dead two years now); the Weimaraner, Stitch, wrinkles her nose in disgust and goes to bed. Max will eat Stitch's too, gladly.

Once the tomatoes have been carried to the stove and put on to simmer and the houseplants have been watered, it's time for outdoor or desk activities, and the kitchen is quiet until noon. Then it's dog-feeding time and juice-bottling and fresh-pot-of-coffee time. Frantic activity. Dogs dashing about madly, hopefully. After a while, all's quiet until the middle of the afternoon, when the family starts straggling home. All the cats come in (and someone remembers to pitch Small out). The kitchen hums. Snacks. Tom's friends in and out. I start getting organized for dinner. Barn chores. Maybe Bob visits. Bud's home. Everybody's in the kitchen. Small again, too.

Bud decides to put a new rope-pull on the lawnmower. Not much choice; the old one is broken. He has a workbench, but prefers the kitchen table. I go to the sink, so I won't be able to see the blood when the spring in the armature (I think it's an armature) gets away from him and cuts a knuckle to the bone. We leave the kitchen briefly to bandage the finger, and then we return to mop up the blood. Bud repairs the floor where the spring cut the linoleum.

Dinner is served in the dining room. That's on the other side of the sitting room, well removed and out of sight of the chaos that reigns in the kitchen.

Usually by 7 or 8 the kitchen is tidy again—unless there's an urgent request for cookies. By 9 or 10, though, someone (it varies) is at the table, reading and snacking. That's the usual kitchen schedule, unless we have guests. When there are guests, you can bet *they'll* be in the kitchen too. On casual evenings, they'll be there until dinner is served. On more formal occasions, we usually manage to spend at least a little time in the sitting room or living room before dinner.

There's not a straight line in the entire place. The stove isn't level. How could it be? The *floor's* not level. The inlaid linoleum is light colored and not of the permanently shined variety. It's hardly a practical floor for an active family tracking dirt and debris in from garden and barn.

There are so many doors it's mind boggling. The pantry door must be left ajar in winter or the pipes (and the canned goods) freeze. We recently tiled the wall behind the stove, and that makes it easier to clean up splashes from exuberantly cooking foods. The shelves are impractical too—glassware not used daily becomes shockingly dusty in no time at all. The cabinets, however, are splendid. Stained barnboards are pleasant to look at, easy to keep attractive. The view from the windows is stunning at all times of the year.

We'd like to put a woodburning cookstove where the bookcase lives now. That would add to what we consider the kitchen's charm, but it would inevitably add to the confusion and problems. The dogs will quarrel about whose turn it is to sleep under it, and there'll be ashes everywhere. And wood. And the problem of where to put the books— they have to be handy. I like to think that the strangeness of the whole mechanism is itself a virtue. Keeps you on your toes. And all that walking from one outpost to another is good exercise, helping to compensate for the calories produced in our kitchen and so ardently consumed by the household.

And the garden? It should come as no surprise, considering the nature of our establishment, that the garden is a long way from the house. The house itself is surrounded by lawns and ornamental plantings—all mere show. You want anything as mundane as a cabbage, you're going to have to go out through the breezeway and down the slope beside the barn and past it to the vegetable garden. But that's okay; it's a nice walk. So I can't see the garden from the house. Much of the time that's a blessing. It's designed to produce edibles, not to gratify aesthetic cravings. By fall it's distinctly scruffy looking and needs a lot of attention. Which I don't intend to give it. Better I shouldn't be reminded of my shortcomings.

The garden is immense, 85 by 100 feet, but getting smaller. That bit back by the pasture fence will be lawn next year. Better that Tom should be mowing than I cultivating. Besides our family is shrinking, and our other projects are multiplying.

This garden lies at the foot of a slope. The former owners selected the site, not I. The foot of a slope is not the best place for a vegetable garden. Although the drainage is excellent, the area is a natural frost pocket. My mistake was enlarging the garden the year we moved here. I planted rhubarb at the front edge as a border; it is too much rhubarb for any practical purpose. Behind the rhubarb lies the asparagus bed. On the east side, a strip of lawn about ten feet wide separates the garden from the barns and paddock. To the west side, a couple of butternut trees and a patch of naturalized hemerocallis, asters, and monarda butt up against the compost heap at the front corner. Behind that, the raspberries sprawl untidily. The grape arbor is beside the raspberries, with a narrow strip of lawn between them. More lawn lies beyond the grapes and borders the garden south of the raspberries.

What grows where in the part of the garden that is annually tilled varies from season to season, in accordance with good gardening practices. Here and there, among the vegetables and herbs, are rows of flowers. The flowers started with the marigolds and nasturtiums that were a gesture toward pest control. They looked so attractive that the next year I planted tender bulbs and tubers left over from the ornamental gardens and sowed rows of annual flowers for cutting. For my own convenience, I'd prefer to have all the salad vegetables right behind the asparagus, but in practice they're scattered all over the garden. Since the garden is about ten miles from the kitchen, fifty feet one way or another doesn't make much difference.

The herbs? Well, that's another story. There's mint, of several kinds, everywhere. Beside the barn, front and side. Both sides of the house. Dill? To be honest, I never plant dill; it reseeds itself prodigiously, and I let it grow where it wants to grow, provided it's not in the way. That explains why there's some in the formal garden, some by the compost heap. The basil is in the vegetable garden, beside the tomatoes. Parsley, at the moment, beside the rhubarb. Tarragon there too. Oregano up by the dianthus, next to the Japanese maple. Can't remember where I put the rosemary, but the sweet woodruff is over there by the paddock, and you can't walk three yards without stumbling over yet another clump of chives.

I did have a proper herb garden. A couple of times, actually. In theory, I approve of them heartily. And may yet try again someday. In practice, for me, they're a problem. Question of temperament probably. If you're seated comfortably, I'll tell you all about it.

I've been growing herbs, in moderation, as long as I've been gardening at all. Which is long enough that I'd just as soon not go into it, if you don't mind. I started with the usual things—parsley, a clump of chives. All very diffident.

Then we built a house in the woods and hacked out enough trees to make a nice garden. Just about that time, a nearly religious fervor for herbs began to become apparent in the gardening magazines. A veritable renaissance of interest, a mystique. Ever susceptible to such influences, I began to plan an herb bed. I'd been devoted to using herbs in cooking right along, so I was well aware of the gourmet's respect for fresh herbs, as opposed to that dried, second-rate stuff I was dragging home from the grocer's shelves. An herb garden! Just the ticket, situated so that I could see it from the window above the kitchen sink. Imagine: a border of box, brick paths! Oh, wow!

That first herb bed should have taught me that I wasn't cut out for the occupation, but it merely strengthened my resolve to persevere. I chose the sunniest spot of our wooded plot and began to acquire herb plants. Sage, oregano, thymes, mints, horehound, and other common herbs grew acceptably despite the problems inherent in woodsy soil.

The plants were interesting too, in a modest way. One thing about an herb bed becomes clear immediately. It's pleasant to wander through it, sampling or bruising leaves and sniffing avidly. But especially from a distance, there's not much to look at. No wonder designs evolved for knot gardens. No wonder some were framed with charming hedges, intersected with dainty paths! Even less wonder that some calloused souls simply plunked herbs into the vegetable garden.

The herb bed was so disappointing visually that I hedged it with miniature roses. Box wouldn't survive our winters and besides, I needed more help than box could provide. In the broad sense I wasn't actually cheating; roses are herbs, once grown as much for fragrance and hips as for the beauty of the blossoms. Mine served strictly for decoration. They performed satisfactorily and emphasized the dreariness of the interior of the bed splendidly.

Several mints, a forlorn sage plant, and some lemon balm survived the ravages of the following winter. I surveyed the ruins dispassionately and planted flowers, hardly nodding to the guilt feelings that besieged me.

We moved (not because of the herb bed), and the new house we bought boasted a bed planted mostly to herbs—chives, parsley, dill, mint, yarrow. Printed stakes identified the dessicated remains of less sturdy herbs. I replaced them, firmly, with lilies. Insidiously, however, I began succumbing to the idea that we *ought* to have an herb garden. We had gradually acquired a number of culinary herbs, which were scattered all over the farm. It would be convenient to snip what was needed for a meal from a single location, preferably one handy to the kitchen. The spot I chose, a mere 168 steps round trip, from the kitchen sink (I just paced it off), was visible from the west kitchen window. That was my first mistake. That misbegotten bed at our former address had been visible from the kitchen window too. If there's one bed that gets my constant attention, it's one visible from that room in which I spend so many daylight hours.

Leaving the scattered herbs where they were for the time being, I planted others in the new bed: marjoram, cumin, salad burnet, various kinds of thyme and basil, lavendar, caraway, borage, sage, and others.

As an appealing but edible concession to aesthetics, I added a border of Alpine strawberries.

The site was sunny, the soil fertile, the drainage admirable. The herbs flourished. The borage became enormous, produced quantities of charming blue flowers over a long period of time, and then collapsed in limp exhaustion all over the horehound. Shortly thereafter, scores of seedling borage plants emerged in every open spot, crowding out quantities of less robust plants. A bed next to the herb bed sparkled with poppies, carnations, pinks, and alyssum, every blossom in stark contrast to the fragrant but insipid-looking neighboring bed. I racked my brain for something commonly considered an herb that would brighten the bed. Nasturtiums! Violas!

Any perennial herbs that survive the winter are entirely welcome to stay in my ill-fated "herb garden," but the annuals will be grown in the vegetable garden. I've had it, for now anyway. Like many other gardeners and cooks, I've been fascinated by the *notion* of an herb garden. Visiting a nursery or herb garden—or even reading about one—has sent me scurrying to my desk to compile lists and sketch diagrams. Maybe someday I'll achieve one of the polite herb gardens. I know my limitations well enough to realize that a knot garden or even a wagon wheel with different herbs planted between the spokes is out of the question. My *mind* isn't that tidy, much less my garden. And there are too many herbs that behave like weeds. I've become offended by the aura of reverence accorded herb gardens. (I've snapped at several old friends and have been barely able to conceal my scorn for the plans of novice gardeners.) My affection for certain herbs remains intact, but let's forget the mystique business. Herbs are plants. Some handsome, some on the scraggly side. Their appearance is going to determine where they live in my garden. Hang convenience and tradition.

So there you are. A kitchen, a garden, a certain amount of prejudice and irreverence. That's all you need. Wise novices will think small with the garden. (I know, never having achieved modified novice status.) Expansion of the garden can come—if at all—once you decide whether you want to store food for the winter, once you get the hang of growing your own produce and have decided how much time you're willing to spend in the activity. Start with the vegetables or fruits you like best. Add novelties at a rate you can handle comfortably so that neither kitchen nor garden becomes your master.

The vegetables and small fruits I've selected for consideration reflect both my family's tastes and our gardening situation. I've ignored brussels sprouts and leeks, both of which grow magnificently in our garden, because they're greeted with undisguised ennui at our table. I've ignored melons and lima beans, both of which we all dote on, because in our climate they require efforts I'm not willing to make. After years of trying to grow them, I've decided I can't face any more hopes blasted by frost, whether it comes in June or August.

We live in western Massachusetts, in the foothills of the Berkshire Mountains. Here it's considered safe to plant warm-weather annuals such as tomatoes at the end of May, and we feel mildly offended if frost kills them before Labor Day. But elevations in our town differ enough that some parts of it have a growing season two or three weeks longer than others. In addition, all gardeners have to take their own micro-climates into consideration. My basil has been nipped on mornings when my neighbor's garden has escaped frost completely. One of the most attractive features of our climate is our cool evenings. Even following hot days (we think anything above 85°F. is hot) we can usually count on pleasant sleeping temperatures at night—pleasant for us, but not necessarily for the plants.

You can, by using the proper techniques and carefully selected varieties of plants, grow almost anything you want, almost anywhere. It all depends on the effort you're willing to expend. I'm not willing (except in fits and starts) to go the cloche route or any other way that complicates my life unnecessarily. Besides that, I'm beginning to believe that adapting a plant to grow where it normally doesn't may be a mistake. Occasionally, lured by the copy in the seed catalogues, I try the latest northern adaptation of some warmth-loving vegetable or fruit we favor. This past summer it was cantaloupes and watermelons again. We had plenty of ripe melons, both kinds. They were beautiful in appearance; their aroma was heavenly; their flavor was nonexistent.

The selection of recipes is based on the premise that a gardener-cook is, by definition, a busy person. If you care enough about quality to grow some of your own food, however, you welcome ideas for preparing it. You don't find here the kind of exhaustive (or maybe it's exhausting) instructions encountered in the magazines devoted to *haute cuisine*. Another prejudice. I don't care about the correct, the traditional method. The easy one is the one that appeals to me; if it looks too complicated, I know I'll never get started.

Similarly, the recipes don't demand rigid attention to ingredients. I use nothing but dark-brown sugar when a recipe specifies brown sugar. Even if it specifies light-brown sugar. That's a personal preference, and perhaps you wince at it. Use what you choose; the results are supposed to appeal to *your* palate. Nor do I specify "fresh lemon juice" or "home-made chili sauce." Doubtless a fault, but I thrive on the slapdash and convenient. Besides, who's to know that the homemade chili sauce in question is superior to a given store-bought brand?

Be flexible. So the celery casserole lists walnuts as an ingredient, and you're fresh out. Maybe you don't even *like* walnuts. So try toasted slivered almonds. It calls for a can of condensed cream soup, and there's none left in the pantry. Make a white sauce of an appropriate consistency and flavor it to complement the other ingredients. No, it won't be the same as the original recipe. Who cares? Good cooking demands either strict attention to the rules and the recipe or a combination of creativity and good sense. Anyone interested enough in gardening and cooking to read about them in combination is clearly capable of either approach.

The gardening suggestions assume a knowledge of basic skills too and reflect not the *right* way to go about growing a given plant, but *one* way to approach it. Usually, the easy way; always a way that has been successful for me.

CHAPTER 2

Rhubarb's Up

After a long winter I anxiously await the melting of the snow. The first warmish day finds me prodding around in the gardens, looking for confirmation that spring is coming. The winter aconites, the snowdrops, the crocuses are duly noted and admired. Then I make my way down to that barren patch that (soon, I hope) will have to be tilled and examine its nearest edge. I brush away the leaves that have lodged among the debris from last fall—and there's a pink bud just emerging. My triumphant announcement can be heard for miles.

Rhubarb

Rhubarb is almost as common to the spring landscape as the dandelion. It's among the first plants to poke its nose through the chilly soil in spring. When treated well, rhubarb plants will begin production in April or May and continue until early fall. Just a few plants will supply the needs of a moderate-sized family with a moderate-sized appetite for the stuff. Plant some in the spring, and you'll start reaping the annual harvest the next spring.

Or at least that's the way it's supposed to work. Our present rhubarb bed was planted one spring and produced so handsomely that when it re-emerged the following spring we still had bags of rhubarb stalks in the freezer and a couple of jars of sauce on the shelves. Part of the row came from plants grown from seed the previous year, part from root divisions. All the plants had been living in a different part of the garden— an inconvenient part. I moved them as soon as their pink snouts revealed their whereabouts. The books say that freshly moved rhubarb can't be harvested that year, or shouldn't be anyway. I think that under certain conditions that information is a snare and a delusion. You can tell by looking at the rhubarb. If it gives indications of a design to take over the world, why not use it? Treat it properly, and rhubarb can be harvested with impunity for months on end—and even after being moved. My plants were dug from one spot and moved to another so quickly that they didn't resent the trip at all. A brand-new planting made under less agreeable conditions might well need a year to establish itself.

Rhubarb with red stems is more popular than the green-stemmed kind, because it looks more appetizing when it's cooked. There's no difference in flavor, whatever the color of the stem. Dig a large hole for the roots—about two feet deep and two feet in diameter—and make sure the bud is on the top side of the root when you plant it. When the hole is filled in, preferably with compost but at least with good rich soil, the bud should be covered with about three inches of soil. Use a thick mulch to conserve the moisture rhubarb likes.

To be tender and crisp, rhubarb should grow quickly. Feed it with compost, aged manure, or commercial fertilizer applied according to instructions. But feed it! You'll understand its need for ample nutrients when you observe its growth. The stalks can be harvested when they are four inches long and two inches wide, but don't remove all the stakes from a plant, because that weakens it. Grasp the stalk at its base and twist gently upwards to remove it. When you harvest rhubarb, dispose of the leaves safely; they contain oxalic acid and are poisonous to people and animals.

Leaves are cooked and eaten in certain parts of the Himalayas, in small quantities and with a certain amount of circumspection, one assumes. Maybe the cooking helps. Anyway, for our purposes, the compost heap is the place for the leaves. Not on the table, not given to the livestock. Cows and pigs are two animals I know of that will eat them if they get the chance.

When your rhubarb decides to send up a flower stalk (you'll recognize it because it's tall, straight, and hollow), cut it off. Ripening seeds take energy that should go into producing stalks for the table. Once the rhubarb has set seed, it tends to think it's done its job for *that* year.

If you don't harvest rhubarb for several weeks, the stalks will become woody and unsuitable for consumption. Pick them anyway and consign them to the compost heap. The pruned plant, if it has been generously fed and watered, will respond by sending up fresh stalks.

Given half a chance, rhubarb can perk up the most jaded appetite. It's versatile too. Known also as a pieplant and wine plant, rhubarb is technically a vegetable—but we prepare it as a fruit. To further cloud the issue, rhubarb was originally used as an herb. The first known recorded description in its long history occurs in a Chinese herbal dating from 2700 B.C.

Rhubarb belongs to the buckwheat family (*Polygonaceae*), the genus *Rheum*. The twenty-five species of the plant include wild, medicinal, garden, and ornamental types. Speaking of ornamental, the common garden rhubarb (*Rheum rhabarbarum*) is a handsome plant. If you let that flower stalk alone, it would produce a showy bloom. The plant is indigenous to eastern Asia. The root was the part used in China and Tibet from early times, primarily as a cathartic. One source asserts that its culture for medicinal purposes began in 1777 in England. Certainly it was known, at least, in England long before that, since the word was used to denote sourness or bitterness as early as 1526. The plant reached Europe primarily through Russia, and its medicinal qualities were widely acclaimed before its culinary properties were appreciated. By the middle of the nineteenth century it was widely used as a food in Europe and England

Rhubarb is a plant that needs cold winters to thrive. Most species originated in the mountains of central Asia and western China. Somewhere, sometime, people discovered that it could be made palatable if sweetened. Probably its appeal was heightened because of the plants harvested in cold climates it's the earliest that can be eaten as a fruit. Unsophisticated peoples doubtless considered it something of a spring tonic too. Why not? The stalks contain vitamins A and C as well as calcium and iron, and they have laxative qualities.

In the Scandinavian countries, rhubarb is often served as a compote. In the Central Asian Republics of the USSR rhubarb is made into jellies and compotes and is eaten raw as a tart snack. (When a friend reported that the children in her neighborhood were snacking on her stalks so enthusiastically that it threatened her sauce supply, my sons refused to believe it. It took us a long time to convince them that the plant is edible in *any* form; they're still not willing to tackle it raw.) Cooks in Iran make sherbet of rhubarb; the English use it in jam. In our country it's used primarily for sauces and pies, but it also turns up in other desserts, as a meat sauce, and in various homemade wines. It's often used to "stretch" less abundant fruits such as strawberries.

When I was a child I conscientiously avoided rhubarb in any guise, though my family grew and ate it. Then one day, at a friend's house, I was served rhubarb meringue pie for dessert. What could I do? My social sensitivity was developed to the point that I ate it, no questions asked, no comments made. It converted me. Unadorned stewed rhubarb may be an acquired taste, but no previous experience is necessary to enjoy this pie.

RHUBARB MERINGUE PIE

3 cups diced rhubarb 1¼ cups sugar ¼ teaspoon salt 2 tablespoons water 1½ tablespoons cornstarch 3 tablespoons water 4 eggs, separated baked pie shell	Combine rhubarb, 1 cup sugar, salt, and 2 tablespoons of water in a saucepan; place over medium heat and let come to a boil. Dissolve cornstarch in 3 tablespoons of cold water and add to the rhubarb mix. Cook, stirring constantly, until the mixture is clear and thickened. Beat the egg yolks slightly, stir a little of the hot rhubarb stuff into them and then add the result to the rest of the rhubarb. Stir and cool. Beat two egg whites until stiff and fold them into the rhubarb. Pour it all into the baked pie shell. Top it with a meringue made of the remaining two egg whites and the remaining ¼ cup of sugar. Brown it in a 400° F. oven until it's nicely colored, about 8 minutes.

Rhubarb jam is another crowd pleaser, and the recipe has been around for years. I have no idea where it came from, but basically it's gelatin, sugar, and rhubarb, with pineapple. Sounds ghastly, but it's great. Our sons eat it by the galore. Use whatever flavor gelatin strikes your fancy; our sons especially like strawberry, but raspberry, cherry, and others are fine too.

RHUBARB JAM

5 cups of rhubarb, in small pieces 5 cups sugar 6 ounces flavored gelatin 8 ounces crushed pineapple	Cook the rhubarb and sugar together for 20 minutes. Stir in the gelatin until dissolved. Add the pineapple and mix well. Pour into sterilized glasses and seal with paraffin or pour into the kind of jelly jars that accommodate canning caps. Either way, seal. If you can't be bothered with preserving it that way, just pour it into big jars and store it in the refrigerator. In our house it doesn't last long. It's great on ice cream as well as on toast, bread, muffins, biscuits. It's absolutely foolproof, wonderfully fast. I usually double the recipe, which is considered tempting fate with most jams. Not with this one.

We use baked or stewed rhubarb often to accompany a main course. Same proportions apply either way, but if the oven is going to be used to cook some part of the meal, baking is the easier, more economical choice.

BAKED RHUBARB

4 cups rhubarb 2 cups sugar butter 1 teaspoon nutmeg	Slice the rhubarb stalks into ½-inch pieces. Toss them with the sugar and put them into a buttered baking dish. Sprinkle with nutmeg. Cover and bake at 300°F. until tender, about an hour. But if it fits the rest of your menu better, you can bake it at 350°F. for about 45 minutes. For a change, skip the nutmeg and substitute brown sugar for the granulated.

The recipe for crumble was given to me by good friend Pip Stromgren, a transplanted Britisher. It's become a favorite in our family. Pip, always occupied with writing and ballet, doubles the recipe and freezes one dishful before baking it. It's then ready to be an instant dessert, once thawed, on a busy day. What other kind is there?

RHUBARB AND APPLE CRUMBLE

2   cups diced rhubarb
2   cups sliced apples
4   tablespoons brown
     sugar
1½   teaspoons
     cinnamon
1¼   cups flour
6   tablespoons sugar
6   tablespoons butter
	Butter a baking dish. Combine rhubarb and apples, sprinkle with brown sugar and 1 teaspoon cinnamon. Rub together the flour, sugar, butter, and ½ teaspoon cinnamon until fine. Sprinkle it over the rhubarb-apple mixture. Bake at 350° F. for 50–60 minutes.

Anne Judson of Ashfield introduced me to the pleasures of Victoria sauce and rhubarb wine. The sauce, a kind of mild chutney, is served with meats, and you'll find the recipe in any canning book. Why it's called "Victoria" is a mystery to me. Is it for the Queen or because one variety of red-stalked rhubarb is called "Victoria?" I don't know.

Anyway it's a good savory. The wine recipe is not a common one. There are tons of rhubarb wine recipes, almost all of them combined with some other fruit. This one is special because it's rhubarb, period.

RHUBARB WINE

3   pounds rhubarb
1   gallon cold water
3   pounds sugar
¼   teaspoon dry
    baking yeast or
    1 packet wine
    yeast

Cut rhubarb into small pieces and put it into a large kettle or pot. A pressure canner, water-bath canner, or jelly kettle is excellent for the purpose. Bruise the rhubarb thoroughly—for which a wooden mallet is useful. Or a potato masher. Anyway, be thorough. Pour the water over the distressed rhubarb, cover the container, and forget all about it for ten days. (I find it necessary to mark the event on a calendar.) Uncover and remove the mold. It's pretty depressing looking, sort of grayish-green. But it skims off easily. Pitch it.

Strain the liquid into another container and stir in the sugar and yeast. Ordinary baking yeast can be used, but using yeast formulated for wine-making eliminates any danger of a yeasty flavor in the finished product. Anne recommends Montrachet rather than the all-purpose wine yeast, because it is finer and seems to produce a more delicate wine. The packet contains 1 tablespoon of yeast, the same as a packet of baking yeast, and is enough for 1 to 5 gallons of wine (depending on the kind). I use baking yeast. Fie on the consequences; that's what's here. Anyway, cover the product and forget it for another 4 days. Except, of course, to stir it daily.

Strain again and bottle. Cork it loosely. (If the cork is too tight, the gases from fermentation may build up and cause the bottle to break.)

After 2 months add 1 teaspoon of pieces of rock candy to each bottle. (We use old 750 ml. wine bottles. Yes, new wine in old bottles.)

When the wine becomes clear and still (keep checking), tighten the corks. It's supposed to be ready to drink in 6 months, but don't even try. Steel yourself to wait at least a year and a half. Two is better. The flavor resembles sherry. That first year is a stinker, but if you have any faith in yourself, you can keep making more and adding to the store. Meantime, get yourself an interesting hobby and forget the wine.

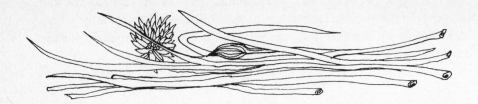

Chives

You'll see signs of life in your clumps of chives about the same time that the rhubarb gets going. Once chives break dormancy, they're off and running. Usually they're the first fresh offering from our garden in the spring.

Not that we chomp a bowl of chives or instantly whip up a batch of cream of chives soup. No immoderate frenzy of seeing what can be done about all those chives. But little snips of chives are welcome in a great many sauces and spreads. Cream cheese, cottage cheese, and sour cream are all likely candidates for the addition of chives. They're useful in salads and stews or sprinkled on soups as a garnish. They're good in scrambled eggs and omelets or atop shirred eggs. There's no satisfactory substitute for fresh chives. You can snip and package them for the freezer, and they'll stay green and moderately flavorful. But they'll be limp and, I think, limited. As far as aesthetic appeal is concerned, I blush to admit that I prefer the freeze-dried ones from the grocer.

You can, of course, evade the issue by bringing in some chives to grow in a pot on a sunny windowsill. That presents its own problems, which we'll get to in a minute.

There's no special problem in growing chives from seed, except that it takes longer than starting from a plant division, and it's a fussy procedure. If you're successful, moreover, you'll have enough plants for your entire county. It makes sense to buy a young plant or accept a start from friend or neighbor.

Chives, or *Allium schoenoprasum* (which translates roughly as "rush leek"), like a fertile site in full sun and a fair amount of water. They're members of the lily family and like their other oniony relatives produce bulbs. Since we use the tops, fertility is necessary to keep them growing vigorously. A mulch is a good idea to retain moisture and suppress competition from weeds. Actually, the worst problem is keeping out grass. Its roots tangle around the chives' bulbs, making it the very devil to get out once it has a firm foothold. Try not to let it get that foothold at all, since the competition isn't good for the chives—and who wants snipped grass on his baked potato?

If you don't keep the chives cut back, eventually they'll produce flowers. The flowers are attractive enough that most people just let the chives go ahead and blossom. You may find infant chive plants coming up here and there if you let the plant set seed. Don't inadvertently cut one of the flower stalks for culinary use. Tough, woody. It's an accepted practice to divide clumps of chives every couple of years, so that they maintain their vigor. Kept in good condition, the clumps are handsome enough to grow in ornamental borders. They have a modest reputation as companion plants for carrots, the growth and flavor of which they're said to improve.

What with one thing and another, interest in companion planting has escalated in recent years. Most of us are increasingly reluctant to control insect pests with chemical sprays, especially in a food garden. So far, empirical evidence on the effectiveness of certain plants for pest control or for promoting growth and health of other nearby plants is scanty. We read or hear about a gardener successfully repelling bean beetles by planting marigolds next to the beans, so we give it a try too. If it works, the bean-marigold combination becomes a permanent feature in our gardens. That's strictly pragmatic. I've never seen a bean beetle in the flesh; no, not even before I started scattering marigolds throughout the vegetable garden. Effective or not, they look nice out there. For all I know, it's like the old gag of scattering bits of paper on the ground to repel tigers in Kansas. "But there are no tigers in Kansas," you say. "None," comes the response. "Remarkably effective deterrent."

Gardening is at least as much art as science.

Now, about bringing some chives in for winter. Take a young plant or, with a good sharp spade or shovel, dig out the outer portion of a mature clump. Put it in a large pot, about five inches in diameter. Most experts agree that the plant should be cut back severely. Some advise sinking the pot in the ground until there's a hard freeze and then mulching it or removing it to the cold frame for three months. At the end of that time, you're to transfer it indoors to a sunny windowsill and water it well.

That will work for some people, but I prefer a different method, chosen because three months after a hard freeze we're likely to have enough snow cover that I'd never be able to find the cold frame, to say nothing of a mulched pot. The point of the procedure is to give the plant a rest period. I pot up chives in September and cut them back. I leave the pot outside near the house, through repeated frosts. If it makes new top growth, I whack it off. When snow comes I bring the pot in and hope for the best. Usually we have chives all winter. I water the plant sometimes with a weak solution of fish emulsion, being careful not to get any on the foliage. (They say the product is deodorized. Ha!) Fishy chives I can live without. But it needs fertilizer, on a regular basis, because we use the foliage regularly. Multiple pots of chives—three or four—would satisfy our requirements better than one, but there's always a space problem. Freeze-dried and frozen chives take up the slack when it's necessary.

It seems eminently logical to move from chives to scallions, but there's one hitch. The two are related, but chives are usually considered herbs and scallions are usually considered vegetables. This might be as good a time as any to address the question of what makes an herb an herb.

Now it's quite possible that you've never stayed awake nights trying to puzzle out just what makes an herb an herb. Nonetheless, you may have wondered idly about the subject now and again. You hear someone say, "Dandelions are weeds." Out of the shadows a voice pipes up, "Oh, dear me, no, pot herbs *and* medicinal herbs. *Taraxacum officinale*, you know. The official remedy. For a number of things. According to the Doctrine of Signatures, its wide distribution alone suggests it as a cure-all." (You don't have voices like that in your shadows? Pity.) Then you'll hear someone else argue that of two members of the same genera, one is an "herb" and one a "vegetable." Quite aside from chives and scallions, one thinks immediately of fennel. (Well, *I* do.) Everyone agrees that the variety sweet fennel is an herb, but the variety Florence fennel, or finocchio, is usually considered a vegetable.

To complicate matters still further, some troublemaker is bound to bring up the subject of spices—and various salts, seeds, and MSG (monosodium glutamate)—grouped together on the grocer's shelves. You've seen books devoted to "spice-and-herb" cookery, and often if the matter is covered in cookbooks at all, it's usually all in the same chapter.

Some writers on cooking sidestep the whole issue by admitting that there is some confusion and disagreement on the subject. Others, rather sneakily, assume that *everyone* knows the difference between spices and herbs.

Well, do we? I took a poll, confined to my own family. Sample size: one. My husband said that there was no doubt in *his* mind about what was an herb and what was a spice. "Herbs are something you grow in your garden for flavoring food. Spices are something you buy at the store for flavoring foods. Spices, by definition, come from exotic places, at great expense."

In said exotic places, are spices automatically herbs and vice versa? "Obviously," said he. And if I buy basil at the store, does it become a spice? "No," he said, patiently. "You *could* have grown it. You can't grow cinnamon. Exotic."

Such peculiar conversations are commonplace in our household as we stand around the kitchen drinking coffee before breakfast. Occasionally curiosity overcomes our indolence to the extent that we drag out the dictionary.

I can report that the dictionary is, to put it mildly, less than illuminating on the subject of herbs and spices. Nothing about fennel at all. According to *Webster's Seventh New Collegiate Dictionary*, an herb is "a seed-producing annual, biennial, or perennial that does not develop persistent woody tissue but dies down at the end of a growing season." Well, stuff and nonsense. Would anyone deny that bay leaves are herbs? They come from the bay laurel, which is either a good-sized shrub or a small tree, depending on your point of view. What about rosemary? And sage? Besides, the definition *would* include many plants that nobody (at all) considers herbs. Such as zinnias, primroses, beets. Okay, does it say anything else? Yep. Let's try the second definition: "a plant or plant part valued for its medicinal, savory, or aromatic qualities." That's better—sort of. But it doesn't actually eliminate cinnamon or cloves. Maybe the definition for spices will help: "any of various aromatic vegetable products (as pepper or nutmeg) used to season or flavor food." Except for the parenthetical remark, that could be an herb too. I tried, therefore, a different dictionary and found the magic qualifier: "one or other of various strongly flavored or aromatic substances of vegetable origin, obtained from tropical plants, commonly used as condiments, etc." Aha! Just as my sample of one suggested: tropical is clearly exotic.

So there we are. That takes care of the spice problem fairly well, even though I've heard people at my table say, "Umm, this chili is *spicy*." Sorry about that, gang; I use no spices in chili. Herbs. *Hot* is what you mean, not spicy. That tropical plant stuff still, unfortunately, doesn't limit herbs sufficiently to help us to understand why there should be disagreement on whether, say, a *rose* is an herb.

To settle the matter, we ought to delve briefly into the history of herbs. Their reputation for usefulness has fluctuated considerably over the ages, but currently we seem to be in a period of respect (not to say reverence, in some quarters) for herbs. Herbs—and spices too—at one time served to disguise the disagreeable condition of food. In winter, it was likely to be bland to a fault, because of the absence of fresh fruits and vegetables. In warmer weather, it was likely to be *ripe* (especially meats), just this side of rotting. Herbs covered a multitude of sins.

Other characteristics of herbs were quite important too. Besides culinary enhancement, they were used for their fragrance, for dyeing fabrics, for medicinal purposes, for pest control, companion planting, magic—and decoration.

In periods of doubtful sanitary conditions "strewing herbs," such as mint, made both private and public buildings somewhat less offensive to the nostrils. Such pleasantly fragrant herbs are still in demand for perfumes, soaps, lotions, and candles. Since roses and violets and such were valued for their scents, they came to be regarded as herbs.

Synthetic dyes are, of course, in wide use, but many craftspeople and hobbyists prefer vegetable, animal, and mineral dyes. Among the plants used are some not commonly considered herbs, except for this purpose: onions, black walnuts, Scotch broom, coreopsis, indigo, blueberry, grape, sumac, sassafras, bloodroot, and goldenrod.

For purposes of healing, many herbs remain in good repute. Mints for minor digestive upsets, digitalis (foxglove) for heart and circulatory disorders, witch hazel as an astringent, aloes for burns, horehound as an expectorant, laxative and cough remedy, hyssop for colds, borage for catarrh, St. John's wort for diarrhea, tansy for tonic, angelica as a stimulant, camomile and poppy as sedatives. The list goes on and on, and many herb plants (including dandelions) remain in the official pharmacopoeia of various countries.

For pest control, folk wisdom recommends basil against flies and mosquitoes, pennyroyal against gnats and mosquitoes, fennel against fleas, garlic and tansy against Japanese beetles, horseradish against potato bugs. Some herbs are considered useful in that they seem to stimulate the growth and improve the flavor of garden plants: basil for tomatoes, camomile for cabbages and onions, chervil for radishes, nasturtiums for cucurbits. It must, however, be noted that a few herbs have a *depressing* effect on the growth of vegetables: dill inhibits carrots, fennel inhibits almost *everything*, hyssop makes radishes dejected.

I think that in time more and more of these propositions will be tested by plant scientists. Folk "wisdom" is based on observations, after all. Even though necessary controls in observation have often been absent, that doesn't necessarily negate the conclusions. Time was, and recently, when both companion planting and herbal remedies were dismissed as mere superstitions, and for good reason. Too much was claimed for individual species. Oregano, for example, was credited with curing everything from indigestion to dropsy, yellow jaundice, and deafness. But the fact is that about a quarter of all prescription medications are made from herbs and other plants (digitalis is an example). Effective pesticides, such as rotenone, are made from plants.

Those are two of many reasons why the practice of companion planting has both curious observers and avid adherents.

It is entirely possible that the association of herbs with magic and religious ceremonies was related to their observed healing properties. Yet interestingly enough, some herbs have had a mixed press. Basil, for example, was considered sacred in India; in Italy it served as a courting herb, or a sign of courtship. But earlier Greeks and Romans thought it would thrive only if "sown amid vile shouts and curses," and some western Europeans thought scorpions were bred by it. What good can be expected of a plant that produces such progeny?

As far as decorative aspects are concerned, some plants widely considered to have herbal qualities are also known and used as garden flowers: arbutus, beebalm, ajuga, calendula, feverfew, foxglove, nasturtium, roses, sunflowers, garden heliotrope, violets, and yarrow, to name a few.

So where does all this leave us in finding a definition for herbs? Right back at the beginning? Not quite. Herbs are best defined by use, and some have multiple uses. Herbs come from temperate, not tropical climes. There's something comforting in the whole idea that one person's weed may be another's salad—or cure for dyspepsia or the source of color for his hand-made sweater. It's nice to have some latitude in such matters. Makes a ready source for stimulating discussions. Or arguments.

Scallions

That matter safely out of the way, let's get back to scallions. Yes, yes, they're used to flavor a multitude of dishes. But they're also munched as perfectly acceptable companions to radishes, celery, and other finger food. They're so versatile and so easy to grow that they're admirable additions to the garden. The nomenclature of various members of the onion family gets a little jumbled at times, but let's plunge in anyway.

I'm unable to resist the enticements of seed catalogues, a condition that frequently leads to disappointments. Once in a while, though, some modestly advocated variety turns out to be remarkably successful in the garden. Honors ought to go to He-Shi-Ko, a perennial onion (or scallion).

The idea of a perennial onion needs a little explanation. You pull the whole thing for the table. But what's the virtue of a perennial plant if the whole thing is to be harvested? Those plants left in the row continue to grow. Once they reach a certain size, they split. *Voila*! Multiple

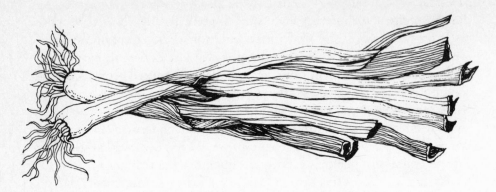

onions where only one had been growing. Selective harvesting can work wonders. But let's start at the beginning.

I decided to try He-Shi-Ko because our entire family dotes on little green onions. Little green onions are a snap to supply in spring. Buy sets and plant them as soon as the ground can be worked. The problem—if a steady yield is your goal—is that they continue growing. As bulbs form, the flavor becomes too robust for most palates. Scallions (bunching onions) or shallots (multiplier onions) are the answer to the contretemps. The latter are actually mild-flavored bulbs which can be used at one stage of their development like scallions. Many scallions eventually form bulbs; He-Shi-Ko does not.

He-Shi-Ko is a bunching onion (that is, scallion) grown from seed. It's supposed to be ready for eating in seventy to eighty days. I planted a large flat on February 22 one year. After three days on top of our antique furnace the seeds germinated, and I placed the flat in the light garden. Off to a rousing start, I thought. At the end of March I put them on the side porch—unheated but covered with plastic for winter, a sort of walk-in cold frame.

On April 12 that year (my memory isn't fantastic; I keep a rudientary garden notebook) I planted the first onion sets outside. What with one thing and another, the He-Shi-Ko never got transplanted into the garden until May 5. They were ready on April 12, you understand, but I wasn't. I put them next to storage onions started from seed. And promptly forgot all about them. Keeping that notebook sometimes convinces me that I'm businesslike, organized. The fact is that I'm haphazard, in a kind of earnest way.

The onions grew satisfactorily, and by late August the tops of the storage onions began to flop over, as is their wont. It was then that I remembered the He-Shi-Ko. They hadn't flopped. The plants were enormous, like medium-sized leeks. "Another great idea shot to hell," thought I. They were surely too big to be palatable. I pulled one, cut off the roots and most of the top and started to clean it, stripping the outer layer of skin. Nestled within the outer covering were four perfect scallions. I checked several other plants and found they'd all been busily dividing. We've literally been inundated with scallions ever since, except when they're buried under snow.

I transplanted the scallions that remained in the row to a couple of flower beds when fall cleanup time came. They're winter hardy, and we have some early scallions ready to eat before onions from sets can be harvested.

If you decide to try perennial scallions, notice that not all varieties of bunching onions available are perennial. Lisbon White Bunching is an annual that ultimately forms small bulbs. White Portugal or Silver Skin is an all-purpose onion, for sets, pickling, green bunching, and storage. The most widely available variety is Evergreen Long White Bunching, which can be wintered over outdoors for early use in the spring. The only other perennial bunching onion I've seen advertised is Kujo Green Multistalk, which I mean to try—some year—along with He-Shi-Ko. Never be lulled into leaving well enough alone.

Use scallions, perennial or annual, like little green onions or whenever a recipe calls for bunching onions or scallions. In some regional cooking—Creole, for example—shallots are used in the way that these green onions are used. Shallots grow in clusters just as scallions do, but bulbs eventually form (little ones), and they're more frequently used in the dry, storage form. All of these cousins are milder in flavor than most storage onions. That's where their usefulness and their limitations come in. What I like about the perennial variety is the total lack of fuss in growing and using them. One packet of seed and we were on our way, evidently forever. Obviously, they eventually set seed—but there you go with a fresh crop coming along, without any effort on the part of the gardener. That's my kind of plant.

Mint

Usually by the beginning of May, in our climate, three other perennial herbs have made enough growth to be usable. (You who garden in kinder regions may scoff at such poverty of garden produce in *May*. We learn to treasure what we have.) The first of these three is mint, which gets a great deal of attention from us beginning in late April because of

Derby Day. Our friends Frank and Mary Wickwire have a party on Derby Day, a party always notable for good company, glorious and abundant food—and mint juleps. Mary and Frank remind all the regular guests that they have a date the first Saturday afternoon in May, and all of us feel obliged to inspect our mint patches. Frank makes a good mint julep. But Bud—well, Bud makes the best I've ever tasted. I've watched him make them for years, but I figured it would be prudent to have him write down the actual recipe because he's such a stickler for detail in this particular matter. I asked for a recipe all right, but what I got was a dissertation. I include it in its entirety. I like to encourage the art of julep making.

The main thing wrong with most Mint Julep recipes is that they give the reader the impression that a Julep is a cocktail (which it isn't) consisting of a water glass full of bourbon to which has been added a couple of sprigs of mint, some ice, and an indeterminate amount of some kind of sweetener. This attitude results in a concoction that has only the doubtful virtue of setting your guests' teeth on edge to the point of welcoming indiscriminately anything that they may be served following the "Julep."

A true Julep is a "cooler." The word itself comes from the Middle English, adapted from the French, adapted in turn from the Arabic, *Julab*, adapted once more from the Persian, *Gulab*, meaning "rose-water." It is defined as "something to cool or assuage the heat of passion, etc.," a 1624 meaning from *The Oxford Universal Dictionary*, revised edition, 1955. Prepared correctly and consumed slowly it is one of the few hot-weather drinks that becomes more refreshing as the consumer approaches the bottom of the glass. It is an eminently civilized drink that, all by itself, justifies the development of bourbon whiskey.

A Julep may be made in either an eight-, ten-, or twelve-ounce glass, as long as the proportions of mint, whiskey, and sugar are correct, and depending only on how long you want the drink to last.

Gather a half-dozen sprigs of fresh garden mint for each drink. (It makes no difference whether you have peppermint or spearmint.) Twist or bruise four sprigs of mint and drop them in the serving glass. Add three teaspoons of sugar. (Most recipes suggest confectioner's sugar; granulated works just as well and perhaps makes a better syrup.) Add a little water (or bourbon if you want to keep the drink inviolate) and muddle with a pestle or the handle of a wooden spoon until the mint is well crushed and the sugar is dissolved.

Pack the glass full of finely crushed ice. Add two ounces of decent bourbon and stir. The ice will collapse and melt a bit. Pack the glass the rest of the way with more finely crushed ice and then add bourbon until there is liquid to the top of the glass. Stir. If you find that you have added a considerable amount of bourbon to fill a large glass (that is to say, one ounce), then add another teaspoon of sugar. Stir until the glass frosts on the outside. Add the remaining sprigs of mint by inserting them into the crushed ice and serve. Each drink should contain its own long-handled spoon so that the consumer can keep the drink stirred as it is consumed.

Juleps have their place, quite inseparable from summer and gardens and horses. (Not everyone will agree with the horse part, but my prejudices insist on a hearing.) But that's far from the end of the uses of mint. We'll get to that once we dispose of the procedures for ensuring a steady supply. Mint has a reputation as a rampant grower. It does best in moist, fertile soil and appreciates a little shade, though it isn't essential. These conditions are so easy to supply that in most gardens the major problem with mint will become one of confinement. In the proper environment, mint will respond so enthusiastically that you may suspect it of having designs on your entire garden.

The mints are shallow-rooted plants that spread by white underground runners called stolons. You may find a mint plant popping up some distance from the original colony. If you pull it up, you'll probably find it's connected to the older group by stolons. Mints produce seeds, but they cross-pollinate so readily that if you want a specific kind for your garden it's best to get a started plant, preferably one you've sampled for taste. Euell Gibbons once remarked that if you were dissatisfied with the taste of a particular mint it was a signal to sample others. That many variations occur.

If you want to keep mint confined, container growing is the best bet. There are, however, places where you may want to allow it to spread. I've established it as a ground cover around the barns because rats, allegedly, dislike it intensely. They seem to be overcoming their aversion wonderfully, but in any case it smells delightful when we or the animals step on it.

So what kind of mint should you grow? There are a number of varieties to choose from. Spearmint (*Mentha spicata*) is the mint most commonly grown for culinary purposes. It has dark green leaves— pointed leaves, hence the name—and produces a lavender or purple flower spike in July and August. To keep a good supply coming along, cut it back periodically. While you're at it, you can tie a string around a bunch and hang it upside down in an airy place to dry for winter use. When the leaves become brittle, strip them from the stems and store them in an airtight container. If nothing else, it's pleasant to open the jar and sniff. Preferably when you're unobserved.

Peppermint (*M. piperita*) is stronger in flavor than spearmint. Paler in color, its leaves aren't pointed, and they're downy. Peppermint is listed as an official drug plant, and hundreds of thousands of acres are planted to the crop in the United States alone. Its oil, produced at an average weight of fifty-three pounds per acre, is used for medicines, cigarettes, cosmetics, and toiletries, as well as for flavoring chewing gum and candy. As a drug it's supposedly effective in treating flatulence, colic, cramps, muscle spasms, dyspepsia, cholera, and diarrhea. A wonder drug, no less.

English pennyroyal, a member of the mint family (*M. pulegium*), has had the reputation of repelling gnats, mosquitoes, fleas, and moths. Like other mints, it's perennial. American pennyroyal (*Hedeoma pulegioides*), however, is an annual and not a true mint. It acquired its common name because its properties and uses are similar to those of English pennyroyal.

The mints originated in the Near East, then spread throughout Europe and North America, where some of them naturalized. In the Middle East, salads are liberally laced with mint. In India, people hang bunches of mint in doorways for fragrance. The foliage of some mints is so attractive that it is at home in floral arrangements too. Because it roots so readily in water, you can easily propagate extra plants by soaking cuttings. And because it thrives in semi-shady areas, mint makes a good houseplant.

Once you've established peppermint and spearmint in your garden, you may want to try some of the more exotic varieties. Apple mint (*M. Rotundifolia*) has small, round, gray-green leaves which are soft and wooly. It's popular in herb-tea blends. Orange mint (*M. citrata*) has a citrus fragrance. Its dark-green leaves are reddish underneath, and it makes an attractive houseplant as well as a good tea. Pineapple mint (*M. variegata*) has handsome leaves variegated with white and cream. Indoors it tends to be a trailing plant, so it's a good candidate for hanging baskets or pots. Its odor is reminiscent of pineapple, and it's used primarily as a garnish or a flavoring for tea. Corsican mint (*M. requienii*) has tiny leaves and is usually used for its fragrance.

Some gardeners use peppermint as a companion plant to members of the cabbage family because it reputedly repels the white cabbage butterfly. It's also said to improve the flavor of tomatoes if planted near them. There's one catch: a vegetable garden is likely to provide conditions so satisfactory to mint that it will become a veritable weed.

Generally, the mints you select for culinary use will be chosen for the particular nuances of flavor you prefer. Since there are such distinctive differences even among mints of the same species, the only rule of thumb is: use those that taste good to you. A sprig of mint tucked into the glass is indispensable to some iced-tea fans. Added to green peas (but removed before serving since cooking makes it tired-looking) it imparts a pleasant flavor. It's often used to flavor lamb roasts, but perhaps appears more frequently in sauces or jellies served with the cooked meat.

Mint jellies and sauces have long been a popular accompaniment to lamb. One simple approach is to combine a cup of chopped mint leaves with just enough boiling water to moisten them. Stir in a cupful of your favorite orange marmalade. For many years I made mint jelly from the recipe given with pectin bought at the grocery store. Still do, in fact, since Tom likes it spread on buttered bread and further embellished with embarrassing quantities of peanut butter. We won't dwell on such depravities. Some years ago our good friend Pip Stromgren gave us a jar of mint jelly that we found especially appealing. Through some misunderstanding, I thought the recipe came from her younger sister, Esme. Actually, it's from her older sister, Priscilla, but some beliefs defy any effort to correct them. To us it remains Esme's mint jelly—and our favorite.

ESME'S MINT JELLY

6	pounds cooking apples
4½	cups water
2½	cups packed mint
4½	cups white vinegar
sugar	
6–8	tablespoons chopped mint
green food coloring, optional	

Chop the apples coarsely, add water and mint, and place them in a large pot. Simmer until very soft. Add vinegar and boil for 5 minutes. Strain. Measure. Return it to the pot and add 1 cup of sugar for each cup of the mint infusion. Stir until the sugar has dissolved. Boil rapidly until a gel is obtained on testing. (I find it easier to be guided by a jelly thermometer.) Stir in the chopped mint, and coloring if desired. (Careful there: in its honest condition the jelly isn't exactly gorgeous, but too heavy a hand with the artificial coloring can result in a visual outrage.) Ladle into sterilized jars and seal with paraffin or with canning lids used according to the manufacturer's directions. This recipe makes a fair amount of jelly. It may be successfully halved.

Carrots, especially young ones, take kindly to mint too.

MINTED CARROTS   *Serves 4*

2	cups carrots, thinly sliced
3	tablespoons butter
3	tablspoons water
1	tablespoon brown sugar
salt and pepper to taste	
3	sprigs mint

Put the carrots in a heavy pot with the butter and water. Cover and cook gently just until tender. Remove the lid and allow any remaining water to evaporate. Add the remaining ingredients. Saute for a minute or two. Remove the mint and serve.

A cup of chopped mint leaves can be added to a tossed green salad dressed with vinegar and oil. A teaspoon of fresh chopped mint mixed with each serving of cucumbers in sour cream makes that summer favorite all the more refreshing. Some admirers of the herb like to combine it with cream cheese as a spread for whole-wheat bread or crackers. It combines nicely with applesauce or baked apples. Mint sherbets and parfaits are refreshing, and creme de menthe is a popular liqueur, whether used as sauce for ice cream, as a cocktail ingredient, or as an after-dinner drink. There's just no stopping. What would we do without mint?

But then, I feel the same way about so many plants that it's ridiculous. Every once in awhile I acquire one that impresses me to the point of awe. Like oregano.

Oregano

I discovered one year, to my acute embarrassment and chagrin, that the herb I'd been so tenderly nursing through winters, using so profligately as seasoning, and sharing with unsuspecting friends as oregano is actually something of an imposter. It's some comfort that this delusion has been carefully nurtured by various seed and nursery companies. Nevertheless, there it is: what I'm growing is *O. vulgare*, considered by the experts to be an inferior variety. Common. Popular. Oh, the shame of it all. I don't think it's quite the sin that palming off Russian tarragon as *real* (that is, French) tarragon is, but it's ignorance of the first order, if not worse. Yes, of course it tasted different. I was prepared to rise above that peculiar problem, secure in the virtue obviously inherent in growing my own oregano. Snob appeal. Naked and unrepentant.

The respectable oregano is *O. heracleoticum*. Like the disreputable stuff I've been using, it's a perennial and native to the Mediterranean area. My oregano grows to about two feet in height and has purplish flowers (and common or not, they look great in floral arrangements, fresh or dried). The leaves are small and oval, dark grayish-green in color. I've read that the flowers can also be pink, lilac, or white. *O. heracleoticum*, on the other hand, is low growing, always has white flowers on a twelve-inch stalk, and must be treated as a tender perennial; that is, like rosemary it has to spend cold weather indoors. While in pursuit of this information, I discovered a faction that calls the common stuff wild marjoram and the real article winter marjoram. Marjoram is a relative of oregano, but those people are just showing off.

It is difficult to get anything but common oregano, but assuming that you're willing to reconcile yourself to *O. vulgare*, there's little problem in growing, drying, or enjoying it. You can begin with seeds or plants and put them in your garden in a permanent location, preferably in full sun. Ordinary garden soil is entirely satisfactory. If you want to cut fresh oregano all summer, you are advised to prune it to a height of a couple of inches before it flowers. Take your cuttings for winter use after it has made its second growth and is ready to bloom. Dry it — or any other oregano species — by hanging it upside down or placing it on a screen in a shady, airy place. And by the way, there's no need to coddle it in cold weather. Stuff's indestructible.

Common oregano formerly held an exalted position as a medicinal herb for both internal and external use. It was said to be effective against everything from convulsions to deafness. (You know how many complaints the herb of your choice can cure.) More recently it has had some reputation as a mild tonic, and its warming qualities have resulted in its use as a liniment. *O. heracleoticum* has to its credit the alleged distinction of chasing bugs away from cucurbits (melons, squash, cucumbers). This, perhaps, is a result of its having a stronger aroma than common oregano does. What one buys from the grocer's shelf is usually imported, and its flavor and fragrance are far more pronounced than the kind that we can so easily grow.

The hunt for *O. heracleoticum* resulted from my having become aware of all those fine distinctions. I studied many catalogues, and the only one I found listing it was Johnny's Selected Seeds in Albion, Maine. I sent off an order to them, intending to regale anyone who would listen with a report of my adventures. Johnny's sent me a letter reporting that they had only *O. vulgare*; their listing was in error. I tried again another year, with no success. True to form, I decided, "Okay, that's it gang." I wasn't cut out to be a crusader. I marched off to the supermarket and treated myself to a large jar of *O. heracleoticum*. I used both kinds, feeling nary a qualm when I reached for the imported stuff. However, I am nothing if not inconsistent. When Johnny's later listed "oregano sp." I couldn't resist sending off for a packet, and as a result I'm convinced that two plants now living in my light garden are *O. heracleoticum*.

I use common oregano from the garden to flavor a lot of milder dishes. To me, it tastes so much like marjoram (*O. marjorana*) that I no longer grow that herb. Especially combined with basil, common oregano is good in any recipe that calls for tomatoes. Well, not *any* recipe. We like it sprinkled on shirred eggs along with a generous dusting of grated Parmesan or Romano cheese. Come to think of it, we like shirred eggs. You may recall my mentioning them before. We seem to be the only people we know who eat shirred eggs. Such an omission from the diet is close to criminal. Let's hear it for shirred eggs.

SHIRRED EGGS WITH OREGANO   *Serves 2*

2 tablespoons butter
4 fresh eggs
2 tablespoons cream
   or milk
salt and pepper to taste
2 tablespoons grated
   Parmesan or
   Romano cheese
2 tablespoons fresh
   or 1 teaspoon
   dried common
   oregano
	Preheat the broiler. Melt the butter over moderate heat in a pan that can safely go under the broiler. I use an iron skillet or a paella pan. Break the eggs into the pan and dribble the milk or cream around the edges. Salt and pepper them. Turn the heat off, too. Sprinkle the eggs as evenly as possible with cheese and oregano. Put the pan under the broiler and cook until the whites are set and the cheese delicately toasted. This always takes longer than I believe it will, but maybe that's just because I watch it so intently to make sure it doesn't burn. I heartily recommend watching it anyway. Burned eggs are not appetizing. Properly shirred eggs make a memorable breakfast.

As for that other oregano, the sharper-flavored *O. heracleoticum*, I dote on it. What's pizza sauce without oregano? Often I use it on the shirred eggs, but only half the amount of *O. vulgare*.

One of my favorite recipes using the stronger herb is probably Greek in origin. Someone told me that. Can't remember who, but it sounds reasonable. The recipe is a stunner. Come to think of it, there's no reason not to use home-grown *O. vulgare* if you'd prefer a subtler version.

ROASTED CHICKEN WITH OREGANO   *Serves 2–4*

1   whole chicken
¼–½ cup melted butter
salt and pepper to taste
2   whole cloves
    garlic, peeled
1   teaspoon dried
    oregano
2   tablespoons lemon
    juice
½   teaspoon dried
    oregano

The size of the chicken can run from broiler to roaster, provided the bird is plump and tender. You might like to cook two broilers or fryers at once, for example, if you're serving 4 to 6 people. I use whatever's in the freezer and proceed from there. The amount of melted butter needed depends on the area of chicken to be basted as well as on your taste. Whatever. Remove the giblets and neck, to use for whatever purposes you like. You won't hear any more from me on that subject. Salt and pepper the cavity and put the cloves of garlic and the one teaspoon of oregano in it.

Place the chicken in a pan and drizzle the melted butter over it. I use a roasting pan with a lid because later on you'll need to cover the chicken for a while. If the pan isn't teflon coated, I usually spray it with a non-stick product before putting the bird into it.

Turn the chicken breast-side down and put it in an oven preheated to 400°F. for 30 to 45 minutes, or until golden. Turn the chicken breast-side-up and the oven to 350°F. and roast for another 30 minutes. Turn the oven down to 300°F. and continue cooking the chicken until it is tender. With a fryer, that will be about an hour. Adjust the time depending on the age and size of the bird(s) in question.

When it's tender, remove the chicken from the oven. Drizzle the lemon juice over it and sprinkle it evenly with ½ teaspoon dried, crumbled oregano. Cover it and let it rest for 10 minutes. Remove it from the pan for carving. The juice remaining in the pan can be served separately in a sauceboat. Put a little hot water—certainly no more than ¼ to ½ cup—in the pan and stir it around to loosen any browned particles sticking to the pan, if you like. I never add water, preferring the sinfully rich juice as is.

This chicken dish is especially gratifying when served with lemon rice. That you make by adding a couple of tablespoons of lemon juice to the water used for cooking the rice. Before serving, garnish the rice with a little finely grated lemon peel. Hard to beat.

One of the particular virtues of the chicken is the leeway afforded by that last period of cooking in a slow oven. If dinner will be delayed, turn the heat down to barely warm until it seems safe to resume active cooking.

Tarragon

The last of the trio of perennial herbs so welcome in the early garden is tarragon. Mention tarragon to any herb grower, and you're bound to be reminded that there's French tarragon and then there's Russian tarragon. Said herb grower is likely to sneer at the mere mention of the latter.

Although both these tarragons have the same scientific name, *Artemisia dracunculus* (Family: Compositae), the European (usually called "French," but occasionally referred to as "German") tarragon normally doesn't produce fertile seeds and so is grown from cuttings and root divisions. The Eastern, or "Russian," tarragon produces seed abundantly. Unfortunately, although it's a vigorous plant, it lacks the oils that account for the aniselike taste and smell of French tarragon.

The word tarragon itself is apparently a corruption of the French name, *esdragon*, itself derived from the Latin name meaning "little dragon." That fanciful name resulted from the appearance of its roots, which coil like serpents. If the plant isn't divided every three or four years, it strangles itself. Nothing quite like a suicidal plant. Is tarragon trying to tell us something? Considering also its refusal to set fertile seed? Is French tarragon the victim of a strong death wish?

Anyway, the herb's long history is based primarily on its culinary uses, although once a poultice of tarragon leaves was thought to heal bites from mad dogs, snakes, and insects. Later on, people believed that wearing a sprig of the herb increased one's stamina.

Grown in sunshine in fertile, well-drained soil, tarragon will reach two feet in height and as much as four feet in breadth. If grown in partial shade, it will survive but tends to be scraggly. It has long, narrow leaves and woody stems and can be grown indoors or out. It's a useful plant, but you won't be overcome by its beauty. Although a mulch is helpful to maintain moisture in the soil, tarragon won't tolerate soggy conditions. Overwatering causes root rot. Let me add, however, that its apparent determination to die doesn't make it a difficult plant to grow. My plant is exuberantly healthy though it gets attention only when I cut some leaves for use in the kitchen. Periodically I cut through the plant with a sharp spade and reset the part removed or give it to some deserving person. The plant doesn't seem offended by this cavalier treatment.

Tarragon vinegar is widely known and appreciated, but the herb is also used to season chicken, veal, fish, white sauces, cheese dishes and green vegetables. A few fresh leaves may be added to salads, but tarragon requires a light touch so that it doesn't overpower other flavors. Dried tarragon has a pleasantly sweet odor which makes it valuable in potpourris or dried bouquets. Be careful to store dried tarragon for cooking in tightly sealed containers, or it will reabsorb moisture. Avoid using tarragon in recipes that call for a long period of boiling, because that tends to make it bitter.

A sprinkle of tarragon is delicious on cooked cauliflower, peas, lima beans, and spinach. It is absolutely essential in tartar sauce and sauce béarnaise, and it imparts piquancy to mustard or mayonnaise. Add it and chopped parsley to a white sauce poured over poached eggs for a change of pace at breakfast.

Any good French cookbook will provide recipes for classic chicken and veal dishes sauced with tarragon. Every once in a while I stun my family with one of these sumptuous offerings. For the most part, though, I take the easy way out. Three or four sprigs of tarragon (½ teaspoon dried) put in the cavity of a roasting chicken cooked without stuffing will impart a distinctive flavor. Adding the same amount of the herb to a gravy served with the bird will enhance its flavor without dominating it. (If you use fresh, remember to remove it before serving the gravy. Its aesthetic appeal is nil.) Here's an easy way to prepare a simple but suitably stylish main course.

TARRAGON CHICKEN   *Serves 4*

½ **cup flour**	Combine the dry ingredients, including the tarragon. Dip the chicken pieces in milk and coat them with the flour mixture. Brown them in the oil and butter over moderate heat. Cover and cook until tender, about 30 minutes. Remove the lid and crisp the chicken before serving it. After browning it, you may instead finish cooking the chicken in a 350°F. oven for about 30 minutes if you prefer.
1 **teaspoon salt**	
1 **teaspoon dried or 1 tablespoon finely minced fresh tarragon**	
¼ **teaspoon ground ginger**	
1 **cut-up fryer**	
¼ **cup milk**	
2 **tablespoons cooking oil**	
2 **tablespoons butter**	

Tarragon has an affinity for fish too. Here's another quickie, useful for days when you pine for something different but just can't face hours of preparation.

TARRAGON FLOUNDER   *Serves 4*

4   **flounder fillets, about 1½ pounds**
2   **tablespoons mayonnaise**
3   **tablespoons melted butter**
1   **teaspoon dried or 1 tablespoon finely minced fresh tarragon**
salt and pepper to taste

Butter a shallow baking pan large enough to hold the fillets in one layer. Combine mayonnaise, butter, tarragon, and seasonings and spread the mixture over the fillets. Bake in an oven preheated to 400°F. for 10 minutes, or until the fish has reached the degree of firmness you prefer. Place under the broiler for a couple of minutes, until the top bubbles.

Although it is an herb that is frequently employed in solitary state, tarragon combines well with parsley and with members of the onion family. It's useful in sauces and stuffings. Traditionally it's regarded as somewhat elegant. Since elegance isn't normally my long suit, I welcome easy ways to achieve it.

Asparagus

And speaking of elegance, that's asparagus. I could cheerfully eat it a dozen times a month, hot or cold, sauced or not. As far as I'm concerned, it needs little more than a hefty pat of butter and a dash of salt. When we moved to western Massachusetts twenty years ago, ten bunches of "skinnies" sold for a dollar. For the fat spears you had to cough up a quarter a bunch. Not only did inflation put a stop to that, but disease descended on the fields of Hadley and its environs. A virus, a vile contagion. Just when we thought we'd nailed down a couple of months of affordable (nay, cheap!) gourmandizing a year.

There's still local asparagus, and it's still good. But that marvelous inexpensive abundance is gone. Forever, presumably. A shame, but out of disaster came an asparagus bed.

You know all about asparagus beds and their reputation for being productive over a period of many years. Twenty-five plants per asparagus-eater is said to produce a fairly satisfying harvest. That's assuming they deign to produce any edible stalks at all, after you've performed gardening chores that make raising strawberries and orchids seem like child's play.

At this point, someone is sure to mention that strawberries and orchids *are* child's play. Okay. Maybe for you. Despite my affection and admiration for both, I've given up growing them on the theory that life is too short for gratuitous hassles, particularly when *easy* projects abound. And that's asparagus, under certain conditions.

The most important of these conditions, I think, is mulch, in copious amounts. Start with seed or one-year roots or two-year roots, depending on how eager you are for harvest. I've tried all three, and for easy results fast, it's two-year roots for me. Forget about trenches and double digging and all those complicated procedures that have persuaded you to avoid growing asparagus.

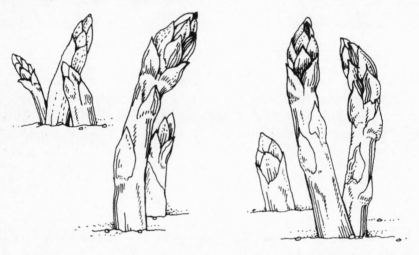

Asparagus roots are fragile, and they spread out tremendously so you need two feet between plants and about four feet between rows. That's measuring from the center of the root mass. Plunge the bare roots in a bucket of water and get to work. Depending on the size of the roots you're working with, it may be just as easy to shovel out a shallow trench the length of your row after the area has been well tilled. The one thing you definitely want to avoid is damaging and crowding those roots. Spread them out. I assume you've chosen a sunny, fertile, well-drained site. Cover the roots with two inches of soil, and mulch. Heavily. Because once weeds get going in a bed of asparagus, you've got big troubles. When we're raking leaves in the fall—what am I saying, "we"? That's our sons' job. Tom's actually, now that Bob has a place of his own. Come to think of it, leaves may be why he left.

Anyway, a lot of those leaves go on the asparagus bed. Mostly maple leaves, but some from birch and fruit trees too. Don't they mat down, smother the asparagus? Not noticeably.

Occasionally during the summer a sturdy weed or clump of grass rises triumphant above the mulch in the asparagus bed. I'm ruthless. Out it comes. And ruthless is easy in a mulched bed, no question about it. Once we finish cutting, and the plants are allowed to grow, I feed the bed with manure, usually horse manure, if I've got more mulch to put on top of the manure. If I'm low on mulch, I wait until fall so the manure will be well covered with leaves. Don't want a cover crop of oats, thank you.

I should mention the harvesting procedure. The first cutting will necessarily be light, and it can be made the next spring after you plant two-year-old roots. Two years for the one-year-old roots, etc. In a word, the plant has to be three years old, regardless of where it spent its infancy and youth. What you harvest should be spears about six or eight inches long and at least half an inch in diameter. When you notice there are few shoots that thickness, it's time to stop harvesting and let the plant develop.

Anyway, that's it. No big deal. (If it were, I'd not bother, because life is too short, etc.) Mulch and manure. If you use a commercial fertilizer or seed-free manure, you don't even have to fuss about putting mulch on top of it right away. And the mulch—well, you use what you have plenty of—spoiled hay, grass clippings, leaves, whatever. Plastic mulch is popular with many gardeners. It will not, obviously, add anything to the tilth or fertility of the soil, and the feeding of the asparagus will therefore have to be heaver than with an organic mulch. I don't use the plastic, despite its numerous virtues. I loathe it with an unreasoning passion difficult to describe.

You know, of course, how to cook asparagus. Steaming is best, tips pointed at the top of the pot. Don't overcook it; time needed will depend on the diameter of the stalks. Over-cooked asparagus is mushy and not to be borne.

So let's assume you've gorged on asparagus in its pristine, unadorned, state, and you're ready for a change. What next? I tend to keep it simple with asparagus, because I persist in considering it a treat and a delicacy not to be tampered with lightly. But there's vinaigrette, hot or cold. Basically, that's cooked asparagus spears with French dressing poured over them, garnished with fresh chopped parsley. One way to keep asparagus fresh in the refrigerator is to stand the asparagus up in water, like a bunch of flowers. If it's fresh from the garden, that won't be necessary, but if you're reduced to buying it today for serving tomorrow, the water treatment is a good idea. It keeps the spears from going limp on you.

Hollandaise sauce is a traditional accompaniment to asparagus too, and it's no problem if you have a food processor. We use it only seldom, having a tendency, all of us, to break out in hives at the mention of so many calories. A blind spot. Anyway, I prefer asparagus topped with fresh bread crumbs lightly sauteed in an equal amount of butter. The texture is in pleasant contrast to that of the spears. Or layer cooked asparagus in a baking dish, each layer sprinkled with the toasted crumbs and grated Swiss cheese. Bake it at 400° F. for 10 minutes.

Asparagus makes a terrific salad too. It sounds—probably is—terribly plebian, but a mound of nicely seasoned cottage cheese on a bed of lettuce surrounded with chilled cooked asparagus tips, wedges of to-mato, and hard-cooked eggs is good. Or take a tender spear—or two or three — and wrap it in the thinnest possible slice of ham, secured with a toothpick. Or substitute a crepe for the toothpick and serve them hot. Or place the ham-wrapped asparagus in a baking dish, dot it with butter, sprinkle it generously with grated Parmesan cheese and bake it in a 400° F. oven for about 5 minutes. That's 5 minutes if all the ingredients are at room temperature.

We never have a surplus of asparagus for the freezer anymore; we've become too greedy. But I used to freeze it in quantity when I was buying those marvelous dime bunches. Simplicity itself. Wash and dry it, package, pop it into the freezer. Is that the correct method? Well, now, experts tell you to wash it and then scald it for 3 or 4 minutes, depending on the diameter of the stalks. Drain, chill in ice water, drain again, and package. One day my friend Kay Martin told me that the grower who supplied her with crates of the stuff said it wasn't necessary. She quit, and so did I. I'm ever eager to pounce on ways to shorten chores and seldom ask troublemaking questions. It works.

Scalding (or blanching) is recommended for two reasons. It destroys enzymes that change the taste and texture of frozen foods during freezer storage, and it prevents loss of vitamins during storage. Our family has not noticed any loss of flavor and texture, and as for vitamins—who can tell, except under laboratory conditions. I'll take my chances.

That gives you a general idea of the possibilities with asparagus. Sorry I can't be more helpful. But then, why gild a lily?

From something aristocratic and indescribably delicate, we go to something common as dirt, something everyone grows. Everyone who grows anything at all. And in keeping with the theme of this chapter, it's a spring-time perennial. Boy, is it perennial. It's completely winter hardy. Each part of it is gastronomicallyuseful. It's ubiquitous. Furthermore, it has a terrible reputation and is widely despised.

What else fits that description (in forty-five seconds, maximum) except *Taraxacum officinale*—that is, the dandelion?

Dandelions

Before you reach for the weed-killer, reflect a moment. The common dandelion, in addition to providing culinary delights, is an effective medicinal plant, considered perhaps the safest and most active plant diuretic and also an aid in treating liver complaints. It is listed in the national pharmacopoeias of Hungary, Poland, Switzerland, and the Soviet Union.

If the presence of dandelions offends your aesthetic sense, it's better to reach for a sturdy trowel instead of reaching for a poison. Remove dandelions from the greensward and serve them for dinner. Aside from other considerations, it's a wonderfully frugal idea. You save the cost of a salad, soup, vegetable, or beverage as well as the cost of the weed killer (its price being only one of its many disadvantages).

It's possible to buy and plant a cultivated strain of dandelion seed. The seed houses that list it proclaim that leaves of the cultivated plants are less bitter than wild ones. You can buy that kind at produce counters in supermarkets at almost any time too.

Dandelions were introduced to the United States, but no one could deny that they have flourished here. They are native to Europe and Asia. In accordance with the Doctrine of Signatures, which attributed significance to wide distribution, the ancients regarded the plant as a cure-all. Sometimes I think they regarded too many plants that way, with little evidence. The dandelion's botanical name translates roughly as the "official remedy for disorders," which covers a lot of ground. It has been used as a laxative, diuretic, hepatic, tonic, stomachic, and, when ground, as a poultice for snakebite. (I tend to suspect that whether or not it was effective in that latter role depended a lot on the snake in question.) In addition to these traditional virtues, dandelions are demonstrably rich in vitamins, including A, B, C, and riboflavin.

All parts of the dandelion can be used in the kitchen. Most of us think of dandelion greens immediately. To escape toughness and bitterness, use only young leaves, before the flower stalk appears. They may be eaten raw in a salad or cooked like spinach. Some people eat the roots as a vegetable or, after complicated preparation, brew them as a coffee substitute. I don't, but I thought you'd like to know.

Just above the root, but still below the soil surface, you'll find the crown, a cluster of naturally blanched leaf stems. It can be eaten raw, in salads, or cooked as a vegetable. Wash it well and then soak it in salted water to get it clean and drive out any lurking bugs. To use it in a salad, prepare a wilted lettuce dressing. To cook as a vegetable, boil the crown for 5 minutes, drain, and season with butter and salt.

The greens themselves are the best known of the edibles available from dandelions. Pick them young enough, and they'll be tender and mild. Wash them and use them raw in the salad.

Using a blender, you can easily make a spread for whole-grain bread or crackers. Use equal amounts of cottage cheese and greens and add half that amount of your favorite nutmeats. Once the mixture is blended, you may need to add a little mayonnaise to achieve the consistency you prefer. Or put the greens in a kettle and pour boiling water over them. Boil 5 minutes, drain, and season with salt and butter or bacon fat. The leaves are also used in tonics and in dandelion beer.

We're still not finished. The blossom itself is also useful. Before the plant blooms, a yellowish mass of closely packed material is nestled in the center of the crown. Cut it out of the crown, cover with boiling water, and cook 3 minutes. Drain and season with salt and butter, for an artichoke substitute. Once the dandelion sends up blossom stalks it becomes too bitter and tough to be palatable. There's still one use left though. The blossoms themselves are picked to make that well-known potable, dandelion wine.

DANDELION WINE

1	gallon dandelion blossoms
1	gallon boiling water
3	oranges
1	lemon
3	pounds sugar

Put the flowers in a 2-gallon container and pour the boiling water over them. We use an enameled pot. Cover it and let stand for 3 days. Strain the liquid into a kettle, add the sugar and the peels of the fruit. Boil for 20 minutes. Return to the container. Spread ½ cake of yeast on a piece of toasted rye bread and place it on top of the liquid. Cover with a cloth and place in a warm room for 6 days. Strain and place in a gallon jug loosely corked with cotton. Keep in a dark place for 3 weeks, decant, cork tightly. The wine may be sampled after 7 months, but it improves mightily with age. Good dandelion wine is smooth and similar to sherry in flavor. The other kind is undrinkable.

Enjoying the harvest of perennial plants in spring goes hand in hand with getting the vegetable garden ready for another glorious season. Well, some of it will be glorious. Nobody ever said gardening was completely reliable. Typically, though, the kitchen garden manages to repay the time and effort expended on it in spite of the vagaries of nature. Which *are* reliable, as vagaries go.

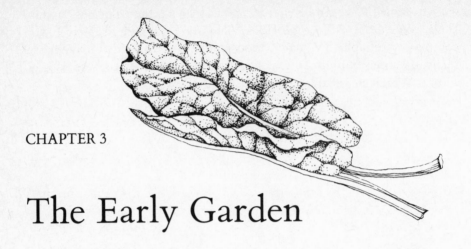

CHAPTER 3

The Early Garden

It's not likely that all the good perennials reappearing in the garden will make you any slower in getting the annuals planted. Any gardener who fusses with perennials is a digger at heart. Don't let that first mild spell, when the fragrance of the good earth warmed by sun tempts you to drag out spading fork or tiller, lead you astray. Sure you're eager to get the lettuce and radishes and onion sets into the ground, but premature soil preparation can be a serious mistake.

Here in western Massachusetts, we till the garden in April. Right; that's a lot of leeway. I have friends who wait until May, and their results are as good as mine. I'm temperamentally incapable of waiting until May. But even impatient as I am, I've learned to wait until the soil is dry enough to work properly. And there's one section of our garden that waits at least a week or two longer than the rest because the soil is heavier there.

Inexperienced gardeners can rely on old hands in their neighborhoods for the signal to begin work. There *will* be individual differences. When you should prepare the soil depends on its structure and the microclimate in your yard. (That's just another way of saying that a sheltered, sunny area is likely to be ready earlier than some other spot.) Soil that is sandy or loamy can be tilled as soon as the frost is out and it's no longer soggy. A heavy soil full of clay won't be ready as soon. Tilling it too early will damage the structure of such a soil. It will cake into lumps, preventing you from making a fine seedbed and therefore making life more difficult for infant plants.

There are several ways to prepare the soil for planting: spading, tilling, plowing, or mulching á la Ruth Stout. Mulch gardening should be started in the fall. The choice of other methods depends on the size garden you plan and the tools available. Spading is entirely effective—and hard work. If you'll be doing it that way, it's best to dig the garden in sections. Since cool-weather vegetables such as lettuce and radishes are planted four to six weeks before heat-loving ones such as tomatoes and peppers, spading the garden all at once will only guarantee that part of it will have to be turned again—or at least thoroughly weeded—before you plant the hot-weather crops. If you're hiring the work done, a complete early tilling will probably be your only choice, but at least you're forewarned. Don't stint on the initial preparation. Unless you've thoroughly prepared the soil, yields won't be up to par and weeds will be a nightmare to control.

Plants need nutrients to grow. All the gardening magazines recommend you test your soil with one of the simple kits available in garden stores to discover the soil's deficiencies. In practice, relatively few gardeners test their soil. I don't know anybody who's done it unless (like me) they received a kit free with a magazine subscription. Our teenage sons thought it was great fun to use. So did I, for that matter. I can't say testing made any differences in my cultural practices that year, though. Most garden vegetables (potatoes are one exception) prefer a neutral or slightly alkaline soil. If yours is acid, you need lime. Ordinary garden lime works slowly, so if you didn't apply lime the previous fall you may want to use the slightly more expensive fast-acting kind in the spring. Then get into the habit of applying lime in the fall, if you need it. Follow the instructions on the label for amounts.

Your garden will need fertilizer too. Aged manures and compost can be tilled into the soil in the spring. If you plan to use chemical fertilizers alone or in combination with organic ones, apply them at planting time according to the instructions on the label. Soil can't be kept in good condition with chemical fertilizers alone. Indeed, there are inescapable problems arising from using only chemicals, and not the least of them is cost. Save leaves, garden and kitchen wastes, ashes, and whatever other animal, vegetable, and mineral matter you can get your hands on. Sufficient organic matter in the soil will help hold moisture, but will prevent a heavy soil from becoming waterlogged. It will nourish the crops too.

I always fret about getting seeds and sets and seedlings planted as soon as possible, and that's silly. The seeds and plants aren't likely to do much growing until fine weather and rising soil temperature nudge them into enthusiasm. Elevation and proximity to ponds or rivers or towns will all affect when you can start planting. So will weather patterns of any given spring. Use the splendid days you get before reasonable planting time to prepare the seedbed and finish the outdoor spring cleaning.

You will have noticed by now that I'm mentioning garden produce more or less in the order in which it's first ready for use. Some of the annual seeds or plants require a long growing season. You'll be nurturing them at the time you're harvesting earlier kinds. Some vegetables are accommodating enough that you can, with a little extra care and a modicum of luck, make successive sowings and harvest them repeatedly. Lettuce is one example.

Lettuces

Supermarket lettuce can't hold a candle to home-grown, and lettuce is easy to grow. It has few disease or insect problems. The only trick is to keep it producing all summer long and into fall.

Basically, there are two types of lettuce; loose leaf and heading. Heading lettuce is further classified as crisp-head (the iceberg ones) and butterhead (Bibb, Boston). Aficionados insist on separate categories for Romaine (Cos) lettuce and endive.

The major problem you'll encounter in growing lettuce is its tendency to bolt. Regular daytime temperatures over 70° F. trigger the setting of seed. Various methods can be used to counter the problem.

First of all, make small, frequent sowings of lettuce, as often as every ten to fourteen days. You're after a steady supply, and once it's ready lettuce doesn't keep well indoors or out. Make sure you *thin* lettuce. Not only will it grow better but for some reason plants properly spaced have less tendency to bolt. The loose leaf varieties should be thinned to stand four inches apart; heading lettuces should stand eight to ten inches apart. The thinnings can provide the earliest salads or can be transplanted if care is taken to keep them watered until they're established. Don't sow the seed thickly; the germination rate is high, and too many seeds will only make the task of thinning more arduous.

Loose leaf lettuce is easiest of all to grow. If the supermarket variety is your only experience of it, you're probably not wildly impressed by this type. But loose leaf lettuce can't take rough handling, and that's one of the reasons why the lettuce you grow in your garden will taste better than lettuce from a supermarket. Because loose leaf lettuce isn't blanched, it has more vitamins than head lettuce. The old variety Black-Seeded Simpson is an early, popular loose leaf. Ruby, a lettuce with reddish leaves, is popular for adding color to salads. For late plantings the Oak Leaf types or Green Ice are recommended, because they bolt less quickly than Simpson or Ruby.

Buttercrunch is my favorite of all the lettuces. It's a butterhead in the same category as Bibb and Boston. It's slower to bolt than other butterheads, and its texture and flavor are incomparable.

The iceberg types generally are more trouble to grow and need better soil to produce firm heads than loose leaf or butterheads do. They're slower to bolt than butterheads, but since they take twice as long to reach maturity as loose leafs and two weeks longer than butterheads, they're difficult to grow where nights get warm early in the season.

To keep a steady supply of lettuce, I find it easier to make the summer sowings in flats, because they can be kept in a cool place where they're sheltered from the midday sun. It's easier too to keep the surface of the soil moist in a flat than in the garden. (But if you have as much as four feet of space to spare in your garden that fits this description, a thin sowing might do well there and will save you some nuisance.) Summer seedlings don't need hardening off, but will have to be kept watered until established after transplanting. And they'll need protection from the sun for a couple of days too. Getting some lettuce started in July will ensure a supply when the tomatoes are at their peak. August sowings will provide fall greens.

Some people grow lettuce as a border to flower beds, or put individual plants in ornamental beds. Well-grown lettuce is certainly attractive, but harvesting it leaves an unsightly gap in the plantings. If space were at a premium, I'd opt for the butterhead variety Tom Thumb, small compact plants that can be grown in window boxes and indoor pots. On the whole, nearly any course of action is better than doing without home-grown lettuce.

That first batch of lettuce to come into the kitchen from our garden is usually Black-Seeded Simpson or Buttercrunch. I strongly recommend setting out started plants as well as seeding directly in the garden. That way you get a real jump on the lettuce season. We're salad lovers, and by May the supermarket greens that had sustained us all winter begin to be a bore. I find myself hanging around the rows of lettuce, anxiously estimating the time for the first harvest. When the day actually arrives, we have a lettuce salad for dinner. Just plain lettuce. (Tom has been known to sprinkle a little sugar on it, a vice he learned from his grandfather.) That satisfies us for a few days, but presently we begin wanting some variety. The first variation on the theme is usually Dutch lettuce.

DUTCH LETTUCE   *Serves 4*

lettuce
4   slices lean bacon
1   teaspoon sugar
¼   cup vinegar
2   hard-boiled eggs,
    chopped
1   sweet onion, sliced

Saute the bacon until it's crisp. Remove it from the skillet and drain it on paper towels. When the fat in the skillet has cooled a bit, add the sugar and vinegar and stir. Tear a medium-sized head of lettuce or an equivalent amount of loose leaf lettuce into bite-sized pieces and put them into a salad bowl. Add the hard-boiled eggs and onion. Heat the dressing to the boiling point and pour it over the salad. Toss lightly. Garnish with crumbled bacon and serve at once.

One cooked dressing that we like on lettuce salads has been in our family for many years. It came to me from my mother, who in turn got it from her cousin Alice.

AL'S COOKED DRESSING

1   teaspoon salt
1   tablespoon flour
1   teaspoon dry
    mustard
1   egg
¾   cup sugar
½   cup vinegar

Mix together the salt, flour, and mustard. Beat the egg well, add the sugar to it, and beat again. Add the salt-flour-mustard mixture and combine thoroughly. Slowly stir in the vinegar. Cook over moderate heat until thick, stirring constantly. If the consistency is too heavy for your taste, thin it with a little vinegar or water. Cool. Store leftover dressing in the refrigerator.

A second dressing we like came from a college friend's mother. It's simple and quickly made, but for some reason I don't have much success with it if I double the recipe. That's okay; it makes enough for a tossed salad for four to six people.

QUICK COOKED DRESSING

1 **egg**	Beat the egg well. Beat the sugar into it. Add the
3 **tablespoons sugar**	vinegar and the salt and pepper. Just a dash of them will
2 **tablespoons**	be plenty. Combine the ingredients thoroughly and cook
vinegar	them over moderate heat, stirring constantly, until thick
salt and pepper to taste	and smooth. This is another one you can thin down a bit
	if you prefer.

Radishes

Radishes are so easy to grow and reach edible size so quickly that they're often suggested as a vegetable for children to plant. I confess I've never had any mature as quickly as all the seed packets and gardening books tell me they should. Maybe you have. A little more than a month is the fastest we've managed. What we have fairly good luck with is keeping them coming all season long, right up to the middle of November in our climate. Our climate is, in many ways, rotten for an avid gardener, but cool-weather crops do well. Hot, dry weather is the enemy of radishes as well as lettuce. I admit I don't know whether the later crops come faster or slower than the spring-sown ones. I tend to lose track, come midsummer. As far as we're concerned, the important thing is to remember to keep planting them, in small numbers but often.

Radishes don't need much space, either. You can plant them about an inch apart in rows a foot apart. No thinning that way, and germination is reliable with radishes. We like the red ones better than the white ones, which I've quit growing. I suspect it's a matter of aesthetics. We've grown wonderfully crisp, sweet white ones, but they just don't look like radishes. The red or red-and-white ones are prettier.

I don't do anything to radishes in the kitchen except clean them and put them, sliced, into tossed salads or, whole, on relish trays. Sorry about that. No exotic dips, not even butter. No radish roses, either. Salt, usually, is their only adornment. This approach doubtless results from a failure of imagination.

Spinach

Talk about busy. This is the time to get the spinach planted too. In my experience, spinach is a fussy crop to grow. It likes cool weather, and we generally have plenty of that, heaven knows. But to produce an impressive harvest, it needs a lot of other conditions, too. Some years we get poor results. I always plant it, though, because I like it so much. When I was a child I actually liked canned spinach. That's devotion. You can imagine my reaction to fresh, tender spinach in a salad, or a soufflé. It's excellent gently steamed, with a hint of lemon juice dribbled over it or garnished with crisp bacon bits.

But more of that later. Growing spinach well requires a certain amount of attention, in addition to a certain amount of cooperation from the elements.

Spinach bolts, and that's the big problem. It makes lettuce look like an amateur in that art. If temperatures are cold for too long after it germinates, spinach bolts. If daytime temperatures are too warm, spinach bolts. When long days arrive, it bolts. If it doesn't grow fast—and that means fertile soil—it bolts. With spinach, timing is certainly important, but the vagaries of weather can play a crucial role in the gardener's results too. From the point of view of the spinach, of course, bolting assures its future. Our defeat is its triumph. When I buy seed I always choose whatever variety is currently heralded as least likely to bolt. For all the good it does me.

If you're to have a sporting chance at a good spinach crop, certain details demand attention. Spinach objects to crowding, and that's one situation over which the gardener has control. Some authorities suggest five-inch spacing; others suggest ten-inches between plants. The latter, under ideal growing conditions, is much to be preferred because it produces big, handsome plants whose outer leaves can be harvested. With any luck at all, it will produce a lot more before the season ends than the other method. Closer spacing usually means removal of the entire plant for harvesting.

There's more than timing and spacing, though, in producing good spinach. A lush crop demands fertile soil, heavy on the nitrogen. Spinach is less tolerant of acid soils than many other vegetables too. It's one of the crops often recommended not only for spring but also for late summer and fall planting. A late-July or early-August sowing is suggested for a fall crop. Seed sown in September or October is intended to produce an extra-early crop the following spring, a technique often used by commercial growers. Summer sowings germinate faster, but at lower percentages than spring ones, so take that into account when sowing seed. I'm afraid I've never had much luck with the summer sowings. I don't honestly know if that's a result of our climate, the cussedness of spinach, or my increasingly slap-dash methods as the summer progresses and harvesting, processing, and other chores begin to demand so much time that cultural procedures get short shrift. At any rate, by then so many of the garden vegetables are ready to eat that I can't get too agitated about my troubles with spinach.

Even when the spinach crop is less than spectacular, there's always enough for some splendid salads. We like a spinach salad with sweet onion rings and sliced fresh mushrooms, tossed with Italian dressing. My favorite for the purpose uses one part red wine vinegar to two parts olive oil, a dash of lemon juice, a generous grating of pepper, and some mashed garlic. Some people prefer to marinate a peeled clove of garlic in the dressing and discard it before serving. That's too subtle for our tastes.

Another salad we like is tossed with French dressing, either the classic or tomato-y kind.

SPINACH SALAD *Serves 4*

1 **pound spinach**
3 **oranges**
1 **sweet onion**
French dressing

Tear the washed and dried spinach into bite-sized pieces. Peel the oranges and slice them thinly. Slice the onion thinly and separate the slices into rings. Toss lightly with French dressing. Be a little stingy with the dressing because of the juice in the oranges.

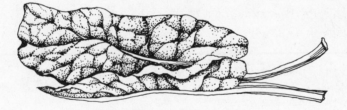

I'm still willing, theoretically, to eat canned spinach, but there's no question that fresh or frozen is prettier, and tastier. It's hard to beat fresh spinach gently steamed. The water still clinging to the leaves after you've washed them is plenty for the purpose, if you're careful to use moderate heat. Four or five minutes is all the time it takes, provided the vegetable is young and tender. Add salt and pepper to taste and a little butter and lemon juice. Like other greens, spinach shrinks rather alarmingly when cooked. One and a half pounds will make four decent servings. An excellent variation on steamed spinach results from adding a sprinkle of lemon juice and a tablespoon of sour cream per serving at the last minute.

If you're in the mood to do something more elaborate, try the following recipe. It's relatively hefty.

SPINACH WITH TOMATO SAUCE   *Serves 4–6*

1 tablespoon butter
1 tablespoon oil
1 onion, finely
    chopped
1–1½ pounds spinach
1 cup tomato sauce
2 tablespoons
    minced parsley
salt and pepper to taste
4 slices lean bacon,
    sauteed, drained,
    and crumbled
2 hard-boiled eggs,
    chopped
	Melt the butter over moderate heat with the oil. In it, saute the onion until it's soft and golden. Add the spinach, washed, drained, and cut or torn into bite-sized pieces. Cover and cook over low heat just until the spinach is tender, about 4 minutes. Add the tomato sauce, parsley, salt, and pepper. Heat through. Toss lightly with the bacon and eggs and serve at once.

If you have a bumper crop of spinach, it's easy enough to put some in the freezer. Blanch it for a minute and a half, cool quickly, drain, and package.

Peas

Every year I toy with the idea of not bothering with garden peas, and every year I end up planting (literally) pounds of them. They're a nuisance to pick and shell, but there just doesn't seem to be any avoiding them. My family dotes on garden peas and complains bitterly when served store-bought ones. ("We're out of real peas already?") Oh sure, I could ignore their anguish. The fact is that I agree with them, despite the unfortunate circumstance of getting stuck with most of the work. The speed with which the members of my family can disappear or become involved in occupations of great moment whenever there are peas to be picked and shelled is one of the marvels of the age.

Did I say "marvel?" "Little Marvel" is one of the varieties I started out with and still sometimes grow. I'm keen on peas that don't have to be trellised. That's a dreadful mistake, because every pea vine I've ever encountered would be better off if trellised. Trellised peas are easier to pick; they're tidier; they're more productive—peas cry out to be trellised. There are no acceptable substitutes. I know. I've tried them all. Nevertheless, there it is. I don't trellis, and I wind up swearing a lot.

There are many varieties of peas that we like. Tom's favorite is the old standby, Laxton's Progress. I like Burpee's Blue Bantam. Some I ignore because of their size. I've learned to forego Alaska because it's not ready enough earlier to compensate for its shortcomings when compared to other peas. I always plant Wando, too, because its quality is excellent and it's quite heat tolerant. I plant it a couple of weeks after the others to extend the fresh-pea season. I never know when to stop.

Peas can be planted as soon as the ground can be worked in the spring. To increase yields first dust the seeds with a legume innoculant, that black powder which encourages the growth of nitrogen-fixing bacteria on the plant's roots. Plant peas in double rows, with about nine to twelve inches between the rows, the seed covered with an inch of soil. Peas don't mind crowding, so I'm generous with seed. The double row and a little judicious mounding of soil around the plants as they grow make the plants support each other a bit. Not enough, but it's a gesture I make. That extra soil also helps keep the roots cool and prolongs the harvest. A mulch is helpful too, because peas need plenty of moisture to produce a flavorful crop. I've never had any insect problems with peas.

The exact time to pick peas is a matter of preference, but I'd rather err (if at all) on the young side. A little experience among the vines soon makes an expert. You can tell by the feel of a pod in your fingers and by its sheen whether it's at the peak of flavor. A bulgy pod is past its prime and won't hold peas as sweet and tender as the skinnier pods. After all the hassle you've gone through to grow them, you deserve perfection.

The beauty of peas from your own garden is much like that of corn fresh from your own patch, though harder to achieve. Corn has the grace to be fast and easy to pick and husk. But like corn, peas are sweet, and their sugar starts turning to starch once they're picked. That's why fresh ones taste so marvelous raw. We eat great quantities of them that way, but as part of a meal I prefer them cooked. (The boys don't.) The first batch of the season is cooked in milk with a pat of butter and a sprinkle of salt. Not a cream sauce, just plain whole milk. The pot has to be carefully watched or it will boil over or scorch, and you know what a mess that is to clean up. You can, of course, serve the peas creamed, or with tiny carrots (cooked separately and combined for serving). Another pleasant change is adding a sprig of mint during the cooking. Don't overdo the mint; a subtle hint tastes better than a too emphatic dose. One recipe I like takes little effort, but yields a delicately distinctive product.

SPRING PEAS   *Serves 4*

2	**cups shelled peas**
4	**green onions,**
	trimmed
4	**lettuce leaves**
2	**sprigs parsley**
½	**teaspoon salt**
¼	**cup water**
3½	**tablespoons butter**
1	**teaspoon flour**

Combine peas, onions, lettuce, parsley, salt, water, and 2 tablespoons butter in a saucepan. Cover and cook over medium heat about 10 minutes. Watch closely and add a little more water if necessary. Remove the lettuce, onions, and parsley and discard. There should be about 2 or 3 tablespoons of liquid left in the saucepan with the peas. Cream together the flour and 1½ tablespoons butter and add it to the peas. Bring to a boil again and serve.

If you have an abundance of peas, freeze them for less fortunate times. Add them to boiling water and blanch for 1 to 2 minutes, depending on their age and succulence. Chill in cold water, drain, and package. You'll be glad you did. I have a friend who says it's unnecessary to blanch shelled peas for freezing. With my usual eagerness to spare myself work, I tried that method with a small batch one year. We didn't like their taste as well as that of the blanched peas, so I reluctantly abandoned the faster technique.

I wish I could learn to leave well enough alone. Reading invariably gets me into trouble. Forget Alexander Pope and his "A little learning is a dangerous thing." A little is just my speed; it's the drinking deep that gets me into hot water.

Take the snap peas for example. The seed catalogues of 1979 presented them as the horticultural triumph of the century, or maybe it was the decade. They could be used like snow peas, like snap beans, like garden peas. Oh, wondrous plant! They were sweet; they were crisp; they were prolific. I ordered a double packet (cautious, but not *too* cautious) and waited impatiently for planting time. Would spring never come? When it did, I planted the snap peas in a tidy double row.

Snap peas were everything the catalogues said they were; the advertisements hadn't exaggerated. The plants were sturdy and bushy, and they were soon covered with lovely purple blossoms. They would have been worth growing for the flowers alone. Pods soon began to form, and as soon as they were two inches long, we sampled them. They were superb. Snow peas? I'd never bother growing them again. Snap peas were so superior that they were literally incomparable. The batch we stir fried for dinner was excellent. When the next picking reached two inches I forced myself to let them alone; let them grow larger, and we'd see if they remained as crisp, as sweet. They actually improved. Not many made it to the table; they were so good we ate them raw, right there in the garden.

Next, we left some on the vines until the peas were well formed within the pods. Heavens yes, they could be cooked like snap beans. Delicious.

We began to wonder about their qualities as garden peas, so we let some get so large the pods were ready to burst, and then we shelled them. (Mostly, I shelled them.) Their quality equaled that of garden peas.

Finally we tried them at the bursting stage, pods and all. The pods remained crisp, the peas tender and sweet. All of us were sold on snap peas. The next year I'd forego snow peas, and we'd grow quantities of snap peas and garden peas.

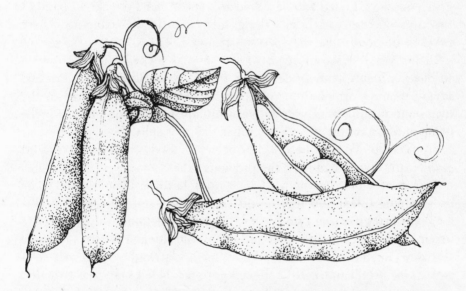

The first indication that something was amiss turned up that fall. Letters started appearing in the columns of the gardening magazines extolling the virtues of snap peas. Recipes were sent in. No wonder; snap peas were a considerable achievement. Two things bothered me: the contributors always mentioned that the snap peas grew very tall on their trellises, and people always mentioned how easy it was to string the pods. That was odd. I hadn't trellised my snap peas. They had been, I thought, 2½ to 3 feet high, and the plants on one side of the double row supported the plants on the other. They sort of leaned to the middle and propped each other up. No problem to pick, that I remembered. I was surprised to hear of peas seven and eight feet tall. My garden is fertile. Why hadn't the snap peas wandered all over it? I hadn't done any stringing of pods either. None of us had noticed any strings. I just snapped the pods off the plant and removed the blossom. Very peculiar.

In the spring of 1980 I ordered half a pound of snap peas. Enough for freezing too, I thought. I planted a long double row. They grew. And grew. And grew. They toppled over each other. They intertwined. They flopped into the aisles between their row and other vegetables growing on either side. They flattened carrots; they clung to onions. Finally they began to bloom. I was eager for the first batch and picked some when they were barely two inches long. Picking them was a nightmare.

But wait! They were just as good as I remembered their being. So what if they had sprawled so untidily? So what if they were a pain to pick? Just a minute. What was that fibrous *thing*? My God, it was a string. Strange. I tried another. And another. After I'd picked a panful I sat down on the grass beside the garden and did the stringing. There could be no doubt that they needed stringing.

The strings on the more mature snap peas picked later were even more prominent. I finally devised a way of stringing that was fast and easy. Snapping off pod between thumb and forefinger nearly to the string and pulling gently downward usually left the pod in hand, the string and cap on the vine. Sometimes the pods split. The pods weren't as pretty as they'd been before the operation. Easy as it was, it was a lot more work than it had been the previous year.

This matter puzzled me for a long time, because I could think of no reasonable explanation for the difference between two crops of the same variety grown in two successive years. Certainly those vines the first year had been healthy; surely I hadn't overlooked the strings. Since that time, new varieties—lower-growing and stringless, or nearly so—have come on the market. I believe I got mislabeled snap peas that first year, perhaps an experimental variety. When I order snap peas now, I buy the shortest vines I can find. Sugar Rae is excellent. At 2½ feet, they're six inches taller than Sugar Ann, but they're much more prolific too. Sugar Daddy is a new stringless variety I want to try. Last summer I grew an experimental one (unnamed) that was dwarfed and stringless.

Snap peas make a good crop, and we enjoy the flavor and texture. With careful preparation, the frozen ones can be nearly as good as fresh ones. Thaw them completely, just barely heat through, and the flavor is superlative.

Actually, strings or no, snap peas are one excellent reason for ignoring garden peas. Yearly I become more impressed with them. They seem to me more prolific than garden peas, but perhaps what's even better is that you eat them pod and all. Instead of having masses of shells for the compost heap or the pigs or whatever, you get the benefit of that extra, delicious food. You can, of course, shell them when they swell to normal pea size within the pod, but why bother when the pods are good too?

We like snap peas raw, very much indeed. When I cook them, I'm careful to be quick about it. Stir frying is a good procedure for them at any stage of their development.

STIR FRIED SNAP PEAS   *Serves 4*

2   tablespoons oil
6   ounces
      mushrooms,
      sliced
1   pound snap peas
salt to taste, about
      ¼ teaspoon
½   teaspoon sugar
2   tablespoons water
	Heat a wok on high heat and add the oil. Heat the oil quickly and then add the mushrooms. Stir fry for 2 minutes. Add the snap peas, salt, sugar, and water. Stir fry for 2 minutes. The water will evaporate. In a pinch, you can use a 4-ounce can of sliced mushrooms or of stems and pieces.

Extra snap peas can be blanched for 3 minutes, cooled in ice water, drained, packaged, and frozen. No, they aren't as good as the fresh ones, but they'll probably beat anything you can buy out of season. I find it, as I mentioned, especially helpful to thaw them thoroughly before cooking them. For our taste, I just barely heat them through. They're fine in the stir-fried method described. Often I simply put the defrosted peas in a heavy saucepan with a generous pat of butter and a little salt and heat them quickly without any additional water. It has to be quick, or they scorch. Or use them as you would snow peas in your favorite Oriental recipies.

Broccoli

An acquaintance of mine had a nasty experience the first time he grew broccoli. He assumed the harvest came after the plant had blossomed. Once the tight green buds open to yellow flowers, of course, that stalk of broccoli has had it. It's the buds that we eat. Remove the stalks that have gone by, to encourage more production.

Broccoli belongs to the cabbage family and is considered by many to be its most elegant member. Similar cultural requirements are demanded by the entire tribe, and similar problems beset them. But unlike cabbages and cauliflower, broccoli continues to produce edible stalks during a long period of time.

A cool-weather crop, broccoli can go into the garden early in the season and will withstand light frost. For the early crop, I set out hardened plants the last week in April. At about the same time I start another flat of seeds in the coldframe. They will grow there until space is freed for them in the garden by the maturing of some other vegetable, peas, perhaps, or spinach, in late June or early July. They'll provide our late crop starting in September.

Where in the garden should the broccoli be planted? Not where it or any other member of the cabbage family grew last year. This precaution will help keep disease and insects at bay. There are several disasters waiting to happen to broccoli, but they can be avoided with a bit of care.

Broccoli is a heavy feeder and dislikes acid soil, so it needs both lime and fertilizer to correct any imbalances or deficiencies in your soil. If cutworms are a problem in your garden, protect the seedlings with cardboard collars pushed an inch into the ground when you plant them. Try to plant seedlings on a cloudy or rainy day—or in the evening—and keep them well watered until they're established. A mulch will help keep the soil moist. Broccoli won't produce a good crop without a plentiful supply of water. The plants get large under proper conditions, so keep them eighteen to twenty-four inches apart. The spaces between the plants can be used to grow lettuce, radishes, or other vegetables that can be harvested before the broccoli needs the room.

A couple of days after the broccoli plants are set out, I put a cupful of dry wood ashes in a circle around the base of each plant to prevent maggots from attacking them. Unless a heavy rain follows the procedure, one application has sufficed for me. The only other pests that have bothered my broccoli are the green worms of cabbage moths, which I control with *Bacillus thuringiensis*, a safe pesticide available under various trade names (Dipel, for example). If you use chemical controls, be careful to follow instructions on the label. *Bacillus thuringiensis* can be used up to the time of harvest and will not harm pets or bees. I have seldom found more than one application necessary. If the worms succeed in denuding a plant, though, that will kill it. Once the buds form the worms don't seem to do them much harm, but the worms do creep into the clusters and match their color so exactly that you should soak the head well before cooking it, to evict the pests. Steamed caterpillars usually offend diners.

Once the central head of broccoli is harvested, the plants will continue to set buds on the branches as long as night temperatures stay below 70° F. If you have the room, you can leave the plants in the garden all summer, and they'll continue to produce or resume production as the nights get cooler. I do a second planting, to give us the big central heads again in late August and September and to ensure a plentiful supply for the freezer. (Canning is inappropriate for broccoli.) The plants will continue producing as long as daytime temperatures stay above freezing.

Fortunately, there are plenty of things you can do with broccoli, starting with raw broccoli. Here again, the thorough washing is a must. If there's anything worse than fishing a cooked worm out of the water in which you've cooked broccoli, it's having a live one poke his head out of the buds after you've dunked it in the clam dip. The same principle applies when you're adding broccoli to a salad.

Broccoli is enjoying a vogue, and small wonder. It's delicous raw or cooked. You can steam it, stir fry it, dip it in a batter and deep-fry it. Don't, for heaven's sake, overcook it. Just barely tender is best, and undercooked beats overcooked by a mile. Once steamed, you can serve it in a cream sauce, with Hollandaise, with a dash of lemon juice, or merely with a pat of butter and a little salt. We're particularly partial to broccoli with cheese. The cheese can be an actual sauce, of course, and that's great eating. I think I prefer it simply dressed with a generous topping of grated cheese. Almost any cheese you like will taste good with broccoli. Our favorites for the purpose are Parmesan, sharp cheddar, and Swiss. Very easy and very good. When I want to call the attention of the family to how much thought I put into meals, I use the following recipe.

BROILED BROCCOLI   *Serves 4*

1½–2 **pounds broccoli**
1 **cup warm cream sauce**
1 **teaspoon grated onion**
½ **cup bread crumbs**
¾ **cup grated sharp cheddar**
butter

Cut the broccoli into manageable pieces and steam it lightly until crisp-tender. Drain. Arrange it in a buttered shallow baking dish, preferably in a single layer. Mix the grated onion into the cream sauce, seasoned to your taste, and pour it evenly over the broccoli. Sprinkle with bread crumbs (whole-wheat bread is especially nice) and cheese. Dot with butter, if desired. Place it under the broiler until it's bubbly and golden. If you're using the oven for cooking another part of the meal, you can skip the broiler part and put the broccoli into the oven until the cheese melts.

Freezing broccoli is a matter of blanching four-inch clusters for about a minute. Remove first any overlong or tough parts of the stalk. Cool in ice water, drain, and package. (Sometimes I don't blanch it at all. The family has yet to distinguish a difference in taste or texture between blanched and unblanched vegetables.) Despite instructions on frozen-food packages from the supermarkets, I like to thaw broccoli (and most other vegetables) before cooking them, if my schedule permits. When cooking, I add just enough water to prevent the broccoli's scorching. Depending on how it's eventually going to be served, I may add a lump of butter, too, and a sprinkle of salt.

Parsley

Snobbery is rampant in horticultural circles. ("You grow forsythia? Really, don't you find it coarse?" or: "Petunias? Aren't they a little vulgar?") But yesterday's cast-off will eventually again become the current darling, as surely as today's rage will soon know its own oblivion. One recourse to this serfdom to botanical fashion is to develop a little tolerance and detachment and to learn some objective facts about what we grow.

Parsley is an example of this tendency to consider certain plants fashionable. Just now, Italian (flat-leaved) parsley is enjoying a vogue and is considered by many gourmets to be vastly superior to the more familiar curled parsley. Both of these are varieties of *Petroselinum crispum*. The Burpee catalogue calls Italian "the preferred parsley in Europe." A third type, Hamburg (*P. crispum tuberosum*), is grown for its root rather than for its leaves.

Fearlessly, I prefer the curled leaf of old to the flat of now, considering it both more attractive and versatile. But full disclosure demands the admission that the flat type has a more pronounced or robust flavor, or at least a different flavor.

Both flat and curly parsley respond to the same cultural practices. Parsley is hardy and can be sown early. It's notoriously slow to germinate. Some experts suggest soaking the seeds before sowing them. I don't. Those small seeds are the very devil to handle after they get wet. Thalassa Cruso's method is splendid: sow the seeds dry, in a shallow trench, and hustle into the kitchen for a kettle of boiling water. Pour it evenly over the seeds; cover them lighly with soil. Her system works. So does planting the seeds and waiting.

Flats of parsley seedlings can be bought in spring, but transplanting them must be done carefully. Parsley develops a long taproot which is fragile when the plant is young. Make sure you don't break it off when you transplant. You can start seeds in the house, but be prepared to spend some time caring for the young seedlings once you move them to the garden. I like to plant them where they'll be undisturbed over the winter.

Parsley is a biennial. That is, it will live over the winter, but during its second season, it will send up a flower stalk. Even though most of the plants' energy will be pumped into seed production that second year, healthy plants will provide you with a steady supply of leaves early in the season. For a sure supply, plant seed every year. New plants will be in production by the time the year-olds become bedraggled. If you plant it in the same place every year, you'll probably get volunteer plants too.

About the beginning of August I put a few seeds in each of two six-or eight-inch pots so that we'll have fresh parsley indoors over the winter. They get put back outdoors in the spring, and with the help of the wintered-over plants out there already, they supply us with fresh parsley until the new crop comes along in June.

Parsley demands a fertile soil and plenty of water. Harvest the outer leaves first, being careful not to damage the growing center. Snap or cut the stems near the base of the plant.

Parsley is rich in calcium, riboflavin, niacin, thiamine, and Vitamins A and C. Its traditional medicinal properties were substantial, ranging from the treatment of insect bites, kidney disorders, and eye ailments to the veterinary care of pond fishes. Today herbalists regard parsley highly as a diuretic and, because it is so high in vitamins, for the pain of arthritis. Most of us are more likely to regard parsley as a culinary necessity, if only an ornamental one. That's a shame, because in addition to its other considerable virtues, parsley works wonders as a breath freshener, even when sent up against such formidable opponents as garlic or onions.

Surplus parsley is easily dried for winter use. Remove the long stems and place the leaves on a baking sheet in a *slow* oven, no more than 250° F., and watch carefully until the drying is complete. It's impossible to give exact time requirements, because too many variables are involved. Parsley can also be frozen, for cooking later. Simply package and freeze. It will retain its color, but will be too limp to use as a garnish. That's why the potted plants on the winter windowsill are so handy.

The healthy parsley plant is handsome, whether in a pot or as part of an ornamental border. Potted plants left outside will need some protection from the midday sun and plenty of water. Indoors, potted parsley does well in a cool, sunny spot or in a light garden. A pair of plants is all we need in winter to supplement the limp but lovely parsley in the freezer and the dried parsley in the pantry.

Getting the early spring garden planted is pleasurable activity. The beginning of a new season finds gardeners eager to get going on that ideal garden imagined during the comparative inactivity of the winter months. With both energy and enthusiasm at peak strength, it's easy to keep abreast of chores. It helps that only a fraction of the garden is planted and demanding attention. The satisfaction of spring gardening can lead to a false sense of security or encourage grandiose plans for the summer garden. Frequently it does both.

CHAPTER 4

Summer's Here

Some of the early garden vegetables will not yet be ready for harvest when you begin planting the summer garden. Indeed, some of the heat-loving plants will have been seeded indoors—by you or your supplier—long before you ever open a row in the outdoor garden. The rationale I offer for the order in which I approach these various plants is simply the time at which they're most likely to be ready for the table and clamoring most vigorously for your attention. I freely admit considerable over-lapping and a certain arbitrary procedure. Broccoli, planted early, will produce all season long under suitable conditions, yet it's possible that the cabbage and cauliflower will be ready for harvest around the same time as broccoli. By staggering planting dates and using different varie-ties, you can harvest cabbage until long after frost. By the same token, beets and carrots and potatoes can be dug or pulled much sooner than late summer. Not only *can* they be dug or pulled, but some of them ought to be, to provide an early treat and to get variety into your menus.

I associate garden produce with their seasons. No matter how many tomatoes we salvage before frost, no matter that with a certain amount of care they may ripen well into December even in our rugged climate, tomatoes evoke images of hot summer days. Pumpkins mean fall and pies and Halloween. And so it goes. Having confessed myself a victim of this mental tyranny, I ask you to imagine a warm, sunny day, after the threat of frost is past. It's time to plant some beans. That means it's time to plant a staggering number of other things too, but let's start with beans.

Beans

Consult any encyclopedia, and you'll learn that the bean is a prolific, easy to grow, adaptable legume that has served as a staple food for humans and cattle from prehistoric times. Any garden book will give directions for growing beans in your backyard—and warn you to take it easy lest you suffer the phenomenon known as "bean glut." That makes it all the more astonishing to read the United States Department of Agriculture's gloomy articles on the more than fifty diseases that attack beans of various kinds in this country and the millions of dollars in losses suffered by farmers each year as a result. Considering everything, we're obviously duty-bound to enjoy every bean we can lay hands on.

Beans belong to the legume family, that large and valuable group that also includes peas, clover, alfalfa, and peanuts, as well as certain ornamental plants. Beans are not only undemanding, but there are so many varieties available that you're bound to find at least one kind that appeals to you.

The beans we're concerned with first are the haricots of French cuisine, beans that are eaten immature, pod and all. Despite the best efforts of plant breeders, home economists, and government bulletins, the haricot is known to most English-speaking peoples as the string bean. The experts would much prefer that we call it the snap bean, or even green bean and wax bean, in recognition of the labors that have genetically removed the "strings" from most popular varieties. Formerly, this objectionable tissue had to be eliminated by the cook (with the aid of generations of despondent children). Some few popular pole beans develop strings as they mature, but for the most part strings are a thing of the past, and we can skip that part of old recipes admonishing us to "Select beans as nearly stringless as possible. Test by gently pulling off tip end."

We'll begin with bush snap beans, the most widely planted in home gardens. This group consists of four different but closely related beans: green, yellow, purple, and wide-podded Italian green beans. From planting to harvesting usually takes seven to nine weeks, depending on variety. Picking them while they're still young and tender not only provides better tasting beans but also more of them. Not allowing the seed to mature encourages the plant to continue blossoming and producing.

Generally, beans are planted about two to three inches apart in one-inch furrows and covered with soil well tamped to encourage germination. If the soil is still too cool, they'll probably rot before germinating, so be careful where you put your first planting. They should go into well-drained soil, because it warms up more quickly than a wet area does. Some catalogues suggest thinning the bean plants when they are two to three inches high to stand five or six inches apart in the rows, but it isn't necessary. Just make sure you leave enough space between rows to allow picking.

Normally beans are sown in two or more successive plantings to ensure that fresh ones come in over the entire summer. Check the length of time the last variety sown takes to reach maturity so that the crop will be ready before the first expected frost in the fall. Some gardeners pull up the plants after their first harvest and use that space for another crop. If you keep the beans picked, however, the plants will bloom again and produce another, though somewhat smaller, crop. I find that method a lot less trouble than making new plantings, but if you choose to pull up plants, be sure to pick all the beans on them, removing even the ones too large to be flavorful. These large, tough pods can be composted, fed to livestock, or strung on a thread and hung to dry as "leather britches" in any airy place. In the winter you take them down and put them to simmer for hours with a hambone and diced onions.

We usually grow all four types of bush beans. The yellow and purple ones are easy to pick because their color contrasts sharply with the foliage. Purple beans are less likely to be bothered by bean beetles (which evidently don't recognize them as edible) and are also more tolerant of cool soils than other varieties. They make a good first planting, especially if you have any doubts about the warmth of the soil. Their pods turn dark green when cooked. Green snap beans seem to be the general favorite even though the yellow ones are more prolific. The flat, wide-podded, Italian green beans are celebrated for their "beany" flavor.

Most catalogues advise sprinkling beans with a legume innoculant before planting them, just as you are advised to dust the peas you planted. You can sprinkle the black powder on dampened seeds before putting them in the ground, or you can sprinkle it on the seeds in the row before covering them with soil. The innoculant's purpose is to encourage the growth of nitrogen-fixing bacteria on the plants' roots. That increases yields and helps enrich the soil as well. Like other legumes, beans take free nitrogen from the air and convert it to a form available in the soil, one reason beans grow well in average soil and help to improve its fertility.

Snap beans are popular with most people. Although during the winter months we rely on canned or frozen ones, when fresh beans are available, there's no reason to settle for less. Eschew the elderly ones and opt for tender, brittle beans that break readily with a *snap*. The size you choose will depend on your taste, but most bean lovers will agree that snap beans are most flavorful before the bean itself is fully formed within the pod. Tiny beans a couple of inches long make a pleasant treat now and then.

Most of the recipes I've chosen can be made with fresh or frozen string beans. Canned beans may be used to good effect in those recipes that don't rely on crispness. So although any vegetable tastes better fresh, these methods needn't be considered solely summer techniques. But during hot weather don't forget that crunchy garden-fresh snap beans are excellent raw, in salads or as a finger food with a dip.

For occasions when you want unadorned snap beans, cut them into pieces the size and shape you prefer and drop them into a little boiling water. For best flavor cook them only until they're barely tender—certainly no more than fifteen minutes, but timing will depend on the size of the pieces as well as the age of the beans. Season to taste with butter and salt and pepper. You can vary the preparation easily by substituting bouillon for the water and salt. To preserve nutrients and flavor, use as little liquid and as short a cooking time as possible. Green beans are appetizing when dressed just before serving with grated cheese—Parmesan, Romano, or sharp cheddar are good choices—or with drained, crumbled bacon. Remember too that string beans are excellent candidates for stir-frying and tempura.

Most snap bean recipes specify green beans, but I'll start with one I developed specifically for wax beans. In fact, I use whatever color beans I have at the time. Green, wax, purple, or Italian can be used in any of these recipes.

SWEET-SOUR WAX BEANS   *Serves 3–4*

1	chicken bouillon cube
¾	pound wax beans, cut up
½	cup water
1½	tablespoons butter
1½	tablespoons flour
2	teaspoon sugar
1	tablespoon vinegar
½	cup water

Dissolve the bouillon cube in ½ cup boiling water, add the beans, and cook until the beans are almost tender and the broth nearly evaporated. Add the butter. Mix the remaining ingredients, stir them into the beans and cook gently until thickened.

Here's a relatively standard recipe with one of its possible variations.

GREEN BEANS WITH BACON   *Serves 4*

1	**pound green beans, cut up**
½	**cup water**
¼	**pound bacon**
1	**onion, diced**

Cook the beans until tender in boiling water. Meanwhile, saute the bacon until it's crisp; drain on paper towels. Saute the diced onions in the fat remaining in the skillet and remove them with a slotted spoon to drain. Drain the beans and toss with the bacon and onions. Salt to taste.

The recipe can be varied easily by adding 2 teaspoons of sugar, 1 tablespoon of vinegar, and ¼ cup water to the bacon fat. Bring the mixture to a boil and pour it over the drained beans. Garnish with the bacon.

The following recipe is festive and colorful. It tends to make family and friends think highly of your character.

GREEN BEANS WITH PIMIENTO   *Serves 4*

1	**pound beans, cut up**
½	**cup water**
6	**slices bacon, fried**
1	**ounce pimientos, cut up**
½	**cup canned French fried onion rings**
½–1	**teaspoon seasoned salt**
½	**cup sour cream**

Cook and drain the beans. Toss with the drained, crumbled bacon, the pimientos, onions, and salt and place in an ovenproof casserole. Spoon the sour cream into the center of the beans and bake at 325° F. for 10 to 15 minutes. (If you aren't using the oven for another part of the meal, you needn't turn it on just for this dish. As an alternative to baking, take the sour cream out of the refrigerator in time to take the chill off it. Place the tossed ingredients in a serving dish. Spoon the sour cream lightly over them and serve.)

During the fresh-bean season, tomatoes will be ripening too. Take advantage of them while you can to prepare this delicious dish. It's Spanish in origin.

GREEN BEANS WITH TOMATOES   *Serves 4*

1   **pound green beans,
     cut up**
1   **teaspoon salt**
½   **cup boiling water**
1   **onion, chopped**
1   **clove garlic,
     minced**
2   **tablespoons
     cooking oil**
4   **medium tomatoes,
     chopped and
     seeded**
1   **tablespoon minced
     parsley**
2   **teaspoons sugar**
freshly ground pepper

Cook the beans in the salted water, covered, until barely tender and drain. Meantime, using a heavy skillet, saute the onion and garlic in the oil until soft but not browned. Stir in the tomatoes, parsley, sugar, and pepper and bring to a boil. Cook, uncovered, until most of the liquid evaporates. Stir the beans into the mixture and cook just until the beans are heated through.

Purists insist that the following dish can be made only with fresh beans. No question that it's superior that way, but we like it well enough to keep it in the repertoire even when I have to use frozen beans.

OLD-FASHIONED GREEN BEANS   *Serves 4*

¼   **pound bacon**
1   **pound green beans,
     cut up**
1   **cup water**
salt and pepper to taste
6   **green onions**
2   **medium-sized
     potatoes,
     preferably new**

Dice and lightly brown the bacon in a heavy pot. Add the beans, water, salt, and pepper. Cook for a few minutes and then add the onion, sliced. Include a few slices of the tops. Pare and dice the potatoes and add them. Cover and cook for half an hour. Whatever you do, don't drain away the liquid. Serve in sauce dishes and provide good crusty bread. Corn breads compliment this hearty concoction well.

The next recipe is one that can, come winter, be made with canned beans. If they're home canned, don't forget that they must be boiled for 15 minutes before using to prevent danger to consumers. There's the reason you must be a little careful in choosing recipes for canned beans-their texture is decidedly soft. This recipe works well with fresh, frozen, or canned beans. It's so good I usually double it to make sure there'll be leftovers to serve cold the next day.

GREEN BEANS WITH HORSERADISH   *Serves 4–6*

1	pound beans, cut up
1	large onion, chopped
¼	pound ham or bacon, chopped
1	cup water
¾	cup mayonnaise
2	hard-cooked eggs, chopped
1	teaspoon Worchestershire sauce

garlic salt to taste
celery salt to taste
onion salt to taste
pepper

1	tablespoon minced parsley
1	tablespoon horseradish
2	tablespoons lemon juice

Cook the beans, onion, and ham or bacon in the water, covered, for at least 30 minutes. While they cook, blend the mayonnaise with the remaining ingredients and leave at room temperature until the beans are ready to serve. (Be sure, in hot weather, to refrigerate mayonnaise and foods dressed with it, immediately after serving.) Drain the beans and put them in a serving dish. Spoon the mayonnaise mixture over them.

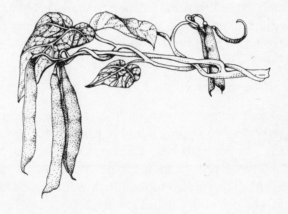

That's just the merest sampling of ways in which to serve snap beans. Freezing is the easiest and generally the most satisfactory way of preserving extras for later use. I prefer doing it in small batches whenever possible. However many beans from a given day's picking don't get used get frozen. I package tiny ones whole and cut the larger ones into pieces about an inch and a half long. I separate the beans from the plants when picking them by using my thumbnail to cut off the stem end. A quick rinse under cold tap water removes the blossom. I gave up tipping them years ago; the tips are entirely edible and removing them is an exercise in aesthetics that I'm willing to forego. Scald beans for 3½ minutes, drain, chill in cold water, drain again, and package.

Once in a while, if freezer space is limited, I can beans. Since they're one of the low-acid vegetables, a pressure canner is essential. Carefully follow the instructions in the booklet that came with your pressure canner. Time for processing vegetables may vary according to the size of the jar as well as with the specific vegetable being preserved.

It's easy to grow too many beans, even if you preserve them for later use by freezing or canning. If you suspect that you've got plenty stashed away and still the beans keep producing, simply stop picking. If you don't need the space for another crop, leave them alone. With just a little cooperation from the weather and some work on your part, you'll have soup beans. When about three-quarters of the foliage has withered, pull up the bean plants and bring them under shelter to finish drying. Shell the beans and store them in a covered container. They must be completely dry, or they'll mold. If you want to be certain to avoid problems, spread them on baking sheets. Place them in an oven that's been turned off after being used for some other purpose. The retained heat is usually sufficient to dry the beans. Another possibility is to store them in the freezer after they're shelled. That's a possibility I'm seldom willing to entertain, because at the time they're ready the freezers are bulging.

Pole Beans

Once you've grown bush snap beans, you may decide it would be interesting to branch out. The choices for such an adventure are awesome. Some snap bean aficionados insist that the bush varieties can't compare to pole beans in flavor. Moreover, some gardeners believe that the vegetable patch looks a little naked without pole beans. There are certain definite advantages to pole beans, even if you're unable to distinguish their taste from bush beans. They're blessedly easy to pick; your back will thank you for the idea. They require less garden space.

Various techniques can be used to give the plants something to climb. Our favorite is a tepee of saplings; they are pushed firmly into the ground, where they describe a rough circle, and at the top they are pulled together and tied with twine. You think it's odd, perhaps, that I fail to trellis peas and yet go to the trouble of growing pole beans. For the most part the garden is my turf. The attention it needs comes, if at all, from me. The rest of the household can be counted on to enjoy the results but generally refrains from becoming involved in any unseemly manner. Hence, for the most part, I feel free to consult my own preferences in selecting varieties to grow. But the fact of the matter is that Bud dotes on pole beans and willingly erects their support.

There's a stand of sumac at the end of our property. He goes out there with a machete and whacks off a batch of them to use for poles.

He even goes so far as to plant the beans, a phenomenon so out of
character that the rest of us stand around to watch. From there on, it's
up to me, but from there on it's simplicity itself.

One year Bud followed the advice of a neighbor who suggested using
a central pole from which four lengths of twine radiated. The twine is
pegged to the ground and serves as the support for the vines. I hated the
method. I believe it took Bud longer than erecting the sapling tepees,
though it's supposed to be an "easy" method. The blasted pegs pulled
out; the twine came loose; the twine broke. Our neighbor routinely uses
the method, successfully. Perhaps we're terminally inept. You can, of
course, grow pole beans on a fence, trellis, or netting as easily as on a
tepee. We're sticking with the tepees from now on. It enhances the
garden visually; it looks business-like and traditional.

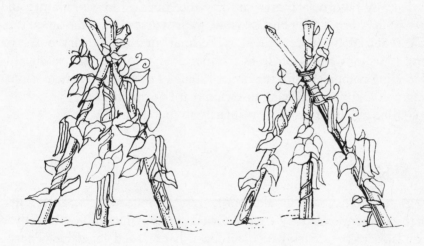

The Indians used their corn plants as bean supports. I tried that too. It
was one of my more disastrous experiments. The resulting tangle made
picking a real chore. Whatever you decide to use, plant three to five
beans at the base of each support, and you're on your way. Pole beans
take a little longer to reach maturity than do bush beans. Count on nine
or ten weeks.

I usually plant marigolds near any kinds of beans. They're said to
deter bean beetles. We don't have any bean beetles (maybe the tiger-
repelling business again), and the marigolds add a pleasant accent to the
vegetable garden. Either reason is a good enough one to plant marigolds.

If we lived in a kinder climate, we'd grow lima beans too. The
planting, care, and feeding of all the varieties of beans are similar, but in
short seasons like ours, attention must be paid to the length of time a
vegetable requires to reach maturity. Enticed by the catalogues, I planted

bush limas year after year. Bush limas take at least ten weeks to produce from seed, and pole limas take two to three weeks longer. Moreover, limas need warm soil to germinate and reliably warm weather to grow well. Occasionally we got an excellent crop; more often it was poor to mediocre. A couple of times we got none at all, so I reluctantly accepted the limitations of my particular garden.

We have had regular success with dwarf horticultural beans. Seedsmen say they can be used like snap beans when they're young, but I don't recommend it. At the green-shell stage, which they reach two to three weeks before bush lima beans, we're willing to accept them as a substitute for limas. At the dry-shell stage they're extremely attractive, mottled red and cream.

Dry shell beans add still another dimension to bean growing. In our garden, my favorite varieties are iffy too; they're slow to mature and slow to dry. From my point of view, their worst fault is the amount of time required to process them. Threshing, or shelling, dry beans by hand is tedious and soon loses its appeal; in addition, the season for processing coincides with the time of some of our most frantic personal activities. Despite a gnawing suspicion that I'm copping out, I've decided to confine our bean growing primarily to snap beans.

Cabbages

"A cooked cabbage should bear no resemblance to a discarded wig." That statement nailed my attention when I found myself blessed with an abundance of the somewhat contempuously regarded vegetable. There's considerably more to cabbage than you might believe if your experience with it has been limited to cole slaw and boiled dinners.

Cabbage belongs to the Brassica, or cole, group of vegetables, which also includes kohlrabi, broccoli, Brussels sprouts, kale, cauliflower, and collards. More distant relatives are radish, turnip, and rutabaga, all of them belonging to the Crucifer plant family along with Chinese cabbage, watercress, mustard, and any number of weeds. Various kinds of cabbage have been in general use since 2000 B.C., making it one of the oldest domesticated vegetables on record. It's descended from a wild plant, *Brassica oleracea*, which is native to Europe.

There are numerous reasons for this long history of use. A lot of cabbage can be grown in a relatively small area. This economical use of space thus guaranteed it a position as an important vegetable for the poor. Its versatility further recommended it; cabbage can be eaten raw or cooked in a great variety of ways. Man discovered early that cabbage can be stored for relatively long periods of time, either pickled as sauerkraut or raw. Either way, it remains an important source of vitamins and minerals. In addition, the crop produces over a long period of time—from early summer in climates such as ours until late in the fall. That's a lot of pluses for one modest vegetable.

Scores of varieties of cabbage are easily available, but they fall into one of five general categories. The conical-headed is the earliest cabbage. Round- and flat-headed types mature later in the season and are better suited for fresh storage. Savoy cabbage is crinkly leaved. Red or purple cabbage spans the season and stores well. Of the five, the conical or Wakefield is least likely to appear in supermarkets because it is rather small and tender, and if left too long in the field it will split. Its flavor is excellent, so it's long been a favorite with home gardeners.

I usually grow four or five varieties of cabbage, started in flats to be put into the garden at appropriate times. If you buy started plants, your choices may be limited. Except possibly for the Wakefield and Red Acre types, I'm not sure I'd recommend cabbage for small gardens though. It takes up space for a long time and good cabbage is relatively easy to come by, simply because most types are sturdy. Unlike broccoli, it can't be harvested repeatedly. Once you cut the head, that's it. A couple of scraggly button heads may grow from the stump, and although they're good eating, they can't be considered a significant return for garden space. Cabbage is a heavy feeder. Growing good heads requires fertile soil and plenty of water. It will not produce well in acid soil. Hot weather may cause the heads to split.

The list of disasters waiting to happen to cabbage in the garden is staggering enough that many gardeners don't want to bother with the plant. Actually, a little foresight will prevent most of the problems. One of the most important precautions is to avoid planting cabbage and its relatives in the same place where they grew the previous year. This procedure will prevent the soil-borne diseases, most notably club root, from destroying the plants. A sprinkling of wood ashes around the plant will deter maggots. Cabbage worms can be controlled with *Bacillus thuringiensis*, the same pesticide used for broccoli and other members of the cabbage family.

If space is no particular problem and you're willing and able to meet cabbage's demands, you can keep a steady supply coming in until after hard frost by planting early, mid-season, and late varieties. In the fall, we cut firm heads of late and red cabbage and put them in an airy place until they "paper." (The outer leaves become dry.) Then we pack them in dry leaves in sturdy boxes and store them in a cold, frost free location. We have fine, fresh heads until early April.

Cabbage gives off a distinct, rank odor when stored in this way, so we use the bulkhead for the purpose. I have heard of people using a cool basement, but one runs the risk of rising fumes suggestive of living on top of a compost heap. We usually make kraut from surplus early cabbage, since it doesn't store well. Stuffed cabbage leaves, which freeze nicely, are still another possibility.

Cole slaw is a standard favorite that lends itself to many variations. Some people insist on shredding the cabbage by hand and then pounding it; I use a food processor or the blender, depending on the effect I'm after. For a coarser effect the food processor is decidedly superior; for grating—whether it's cabbage, carrots, or apples—I prefer the blender. At times I add carrots, apples, raisins, or crushed pineapple to cole slaw, individually or in various combinations. Once in a while I toss in some halved dry roasted peanuts at the last minute. Or add a heaping table-spoon of good picalilli to the dressing for cole slaw to be served to three or four people. Red cabbage makes excellent slaw, alone or in combina-tion with green cabbage. Grated raw cabbage is used in molded gelatin salads by those who like molded gelatin salads. Most of them offend me and the rest of the family.

You doubtless have your own favorite cole slaw recipe. The one I include strikes me as a shredded cabbage salad rather than straight cole slaw, for reasons that I don't really apprehend. It's probably the dressing, but the soaking process has something to do with it too. For this one, I shred the cabbage with a knife, though the food processor would proba-bly serve as well.

CABBAGE SALAD
WITH SOUR CREAM DRESSING

5 cups red or green cabbage, thinly shredded	Soak the shredded cabbage in ice water for an hour. (I don't recommend Savoy for this recipe; any other kind works well.) Drain it thoroughly. Mix the other ingre-dients, pour them over the cabbage, and toss to distribute the sauce evenly. This is a bulky salad.
1 cup sour cream	
1 tablespoon grated horseradish	
4 tablespoons grated Swiss cheese	
½ teaspoon salt	
½ teaspoon pepper	
1 teaspoon dry mustard	

For some reason hot slaw isn't as popular with most people as cole slaw. It makes a nice change. You may use raw or cooked cabbage in preparing it. If you cook it, boil the shredded cabbage in salted water for no more than 5 minutes and drain it before adding the dressing.

HOT SLAW   *Serves 6*

4 slices bacon, diced
2 tablespoons brown sugar
1 tablespoon flour
⅓ cup vinegar
½ cup water
½ teaspoon salt
½ teaspoon pepper
5 cups shredded cabbage
1 small onion, minced

Fry and drain the bacon. Blend the sugar and flour into the slightly cooled drippings. Gradually add the vinegar, water, salt, and pepper and cook until thickened. My measurements for pepper are always approximate, because I use freshly ground, straight from the mill. And I go a little easy on the salt, not minding if those eating my cooking add some at the table. When the dressing has thickened, add it to the cabbage with the onion and bacon and toss thoroughly.

Cooked cabbage needn't be boiled. It should never be overcooked; that way lies a limp and unappetizing vegetable. Frying produces a delicate and delicious result too, as long as you're careful to use moderate heat.

FRIED GREEN CABBAGE   *Serves 6*

1 medium cabbage
¼ cup water
¼ teaspoon caraway seed
1 medium onion, minced
5 scallions, chopped with their tops
4 tablespoons butter
½ teaspoon prepared mustard
½ teaspoon salt
½ teaspoon pepper
1 teaspoon lemon juice
3 tablespoons sour cream

Cut the cabbage in quarters and soak it in salted ice water for 30 minutes. Drain, shred coarsely, and steam it in the water with the caraway seed for 5 minutes. Drain. Fry the onion and scallions in the butter for 1 minute. Stir in the mustard, salt, and pepper. Immediately add the drained cabbage and fry gently for 5 minutes. Add the lemon juice and sour cream, mix quickly and serve.

FRIED RED CABBAGE   Serves 4–6

1	**medium red cabbage, shredded**
1	**medium onion, chopped**
3	**tablespoons bacon fat or butter**
½	**teaspoon salt**
½	**teaspoon pepper**
1	**cup red wine**
2	**apples, diced**
2	**tablespoons brown sugar**
1	**tablespoon cider vinegar**

Shred the cabbage and soak it in ice water for about 30 minutes. Drain. Sauté the onion in the fat until the onion is soft. Add the cabbage, salt, pepper, and wine and simmer for 5 minutes. Add the apples, brown sugar and cider vinegar and simmer for 10 minutes more. All should be tender, not mushy.

Sauerkraut isn't difficult to make, but it involves a certain amount of nuisance and daily attention for a while. The cabbage should be cut finely and uniformly. Pack it firmly into glass jars of whatever size is best for your needs. Add salt at the rate of a rounded teaspoonful to every quart. I use kosher salt. Fill the jar to just above the neck with boiling water and put lids on, but don't seal them. Put the jars on a tray or folded papers because as the cabbage ferments, liquid may overflow. Ideally, the jars should be kept at 70°F. for 10 days, or until bubbles stop forming. Fermentation is then complete. I like to check it daily, because sometimes a film develops on the top. I remove it and check the brine level. Jars can be topped up with a weak brine made of a quart of water and 1½ tablespoons salt. The cabbage should be submerged at all times— some kraut makers put a cheesecloth pad, held in place with toothpicks, tucked into the jar. I don't; any shred of cabbage that rears up over the brine is removed as soon as I discover it.

When it stops fermenting, the kraut is ready to use. At that point I process it, just to be sure. Directions for processing sauerkraut vary somewhat in entirely reputable sources, reaching the same destination by different routes. Consult your favorite canning manual for procedures.

Aside from its more usual appearance with roast pork and mashed potatoes and such, sauerkraut makes a dandy salad. Drain it and save the juice. Mix the juice with ¾ cup sugar and ¼ cup distilled vinegar and bring it to a boil. Take it from the heat as soon as the sugar dissolves and let it cool. Meantime, chop celery and bell peppers and onions and mix them with the drained sauerkraut. Pour the cooled dressing over the salad and refrigerate until you're ready to serve it. One of the beauties of this salad is that it keeps beautifully for days. Theoretically it keeps for two weeks; it's never lasted that long at our house. I especially like to serve it in winter when fresh salad makings are sometimes of questionable quality.

Cauliflower

Before leaving the cabbage family and turning to less demanding vegetables, a defense of cauliflower is in order. Cauliflower has a reputation for being difficult to grow. Actually its requirements are quite similar to those of cabbage, with one important difference. Most cauliflower has to be blanched in order to produce tender white heads. The heads, called the curds, are actually masses of undeveloped flowers. Sound familiar? Well's it's a close relative of broccoli and, in fact, has been crossed with broccoli to produce a new variety that has attracted many staunch advocates. It needs no blanching, and its purple curd (which turns green when cooked) seems to confuse the bugs. It has the same effect on uninitiated diners.

I was surprised to learn that cauliflower has a long, long history. It may have originated in Asia Minor. The Romans grew it, and sometime during the Renaissance it was carried across the Alps and introduced to northern Europe. It was first grown on Long Island during the seventeenth century, a bit of horticultural history that was news to me. I've encountered numerous references about how dull a vegetable cauliflower is, which came as a shock. I'm the only really enthusiastic cauliflower consumer in our family, but I don't think the rest of them consider it dull. ("Yech" and "ugh" maybe, though they're too well-trained to say so, but not "ho-hum.")

Anyway, I haven't grown purple cauliflower—yet. People who should know consider it more reliable than the white varieties. As for the blanching—well, sometimes I do and sometimes I don't. It's a simple process. Just use a rubber band or a twist'em or a piece of twine to gather a couple of leaves together over the developing head. The only problem is that it must be done on a dry day, or the head will rot. Hence, when the weather isn't cooperative, I don't bother. And yes, the unblanched heads are something less than snowy. At least you know when they're ready. If you've tied the leaves, it's a guessing game, which I've been known to lose. Sometimes I forget to check the crop, possibly a symptom of creeping senility. I prefer to think it's a result of having a lot of interests. "Self-blanching" varieties are on the market now, and they'll tempt busy gardeners just as the purple ones do.

Sometimes cauliflower doesn't head, and the entire planting is a washout. Hot nights are the culprits, apparently, so if your area is subject to that condition—and most of the Midwest is—you may decide it's the better part of valor to grow it as a fall crop. You may even decide that it's reputation is justified and elect to forget the whole nasty business and buy some at a roadside market instead. Which is exactly what I do, when calamity strikes my cauliflower.

I'd be loath to do without cauliflower, raw or cooked, in spite of my family's polite indifference. They decline to eat it raw, but many of our guests are as fond of dunking it in dips as I am. And as for cooking it, I manage to sneak it to the dinner table in a number of disguises. Steaming it and serving it with butter satisfies me, but doesn't impress Bud and the boys. They're slightly more receptive (not a whole lot, but I've learned to grasp at straws in certain matters) when I grate generous amounts of sharp cheddar over the buttered cauliflower in its serving bowl. Put enough cheddar on it, and my family will eat nearly any vegetable without complaint. Alternately, I sometimes put freshly cooked cauliflower in a buttered ovenproof dish, dot it with butter, and sprinkle it lavishly with grated Parmesan, Swiss, or cheddar. Heat it as 450°F. until the cheese melts.

Another simple treatment is the following one.

SAUTÉED CAULIFLOWER   *Serves 4–6*

1 **head cauliflower** 2 **tablespoons butter** 2 **tablespoons oil** 1 **clove garlic** ½ **teaspoon nutmeg**	Break the cauliflower into pieces and steam it gently, until it is barely tender. Drain it. Melt the butter with the oil in a skillet over moderate heat. Drop the peeled clove of garlic into it. Sauté the cauliflower briefly, put it in a serving bowl, and sprinkle it with the nutmeg.

Properly accompanied, cauliflower can come to the table as the main dish of an informal meal. Prepare and serve the following recipe in a casserole straight from the oven or in an attractive electric skillet.

CAULIFLOWER AND HAM   *Serves 4*

1	medium head cauliflower
1 or 2	ham slices, ½ inch thick (about 1½ pounds, total)
3	tablespoons butter
½	teaspoon salt
3	tablespoons flour
1½	cups milk
4	slices Swiss cheese
4	thick slices bacon

Break the cauliflower into pieces and steam it until barely tender. Trim any excess fat from the ham and cut it into 4 servings. Sauté it in a skillet greased with ham fat until it is tender and lightly browned. Meanwhile, melt the butter in a saucepan and salt it. Go easy on the salt because the ham and bacon are salty. Remove the saucepan from the heat and blend in the flour and then the milk. Cook over moderate heat until thickened. Put the ham in a casserole and arrange the drained cauliflower on top of it. Pour the cream sauce over all. Place cheese slices on top. In a separate skillet, sauté the bacon until it's almost crisp. Arrange the drained strips on top of the cheese. Bake in a 350°F. oven until the cheese melts and the bacon is crisp. On hot days, or if for any other reason you don't want to use the oven, the whole business can be made in an electric skillet. Sauté the ham and remove any excess fat from the skillet. Then proceed as above. Cover the skillet and cook just until the cheese melts. If you use the skillet method, I think it works best to cook the bacon until it's crisp and drain it on paper towels. Garnish the dish with bacon just before serving. Covered, the bacon may become limp.

Call ordinary creamed cauliflower delicate if you like, but I think it's too bland to be believed. It can be perked up though.

CREAMED CAULIFLOWER   *Serves 4–6*

1	head cauliflower
½	pound mushrooms
3	tablespoons butter
½–1	teaspoon salt
2	tablespoons flour
1	cup milk
½	cup grated cheese (optional)
2	tablespoons minced fresh parsley

Steam the head of cauliflower whole or broken, as you prefer. Meantime, sauté the sliced mushrooms in 1 tablespoon of butter for a few minutes. In a saucepan, melt 2 tablespoons of butter. Salt it and then stir in the flour, off the heat. Add the milk, a little at a time, return it to the heat, and cook it gently until it's thickened. At this point, add the grated cheese, your choice (I usually use cheddar or Swiss). If the last time you served cauliflower you used cheese, I'd skip it this time around. Add the mushrooms to the sauce. Put the steamed cauliflower in a serving dish and pour the sauce over it. Sprinkle it with parsley. Drained, canned mushrooms can be substituted for fresh ones.

Swiss Chard

I mentioned hot days. When summer weather comes, the spinach is finished. All is not lost. There's no denying the desirability of spinach, either raw in salads or prepared as a delicate cooked green. Unfortunately, spinach bolts and is fit for nothing but the compost heap as soon as warm weather comes for good. That's when you'll be glad you planted a row of Swiss chard too.

Swiss chard is closely related to beets, and you'll notice a resemblance in the leaves as well as in the seed. Each "seed" is actually a pod that contains multiple seeds, so sow them thinly, a couple of inches apart. You don't have to be in a hurry to get the seed into the ground, as you do with spinach, because chard is heat tolerant. Generally, sources advise you to plant it on the frost-free date in your area, but I usually sow it about two weeks before that time. Planting earlier doesn't seem to bother the chard, and it's more convenient for me. For one thing, on the frost-free date plenty of other plants are supposed to go into the ground. For another, if planted early, chard is ready by the time the spinach is gone.

Seed packets urge you to make successive sowings of chard, but I think that's a waste of time and space. If you continue harvesting chard throughout the season, it will continue producing. One sowing will last until after repeated hard frosts in the fall. If you lift plants and put them in the cold frame, they'll produce until the ground freezes. With protection for the roots (mulch), plants will often start all over again the next spring.

Mature chard plants need six to eight inches of space each, so start thinning whenever the plants appear to be crowded. By the time they are four or five inches tall, you can begin using them for the table. Eventually, if the soil is fertile, the stalks will grow several inches in length, and the leaves will be a foot or more long. We prefer to use them when they are somewhat smaller than that, because the smaller leaves are milder in flavor and more tender.

We serve chard in three separate ways. The smaller leaves, preferably no more than four or five inches long, are good in tossed salads. Next, we substitute chard for spinach in cooked dishes after the spinach has bolted. Again, you'll be aware of the family ties to beets: the aroma of cooking chard could easily be mistaken for that of its relative. I freeze chard for winter use, blanching it for 1½ minutes. Canning works too, but it's a lot more trouble. And not as good, either. Since I don't bother to label packages, it's anybody's guess when I dive into the freezer whether I'll come up with spinach or chard. They're distinguishable in flavor, of course, but we like them both, hence our impartiality.

Finally, there are the stalks. We use these separately from the leaves in much the same way that one would use cooked celery. Our sons prefer the stalks to the leaves. Braised quickly in a little water or bouillon, they're a fine side dish. Once I mistook a package of sliced stems for celery and used them in a poultry stuffing. Strictly speaking, it was not a disaster, but neither was it a culinary triumph. Some cooks tell you to use the stalks as you would asparagus. They don't mention that it will never be mistaken for asparagus. Chard stems are chard stems, and they're palatable. Asparagus they ain't. There is a red-stemmed variety of Swiss chard, sometimes called rhubarb chard, which is identical in all but color to the white-stemmed kinds. It's pretty and looks something like beet greens. There's that family resemblance again.

From one packet of seed we literally harvest bushels of chard. To keep the plants producing, cut off the outer leaves periodically, even if you don't intend to use them. Some people harvest chard by cutting the entire plant from one to four inches above the ground. It will eventually produce again after that treatment, but it takes a lot longer than if only the outer leaves are removed. That's not surprising; such cavalier treatment tends to alarm a plant. The technique isn't half bad though, if you plan to be away from the garden for a number of days or weeks. It ought to ensure a plentiful supply of greens when you return. And you'll have a big batch to freeze if you attack the entire row.

Like beets, chard is a biennial, so it won't set seed the first year—the very reason it doesn't bolt when hot weather sets in. Chard responds well to a mulch in dry weather. In good soil it grows so luxuriantly that weeds don't stand a chance once it gets going. Insects are no problem either. You may find an occasional leaf that's been nibbled here and there, but no significant damage. Like the other greens, it demands nitrogen in the soil. If the growth of your chard seems slow, feed it.

Swiss chard is a valuable source of Vitamins A and C and iron. It's easier to grow than spinach and is of great use even in small gardens because it produces abundantly over the entire season. I'm not including any specific chard recipes because I use spinach recipes for chard. The major difference between the two is that chard has a sturdier flavor than spinach does. What I really appreciate is its robust growth. Come to think of it, chard may well be one of the reasons that my late-summer planting of spinach has never been successful. I'm just not willing to go to a lot of fuss—not then, not when there are so many delicious garden products ready for use and preserving. Since greens are available, waiting to be harvested, I'm willing to accept them as a spinach substitute, even though they're decidedly second best, especially for salads. Spinach is superb, but let's not be rigid. We have enough problems. The zucchini is maturing.

Zucchini

Zucchini is the only summer squash I grow. That's the result of a conviction that it's the only one worth eating. I've grown crookneck and straightneck and patty pan, and you can have them. Prejudice, I guess, but there it is. One year, seduced again by the ecstatic copy of a seed catalogue, I planted something called "Kuta" squash. This remarkable plant was billed in large type as a "gourmet's delight". When smaller than six inches, the squash are to be eaten raw, in salads and as finger food. Or you can cook them and enjoy their "buttery" flavor. A little bigger, and they're supposed to have the texture of eggplant, and you're advised to prepare them in the ways you'd prepare eggplant. Still larger ones, like winter squash, are recommended for baking or stuffing.

Well, you can have Kuta squash too. Beware any item that does it all. Chances are it doesn't do anything well. Maybe it can be cooked like eggplant, but it certainly doesn't taste like eggplant. It's the same principle as the chard stems, but I didn't realize it until I was up to my knees in Kuta squash. It is indeed a vigorous hybrid, and oh my yes, it's prolific. Fortunately, the neighbors liked it. So did the cows. Not me. I'll take cucumbers for my salads and pickles, zucchini for my summer squash, acorn and butternut and Hubbard for my winter squash. There is no acceptable substitute for eggplant.

And now back to zucchini. Last summer Walt Zalenski, the Chief of Police in our town, warned residents to lock their cars when they parked. He reported that people who had left their vehicles unattended while returning library books or picking up mail had come back to find the back seats of those vehicles piled high with zucchinis. Walt publicly refused to take responsibility for those careless enough to become victims of this cruel joke. For one thing, the number of culprits seemed too large for ordinary control procedures to be effective.

All over the country, markets in summer display containers full of zucchinis. In countless small towns (in our area anyway) many of the displays have signs reading "Help yourself."

That kind of abundance may lead the uninitiated to despise zucchini. If you have to give it away, it can't be worth much. Even those who enjoy the taste of the vegetable may feel driven to the wall by the prolific fruiting of this summer squash. Entire cookbooks are devoted to its use. One I've seen contains over 250 recipes for zucchini.

Growing zucchini is no problem whatever. Obviously. They're bush, not vining plants. Sow about four seeds in a group or hill and space the hills three feet apart in rows four feet apart. I mention the dimensions because the plants are big. Nobody except a market gardener needs many hills of zucchini. I usually plant four hills, just in case.

The seed companies advise you to make two sowings of zucchini, one after danger of frost is over and the second eight weeks before the expected date of the first fall frost. They hint darkly that you'll be sorry if you don't take their advice. They mutter about squash borers and other potential castrophes. Well, they're in the business of selling seeds. A vegetable that people routinely give away isn't all that hard to grow, right?

I don't mean you shouldn't take certain precautions. I plant a nasturtium seed and three or four radish seeds in every hill of squash, and that goes for any other cucurbits I plant too. Many years ago I read that this simple measure will help keep insects at bay. It works for me. I see bugs on the plants occasionally, and they're too lively to catch by hand. Sometimes I see their egg clusters on the undersides of leaves. That's easy to cope with. I remove such leaves from the plant and put them in a covered coffee can that I keep in the garden for just such situations. I've never found it necessary to make a second planting.

Most cooks assume that zucchinis must be prepared fresh. While gardens are producing more than can be conveniently used, they think of the long months when anyone yearning for zucchini has to buy it at the supermarket.

There are plenty of ways around this dilemma. For most recipes, zucchini is at its best when picked small, about six inches long. Ah, you say, in some respects that process merely compounds the problem since it prompts the squash plants to produce more and more. Don't forget that the blossoms are tasty fare when dipped in batter and deep fried, and using them will certainly reduce the harvest. Better still, there are a number of ways in which zucchini can be preserved for winter use. Pickles and relishes are one option; just substitute zucchinis for cucumbers. Use them young and don't remove the skins. So that gives you plenty of pickles but still no summer squash in December? Okay, zucchinis may be canned. Indeed, I have a number of elderly jars of zucchini on the shelves in the fruit cellar this very moment. They're on the shelves because canned zucchini is distinctly disappointing to anyone who appreciates a crunchy texture. They're edible, but just barely. It's easy, however, to blanch and freeze summer squash. Before you point out that this produces a soggy mess when it's thawed, let me hasten to recommend a couple of techniques that deal with that problem and provide an appetizing result. No, it's not as good as fresh zucchini, but that's true of any preserved food.

One important consideration is to freeze small, young fruits, no more than eight inches certainly. Six is better. Slice or dice them, blanch for two or three minutes, and cool them rapidly in ice water. Drain well and package. To use the product, remove it from its package and thaw it thoroughly in a colander. Squeeze excess moisture from it with your hands. Then you're all ready to use it in frittatas or to sauté it Italian-style with tomatoes and onions. You can season it to taste and toss it with bread crumbs, wheat germ, or Parmesan cheese or a combination of these coatings. Sauté it in butter or oil over moderate heat either in an iron skillet or a teflon or other non-stick skillet. The method provides an excellent product, not mushy in the least.

Herbs play an important role in producing memorable zucchini dishes. Dill weed, basil, oregano, and mint all find their places in certain recipes, depending on what other ingredients are being used.

Despite their best efforts at keeping up with zucchini, gardeners are bound to overlook one now and again when they're harvesting. They may not even discover it until it's a monster eighteen inches long and six or seven inches in diameter. As a matter or preference, when I find one over eight inches long, I leave it on the vine. When it reaches truly impressive size, it's time to harvest it for stuffing. English friends tell me it then approximates the vegetable *marrow*.

Cut down the middle and scoop out and discard the seeds and soft pulp, leaving a shell. Then stuff it and bake it in a moderate oven until the flesh is tender. You'll have to play it by ear—it will take from 30 to 60 or more minutes at 350°F., depending on your choice of fillings and the quality of the squash. You may precook the shells first if you like, then stuff and bake until all is heated through. The trick is to find a vessel large enough to hold the squash. A preserving kettle with a rack in the bottom will usually do the job. Put 1 inch of water in it and gently steam the zucchini until it's tender. It's going into the oven with a stuffing, and you don't want to overcook it. Among the possibilities for fillings are corned beef hash, chili, Spanish rice, or spaghetti mixed with meat sauce. The latter filling should be generously sprinkled with grated Parmesan or mozzarella. Grated sharp cheddar goes well with Spanish rice or chili.

Smaller, younger zucchini may be stuffed too, for individual servings. In addition to the suggestions for the mammoth ones, a mixture of corn and tomatoes, seasoned with basil and topped with grated cheese is delicious. Alternately, try chopped onion, cooked rice, chopped tomato, parsley, and oregano. Favorite stuffings for green pepper cases lend themselves to use with zucchini. Use your imagination—and whatever you happen to have on hand.

Young, tender zucchinis can be sliced into tossed salads or cut into sticks and added to vegetable platters served with a dip. Either the blossoms torn into largish pieces or the squash sliced into rounds can be dipped in batter and deep fried. In short, there are innumerable ways to serve zucchini.

Zucchini frittata is a kind of omelette, and since it's substantial, it makes a fine luncheon dish. We serve it for supper too, usually accompanied by hot Italian sausages, crusty bread, and a tossed salad.

ZUCCHINI FRITTATA   *Serves 4*

1 **cup diced zucchini**	Blanch the unpeeled zucchini in boiling, salted water
2 **tablespoons bread**	for 2 minutes or use thawed, drained frozen zucchini.
crumbs	Drain. Soak the bread crumbs in the milk for a few
3 **tablespoons milk**	minutes. With a fork, blend in the eggs, cheese, lemon
4 **eggs**	rind, sugar, and salt. Stir in the zucchini. Melt the butter
4 **tablespoons grated**	in a heavy ovenproof skillet until it sizzles. Pour in the
Parmesan cheese	egg mixture and cook over moderate heat for 2 or 3
½ **teaspoon grated**	minutes, until the eggs are firm but still moist. Run the
lemon rind	skillet under a preheated broiler just long enough to
½ **teaspoon sugar**	brown the top. Serve in wedges.
¼ **salt**	
2 **tablespoons butter**	

There's carrot cake and banana bread. It was surely inevitable that someone would come up with zucchini bread. This recipe, given to me by a cousin in Ohio, makes a delightful breakfast bread. We especially like it toasted. The loaves freeze well.

EARLENE'S ZUCCHINI BREAD

2 loaves

3 eggs
1 cup cooking oil
2 teaspoons vanilla
2¼ cups sugar
3 cups flour
1 teaspoon salt
1 teaspoon baking
    powder
1 teaspoon baking
    soda
3 teaspoons
    cinnamon
2 cups peeled
    zucchini, grated
1 cup walnuts,
    chopped
1 cup raisins

Cream together the eggs, oil, vanilla, and sugar. Sift the dry ingredients together and stir them into the creamed mixture alternately with the zucchini. Add the nuts and raisins. Pour into two greased loaf pans and bake them in a 350°F. oven for an hour, or until a tester inserted in the middle of the loaves comes out clean.

After the tomatoes begin ripening, we like to use some of them with zucchini.

ZUCCHINI WITH TOMATOES

Serves 4

2 tablespoons
    cooking oil
4 small zucchini,
    sliced
1 large onion,
    chopped
1 green pepper,
    chopped
1 clove garlic,
    minced
2 medium tomatoes,
    chopped
1 teaspoon salt
freshly ground pepper
½ teaspoon sugar
1 teaspoon fresh or
    ½ teaspoon dried
    basil

1 teaspoon fresh or
    ½ teaspoon dried
    oregano
grated Parmesan cheese,
    optional

Heat the oil over moderate heat and add the zucchini, onions, pepper, and garlic. Sauté until lightly browned. Add the tomatoes, salt, pepper, sugar, basil, and oregano and cook gently until the liquid from the tomatoes has almost evaporated. Serve immediately, sprinkled with grated Parmesan, if desired.

Zucchini with tomatoes is robust fare. For times when you prefer something more delicate, try this one.

ZUCCHINI IN SOUR CREAM   *Serves 4*

3–4 tablespoons butter
  6 minced scallions
  4 small zucchini, sliced
  1 teaspoon salt
freshly ground pepper
  ½ cup sour cream
  2 teaspoons fresh chopped dill weed or 1 teaspoon dried dill weed

Melt the butter and cook the scallions in it for 2 minutes. Add the zucchini, salt, and pepper and cook, covered, over low heat until just tender. Pour the sour cream over the vegetables, heat through, and serve garnished with the dill weed. This one cries out both for fresh zucchini and fresh dill weed.

The following is our favorite example of stuffed young zucchini.

STUFFED ZUCCHINI   *Serves 4*

  4 zucchini
  1 medium onion, chopped
  2 tablespoons butter
  1 medium tomato, chopped
  1 cup shredded cheddar
  4 slices drained crisp bacon
  1 teaspoon salt
freshly ground pepper

Cut the zucchini in half lengthwise and scoop out the centers carefully. Chop the pulp and sauté it and the onions in the butter until they're soft. Dump them into a bowl and combine with the tomato, cheese, crumbled bacon, salt, and pepper. Pack the mixture into the zucchini shells. Bake at 350° F. for 30 minutes.

Few vegetables, other than greens, are lower in calories than zucchini. That particular virtue all but disappears when they're cooked in these suggested ways. Remember that raw they're a great snacking food. They contain a fair amount of Vitamins A and C and calcium. Probably zucchini's greatest appeal, though, is the great variety of ways in which it can be served.

Cucumbers

Since we're talking about cucurbits anyway, this is as good a time as any to consider cucumbers. The Roman Emperor Tiberius was so fond of cucumbers that he ordered his gardeners to devise methods of growing them out of season. Things being the way they were in ancient Rome, the gardeners started to work instantly on the project, their enthusiasm and industry considerably enhanced by the suspicion that failure was not compatible with maintaining their health. Their method: growing the vines under glass in large pots filled with decomposing manure. The pots were brought indoors at night. Even now, having fresh cucumbers out of season is an expensive proposition, demanding either facilities (such as greenhouses) unavailable to many or the means to pay premium prices. Later on, someone got the bright idea of preserving cucumbers in vinegar, and practically anybody who wanted to could enjoy them during the winter.

Even back in the time of the Roman Empire, cucumbers were no novelty. They'd been a popular vegetable for about two thousand years, having been grown in the "Cradle of Civilization," Babylonia, in ancient times. That makes them at least four thousand years old as a cultivated crop. Small wonder that you see so many different kinds available in seed catalogues and on the racks.

Cucumbers are definitely warm-weather vegetables. You don't dare plant them outdoors without protection until at least a week after all danger of frost is past. The seed declines to germinate until after the soil warms up, for one thing. Below 50° F., forget it. They'll be slow to emerge at a 60-70° F. soil temperature, fast at 75-80° F. If you want an early crop in the north, you can buy started plants to put in the garden about the same time as tomatoes. All the cucurbits resent transplanting, so try not to disturb their roots. You can start them yourself indoors four or five weeks before planting time. It's best to use two-inch peat pots, with four or five seeds in each. Thin to the two or three strongest once the plants are growing well. Plant them, pot and all, about three feet apart in rows at least four feet apart. Make sure all of the peat pot is buried so that it doesn't dry out and thereby damage the plants. Cucumbers take up a considerable amount of space, but the average family doesn't need many plants. Like summer squash, they're prolific. To save space, you can trellis them or grow them on a fence. Alternately, you can grow them around the edges of the corn patch and let the vines climb the stalks if they choose to. This saves space and corn too, because growing cucurbits around the corn deters raccoons. Apparently coon feet are sensitive to those prickly leaves.

Cucumbers aren't difficult to grow, but they appreciate a fairly rich soil. Although they need considerable moisture to do well, the soil must be well drained. Most plants start producing about two months after sowing and ought to be picked daily to encourage continued setting of fruit. Yes, you might have some insect problems. Those pesky striped and spotted cucumber beetles can chew the leaves off seedlings as fast as they emerge. Try the radish and nasturtium seeds or dust the leaves with rotenone or your favorite insecticidal product to control them, following the instructions on the label conscientiously.

Cucumbers are most often used raw, in salads, or pickled. And as mentioned, many different varieties are available. Not only are there pickling and slicing types, but also European, Oriental, "burpless," and cucumbers bred for greenhouse forcing.

Despite their popularity, cucumbers have long been known to contain allergins that can cause minor digestive upsets in many people and severe discomfort or nausea in others. Those in the first category, at least, can usually get around the problem by using the hybrid "burpless" cucumbers first developed by Burpee, but now available in several varieties from a number of different seed companies.

Most of us don't want to take up room in our gardens with several varieties of cucumbers. What to do if you want both slicing and pickling cucumbers? Pickling varieties are usually small to medium-sized; slicing ones start at around seven inches (at maturity) and go up—and up. Some of the Oriental varieties will reach two feet in length. You can compromise by getting a medium-sized variety of slicer. Use the smaller, younger ones for pickling, the larger for slicing. If you regularly make a large number of pickles, perhaps a second planting a month after the first one will be in order. You can use space left free by early crops such as lettuce, radishes, and spinach.

I've read about non-culinary uses for cucumbers. Some people believe that eating the seeds will slow down or prevent the development of prostate troubles in men. The juice of cucumbers is used in some cosmetics and soaps. Combined with Irish moss, it is recommended for softening the skin.

Raw cucumbers are one of the vegetables on the "free list" for weight watchers. Cucumbers are low in calories and contain no fat whatsoever. Many of the recipes using cucumbers, however, are high in calories because of the dressings used. We often use slices of crisp cucumber in mixed salads, and we consider cucumbers in sour cream a standard, delicious way of serving them. Sour cream gets quite a workout in our household, in fact. But for a change of pace, we enjoy cucumbers in sweet cream. It's especially refreshing on a hot day. So refreshing that it's sometimes a sadly depleted bowl that's put on the table when the rest of the meal is served.

CUCUMBERS IN CREAM   *Serves 4*

2	cucumbers, sliced very thin
¼	cup sugar
¼	cup distilled vinegar
½	cup light cream

Soak the cucumber slices in salt water for an hour and then squeeze them dry with your hands. Mix the sugar, vinegar, and cream and pour it over the cucumbers. Let stand at room temperature for an hour. No other seasoning is necessary or recommended. Serve in sauce dishes.

Another cucumber salad I make is especially good when served with fish.

SWEET AND SOUR CUCUMBERS   *Serves 4*

2	cucumbers, sliced very thin
½	cup sugar
½	cup distilled vinegar
1	large sweet onion, sliced very thin
	salt and pepper to taste
2	tablespoons chopped parsley

Soak the cucumber slices for an hour in salt water and then squeeze them dry. Mix the sugar and vinegar and pour it over the slices. Add the onion slices, salt and pepper, and parsley. Marinate the salad half an hour at room temperature.

Sometimes cucumbers are served cooked, in a light cream sauce dusted with nutmeg or fresh, chopped dill. Sliced and sautéed in a little oil with grated onion, they serve as a garnish for fish. A light hand is needed, and absolutely perfect, solid cucumbers. You may prefer to cut them in strips and roll them in bread or cracker crumbs before sautéeing them. It's worth a try. On the other hand, you may decide you'd rather make pickles.

Bread-and-butter pickles are simplicity incarnate. Some pickles literally take weeks to make and cure; these are ready the same day you prepare them. This recipe makes a small batch of about four pints. I've doubled it successfully. What you don't want to use immediately can be packed hot into hot, sterilized jars for later use. I have packed thse pickles in old-fashioned jars with rubber rings and never had any spoilage. If you use contemporary canning jars with metal lids, you can check the seals. If the seal is incomplete, re-process or refrigerate for use.

BREAD-AND-BUTTER PICKLES   *4 pints*

12	**medium cucumbers**
1½	**pounds onions**
½	**cup salt**
3	**cups distilled vinegar**
3	**cups sugar**
¼	**cup mustard seed**
2	**teaspoons celery seed**
¼	**teaspoon cayenne pepper**

Slice the cucumbers about ¼ inch thick and put them into a glass or stainless steel bowl. Add the thinly sliced onions and the salt and stir lightly. Let stand at room temperature for 3 hours and drain. Combine the other ingredients and bring them to a boil. Add the vegetables and instantly turn the heat down so the mixture barely simmers for 2 minutes. Cool immediately the amount you want to serve. Pack the rest into hot, sterilized pint jars and seal.

Corn

And now we come to a subject dear to my heart. I hope you have room in your garden for corn. Corn on the cob is one of those things that literally gets better every year. Plant breeders have developed corn varieties that keep their quality for days after picking. Time was when, to get good flavor, corn had to be picked no more than an hour before eating it. Some people went so far as to insist that the kettle should be put on to boil before you went out to pick.

There can be no denying that the fresher corn is, the better it will taste. But the new extra-sweet hybrids don't convert their sugar to starch nearly as quickly as older varieties do. That's a real boon to most consumers. Even people who have kitchen gardens often resist growing corn because other vegetables produce more harvest in less space. If you grow your own corn, the choice of varieties is extensive, because you can pick just before cooking and serving.

Picking corn for our family is a ritual that takes about fifteen minutes.

We walk out to the garden carrying a large cauldron. The minute one of us enters the corn patch to select ears, the horses come running to the fence. They get the husks, any empty stalks (a stalk often produces two ears, but they usually don't ripen the same day), and culls. We normally pick more than we can possibly eat at one meal, but I cook it all anyway. There are plenty of things to do with any leftovers.

Even with the new hybrids, even considering the potential hazards, it's worth growing sweet corn. Certainly it takes a tolerably good soil and a lot of garden space,but the rewards are worth all the efforts. Our major problem has always been with wildlife, though an occasional straying cow has wreaked havoc too. There are ways to ensure that you get to keep the harvest for yourself, which means ways to foil the birds and animals.

Though most scarecrows don't seem particularly effective, their presence in many a garden is a reminder of the earliest of corn's pests. Crows and other birds pull the young sprouts from the ground before they have rooted firmly enough to hold their own. Some people hang metalic noisemakers in their gardens. Mobiles of tin-can tops and pie plates used to be popular and even, after a fashion, attractive. Garden centers and supply houses sell owl models to frighten birds too. Research at agriculture experiment stations continues, in the hopes of preventing bird depredations. I've learned to live with them, maybe because it seems inconsistent to ply them with sunflower and millet on the lawns, but declare war in the garden. Once the corn plants form ears, some gardeners cover each of them with paper bags just before ripening time to discourage birds and squirrels. But these are the minor destroyers of corn crops.

The formidable enemy is the raccoon: smart and fast of foot, a good climber, and often unafraid of humans nearby. They have an uncanny knowledge of when the crop is to ripen and will rarely pick prematurely. Because raccoons have sensitive noses some observers think the creatures know by the smell. To confuse them, says this faction, hang a sweaty, vile, and rank shirt or some socks in the corn patch. Another faction says that human hair hung in bags around the garden will ward coons off. Still others suggest putting the dog out there as harvest time nears, moving the doghouse as close to the corn plants as possible. Technological solutions abound too, from floodlighting the corn patch (which sounds to me like aiding and abetting rather than thwarting) to leaving a portable radio playing all night (for those who have no close neighbors or neighbors who are not likely to be close long thereafter).

Fencing is always possible, but not of the type used to repel most other animals. Since coons can climb (and pick locks, many gardeners swear), the fence must be weak, not strong. A chicken-wire fence, surrounding the patch, is what you want, so wobbly that the twenty-pound coon will not be able to climb it. This so-called "corn-cage" is said to work, but it costs a lot of money and time to put up and take down every year. Leaving it up means that you grow corn on that same land every season, an unwise practice. Electric fence is easier, cheaper, and less effective, and is sure to short out just the night you need it. Trapping the animals and carrying them off to be released in some uninhabited spot is not likely to work either. It's just a signal for other racoons to move in to fill the void left by the emigres.

You will have guessed that we use none of these procedures. Our system is simple, and it works. We surround the corn patch with squash, cucumber, and pumpkin plantings. Any plant of the cucurbit family will do. The leaves of these plants deter the coons, the theory being, as I mentioned before, that their prickliness is offensive to those little coon feet. You will recall that pole beans can be planted amongst the corn too. Corn, a heavy feeder, can use the nitrogen that beans fix in the soil, so this is another possible companion for corn. But as far as I know, no one claims that this Indian practice will prevent coon damage. Our cucurbits planted around the perimeter do that nicely, with only one accompanying disadvantage. The vines grow with abandon and to get through the thicket to harvest the corn is a nuisance. That's a small price to pay for safeguarding the corn.

Especially at the beginning of the season, I'd willingly eat corn every day. Most often, I cook it briefly, using relatively little water. I put about two inches of water in a deep pot, bring it to a rolling boil, and dump in all the corn, usually about two dozen ears. The water, of course, doesn't cover all the ears. I cover and cook for only three or four minutes. Barely heated through, you say? Trust me; it's great eating. I remove the ears with tongs and serve them on a meat platter so that any water clinging to the ears drains into the well. Spread with butter and sprinkled with salt and inevitably accompanied by quantities of sliced tomatoes, our fresh corn on the cob is hard to beat.

What about the leftovers? Purists insist that they're worthless. They're wrong. I use them in a number of ways, to the evident enjoyment of people at our table. Because the corn is cooked so briefly, leftovers can be frozen for later use. Remove the kernels with a sharp knife, package, and freeze. What could be easier? Four ears will yield about a cupful of kernels. When serving the corn later, best results are obtained by thawing it in the package. Reheat, gently, using a little butter and salt to taste. With an oven meal, it's especially effective to heat the thawed corn in an ovenproof dish. Dot the corn with butter, cover, and keep it in the oven only until the corn is heated through. It tastes like summertime all over again.

One other way of preparing corn on the cob deserves special attention. We tend to reserve the method for days when it isn't terribly hot, because it warms up the kitchen considerably. We roast it, in the husk, in a 425°F. oven for 40 minutes. Husking is the worst part—use care or you'll have burned fingers. It's a good idea to put the ears, in a single layer, on baking sheets to prevent bits of silk falling through the oven racks during the roasting process. Served with butter and salt, corn roasted in the husk is ambrosial.

We like corn fritters for the main course at breakfast but they make a nice luncheon dish too. Top them with honey, jam, or your favorite syrup. You may use fresh (raw) corn, but the extra ears leftover from dinner work just as well.

CORN FRITTERS   *Makes 12*

2 egg yolks ½ cup milk 1 tablespoon cooking oil 1 cup flour 1 teaspoon baking powder 1 teaspoon salt 1 cup corn 2 stiffly beaten egg whites	Beat the egg yolks and combine them with the milk and cooking oil. Beat in the flour, baking powder, and salt. Stir in the corn. Fold in the stiffly beaten egg whites. Traditionally fritters are dropped by the tablespoonful into hot, deep fat and fried at 375°F. until brown. We prefer them baked in a non-stick electric skillet that has been sprayed with a non-stick product or lightly oiled. Preheat to 375°F. Drop the batter by the tablespoonful and bake until one side is nicely browned. Flip and bake the other side. No, they don't taste just like deep-fried ones, but they're good. It's one way of avoiding some calories we don't want—so we can splurge on something else.

Another delicious use for fresh or leftover corn is shaved corn. The recipe freezes well.

SHAVED CORN   *Serves 4*

3 **tablespoons butter**	Melt the butter in a skillet and add all the other ingre-
1½ **cups corn**	dients. Cover and simmer for 15 minutes. A mixture of
1 **small minced**	red and green sweet peppers makes the dish look espe-
onion	cially attractive.
¼ **cup milk**	
½ **cup sweet peppers,**	
chopped	
1 **teaspoon salt**	
1 **tablespoon**	
chopped fresh	
parsley	
freshly ground pepper	

Corn pudding is rather hefty for a side dish, but it's so good that I'm willing to go easy on the main course in order to serve it. Ideally, it ought to appear with an otherwise light course, such as broiled trout.

CORN PUDDING   *Serves 4*

2 **cups corn**	Combine all the ingredients except the egg whites. Fold
1 **tablespoon sugar**	the stiffly beaten egg whites into the mixture and place
1 **tablespoon**	in a greased 1½-quart ovenproof casserole. Bake 35
cornstarch	minutes at 350°F.
1 **teaspoon salt**	
3 **beaten egg yolks**	
4 **tablespoons melted**	
butter	
1 **cup milk**	
3 **stiffly beaten egg**	
whites	

Fried corn provides a pleasant change now and then. It's quick and easy to prepare.

FRIED CORN   *Serves 4*

4   slices bacon   Fry the bacon until it's crisp. Drain on paper towels.
2   cups corn   Remove all but 2 tablespoons of fat from the skillet.
1   small onion,   Add the vegetables and sauté until lightly browned.
    chopped   Serve with crumbled bacon on top.
1   green or red sweet
    pepper, chopped

Corn relish is justifiably popular but many cooks don't want to spend time making big batches and canning it. Here's a good, quick relish that can be stored in the refrigerator.

CORN RELISH   *About 3 cups*

¼   cup sugar   Pickling syrup: Combine the ingredients and bring them
¾   teaspoon salt   to a boil. Remove from heat.
¾   teaspoon mustard
    seeds
⅝   cup distilled
    vinegar

2   cups corn   Add second batch of ingredients. Bring to a boil again
½   cup chopped green   and simmer for 3 minutes. Cool. Cover and refrigerate.
    pepper (sweet)
½   cup chopped red
    pepper (sweet)
¼   cup chopped celery
¼   cup chopped onion
1   clove garlic,
    minced

It seems only fitting to finish the corn section with two recipes from Latin America, the birthplace of corn. Both are side dishes to be served with meats, and both are guaranteed to stimulate a jaded appetite. The first is Mexican in origin.

The second dish is from Argentina. It's a modernized version, using a blender to purée the corn.

MIXED VEGETABLES   *Serves 4*

1	tablespoon butter
1	onion, chopped
1	cup corn
1	medium zucchini, sliced
1	small hot pepper, chopped
1	cup tomatoes, chopped
¾	cup green beans, cut up
salt and pepper to taste	

Melt the butter in a flameproof casserole and sauté the onion. Add the remaining ingredients and mix. Bake, uncovered, at 350°F. for 30 minutes. Stir occasionally during the baking period.

PURÉED CORN   *Serves 4–6*

4	cups corn
⅓	cup milk
2	eggs
2	teaspoons paprika
½	teaspoon salt
pepper	
¼	cup butter
½	cup chopped green onions
¼	cup chopped sweet peppers
⅓	cup grated Parmesan cheese

Blend the corn and milk at high speed for 30 seconds. Add the eggs, paprika, salt, and pepper and blend for 15 seconds. Melt the butter in a skillet. Add the onions and peppers and cook gently for a few minutes. Pour in the corn mixture and simmer, uncovered, for about 5 minutes. Stir frequently. Stir in the grated cheese and serve.

Tomatoes

Native, vine-ripened tomatoes play such a prominent role in summer cuisine that even the smallest gardens usually boast at least a couple of plants. They're the backbone of our summer garden because we use them extensively all year-round. We preserve juice, sauce, and whole tomatoes by the dozens of quarts. From the time that the plants are set out in late May or early June, we inspect them daily, trying to will them into early production.

July 10 was a day of special significance in 1981. We picked the first tomato of the summer—five weeks earlier than our first ripe one the previous year. It wasn't an isolated event, either. The harvest increased daily, in abundance. By the end of July, we had enough tomatoes to start canning. That may be no big deal where you live. In western Massachusetts, high in the hills, it's pretty good.

Our family consumes tomatoes and tomato products with an enthusiasm bordering on excess. Discovering some way to have fresh tomatoes early in the summer has long had top priority, and I think we've finally found a way to achieve it. That's probably presumptuous, based as it is on a couple of years' crops, but if you're interested in early tomatoes, you may want to try the method sometime. I certainly intend to continue using the procedure that accomplished such pleasant results. No, it didn't work in 1982, a disastrous gardening year for us. June was cold and wet, July hot and dry. Our first killing frost came on August 22. I wasn't ready for it. I am, in fact, morally opposed to the whole idea of being ready for frost on August 22 or any other day in August. Not everything was killed, fortunately, but weather of that kind has a distinctly discouraging effect on tomatoes—and me.

Anyway, let me continue with the early-tomato business. One winter I read about starting tomato seedlings early and, as they grew, transplanting them to successively larger pots. The idea was to have them as large as possible, with extensive root systems, by the time it was safe to plant them outdoors. The article suggested that early-ripening tomatoes be selected for the treatment.

I selected two types of tomatoes, one a patio-tomato variety called Pixie, the other a medium-sized, early-tomato variety called Earlibell. On February 17 I put several Pixie seeds into a large pot filled with damp vermiculite and placed it on the furnace to germinate. (Good grief, where am I going to put flats now that our antique furnace died and has been replaced by a modern oil burner of commendable efficiency? Progress comes dear.) On February 21 the seeds had sprouted, so I moved the pot to the light garden. On February 25 I started a flat of the variety Earlibell.

About the middle of March, all the tomato seedlings were large enough to need transplanting to individual pots. I started with three-inch pots filled with potting soil. Thereafter, I continued transplanting the seedlings every two or three weeks. On April 29 I made the final move and put the whole batch into two-pound coffee cans (with drainage holes punched in the bottom) filled with compost. By the end of April, the side porch and the breezeway were crowded with plants waiting to go into the garden, and every available container in the house was filled with greenery. Guilt feelings about my expenditures at seed houses and nurseries were so rampant that improvisation with whatever is at hand becomes mandatory. Hence, the coffee cans. There were five Pixies and a dozen Earlibell plants.

Some of the tomato plants began blooming shortly after being transplanted to the coffee cans. On May 26 I planted the potted tomatoes in the garden, prepared to cover them if frost threatened. All seventeen had superb root systems, but a few plants were on the gangly side. These I planted deeper than the others, so that part of their stems and the first set of leaves were buried. I left a slight depression in the soil at the base of each plant to catch water, either rainfall or, alternately, whatever I put on the garden. All the plants were blooming profusely; a couple had begun to set fruit.

During that same week I set out other tomato plants. We drove stakes immediately so that their root systems wouldn't be disturbed later on. All the plants did well, but the individually potted ones had not only the advantage of larger size but also the probably greater one of sustaining less shock because they were in individual pots when the were transplanted to the garden. The entire contents of the pot could be put in the ground without disturbing the roots much—no cutting away and separating each one from the other plants in a flat.

In two weeks' time the experimental group had prospered enough that it became necessary to tie them to their stakes. We watched their progress avidly and in the middle of June were rewarded by seeing the fruits begin to lighten and change color. Their production continued all through August. We were scarcely aware when it began to taper off, because by the beginning of that month the more desirable varieties, such as "Delicious" and "Beefsteak," were producing fruit.

We await the first vine-ripened tomatoes from the backyard eagerly. Getting them a month earlier than usual was well worth the extra time and nuisance invested. I'm an optimist at heart. June is supposed to be unreservedly glorious in New England ("then, *if ever*, come perfect days"—italics mine). So 1982 was crummy; there will be better Junes.

Anyway, our first tomatoes to ripen are served in the simplest possible way so we can enjoy their flavor without any distractions. That means chilled, sliced, and salted. The first batches of cherry tomatoes, in bowls on the kitchen counter, provide us with agreeable snacks.

Once the tomatoes are in full production and our initial enthusiasm has diminished a little, we start embellishing them. Since they're served daily, some variety soon becomes desirable. Though we frequently serve tomatoes in combination with other foods, in the recipes following they are the star attractions.

BLT's are deservedly among the most popular of sandwiches. They provide the inspiration for this delicious salad.

BLT SALAD   *Serves 4*

8	slices bacon
3	slices white bread
1	clove garlic, minced
3	tablespoons salad oil
2	tablespoons distilled vinegar
¼	cup onion, finely chopped
¼	cup mayonnaise
½	teaspoon salt
5	cups crisp lettuce
2	tomatoes, sliced thinly

Cook the bacon until crisp. Drain and crumble. Remove all but 3 tablespoons of fat from the skillet. Cut the bread into cubes and add it and the garlic to the skillet; sauté until crisp. Remove and drain on paper towels. Stir the oil, vinegar, and onion into the skillet, remove from heat and cool. Stir in the mayonnaise and salt. Tear the lettuce into bite-sized pieces and toss with the tomatoes, bread cubes, bacon, and mayonnaise mixture.

Served hot or cold, stuffed tomatoes are tempting main dish salads. Fish or seafood salad, chicken salad, or egg salad make good choices for cold fillings. Occasionally I sprinkle grated cheese (not surprising, considering our depraved appetite for cheese) thickly on top of the salad and run the tomatoes under the broiler until the cheese melts. Bits of leftover meat or fish in a seasoned cream sauce combined with cooked vegetables can be used for stuffings too. The sauce isn't supposed to be the filling, just the binder for the other ingredients. Place the filled tomatoes in a non-stick (or sprayed) baking pan or add just a little water to the pan to prevent their scorching. Bake at 350° F. for 10 or 15 minutes. Eggs can be cooked in tomato cases too, for a satisfying luncheon or a light supper. Garlic bread, Canadian bacon, and a fresh fruit dessert served with them will convince everyone you mean well and set a fine table. No need to advertise that it took just minutes to prepare the meal.

EGGS IN TOMATO SHELLS   *Serves 4*

4 tomatoes, medium
   size
salt, to taste
minced or dried basil
4 large eggs
¼ cup grated Swiss
   cheese
¼ cup dry bread
   crumbs
2 tablespoons melted
   butter

Take a thin slice from the top of each tomato. Scoop out the pulp and drain the tomatoes briefly, upside down. Sprinkle the inside of each one with a little salt and basil. Break an egg into each tomato and salt it to taste. Bake them at 350°F. just as you do other stuffed tomatoes. It may take as long as 35 minutes for the whites to set. Sprinkle them then with the grated cheese, crumbs, and butter. Return them to the oven until the cheese melts, just a couple of minutes. Serve them on crisp greens, to the loud huzzahs of the assembled diners.

A few pasta dishes make use of fresh tomatoes. This one is our summertime favorite.

MACARONI WITH SALAD SAUCE   *Serves 4–6*

4 large tomatoes
½ pound mozzarella
   cheese
1 small can black
   olives, cut up
1 can flaked tuna,
   drained
cooking oil
¼ cup chopped fresh
   basil or 2
   tablespoons dried
   basil
½ cup fresh chopped
   parsley
salt and pepper
½–1 pound elbow
   macaroni

Cut the tomatoes into ½-inch slices. Cut each slice into ½-inch strips. Cut the cheese into ½-inch cubes. Combine tomatoes, cheese, olives, tuna, ½ cup cooking oil, basil, parsley, and salt and pepper to taste. Let stand at room temperature for ½ hour. Cook the macaroni in boiling water to which you've added ½–1 tablespoon each of salt and cooking oil. Drain. Add to the tomato mixture and toss. Serve immediately or at room temperature.

I always use the smaller amount of pasta because I like any pasta dish heavy on the sauce and light on the pasta. If your tastes run in the same direction, I strongly recommend reserving the cheese to dump directly into the pasta as soon as it's drained. The smaller volume of pasta I generally use doesn't melt the mozzarella as much as it ought to if the cheese has already been combined with the other ingredients.

An easy way of preparing fresh tomatoes for a side dish is to cut them into ½-inch slices. Place them on a sprayed baking sheet. Put a generous dollop of sour cream sprinkled with seasoned salt on each slice and slide them under the broiler for a couple of minutes. Watch carefully so they don't burn. Sprinkle with minced parsley and serve immediately.

Stewed tomatoes are standard fare, but this recipe, despite its close relationship, is a cut above the ordinary. It demands plump, fresh tomatoes.

BAKED TOMATOES   *Serves 4–6*

6   tomatoes
4   slices bacon
salt
pepper
  1   finely chopped
       onion
  1   tablespoon brown
       sugar
basil
  1   tablespoon
       cornstarch
       (optional)
buttered cubes of
  bread, probably 1–2
  slices
	Skin the tomatoes. Fry the bacon until it's crisp and drain it on paper towels. Remove all but 1 tablespoon of bacon fat from the skillet. Cut the tomatoes into quarters and add them, the salt, pepper, onion, brown sugar, and basil to the fat remaining in the skillet. Over moderate heat, simmer, but don't allow the tomatoes to become mushy. Mix the cornstarch into the liquid if you'd like it slightly thickened. You may not need it, depending on how watery the tomatoes are. Place the mixture into a baking dish with the crumbled bacon. Cover the top with buttered bread cubes and bake in a 400°F. oven until the cubes brown. You may use fresh basil lavishly. If it's dried, about a teaspoonful, crumbled, will be enough.

The idea of frying tomatoes may not sound appetizing, but this method produces superlative results. Any firm tomato can be used, but I always use green ones. You needn't wait until frost threatens, although we often do. Pick a few large, handsome specimens that have not begun to color. If you use ripe tomatoes, it's essential that they be firm. The ones best for slicing will be a washout in this recipe.

FRIED TOMATOES

Serves 4

4 large, firm
    tomatoes, sliced
    ½ inch thick
2 teaspoons salt
pepper
½ cup flour
4 tablespoons butter
2 tablespoons brown
    sugar,
    approximately
finely chopped parsley,
    optional

Sprinkle the tomato slices with salt and pepper and dip each one in flour, coating both sides well. Melt the butter over moderate heat, preferably in a non-stick skillet. Add the tomato slices and sprinkle them lighly with half the brown sugar. Cook for 5 minutes, turn each slice, and sprinkle with the remaining sugar. You may have to add a little butter to the skillet at this point. Cook for another 3 or 4 minutes. Serve garnished with parsley, if desired.

Towards the end of the tomato season, after jars of sauce, juice, and whole tomatoes have filled the cellar shelves, I make tomato preserves and piccalilli if we're running low.

TOMATO PRESERVES

Makes 6 cups

3 pounds very ripe
    tomatoes
¼ cup lemon juice
1½ teaspoons grated
    lemon rind
½ teaspoon
    cinnamon
½ teaspoon allspice
¼ teaspoon cloves
1 package powdered
    pectin
5½ cups sugar

Peel and chop the tomatoes. Simmer, uncovered, for 10 minutes. Place 3½ cups tomatoes, the lemon juice, rind, spices, and pectin into a very large and heavy saucepan. Bring to a hard boil over high heat. Add the sugar and cook, stirring constantly, until it comes to a hard rolling boil again. Boil 1 minute. Remove from heat. Skim the foam from the top. Ladle into sterilized jars and seal with paraffin. If I have no paraffin on hand, I fill the jars almost to overflowing and seal with canning lids.

This piccallili recipe has been in our family for generations. I never make it until fall, when frost threatens, but include it here with the other tomato recipes for the sake of convenience. Sometimes I've substituted four tablespoons of mixed pickling spices for the spices listed and cider vinegar for the distilled vinegar. Both versions are excellent; use what you have on hand.

PICCALILLI   *5–6 quarts*

1	**gallon green tomatoes, thinly sliced**
6	**large onions**
2	**red sweet peppers**
2	**green sweet peppers**
½	**cup salt**
1½	**cups sugar**
1	**tablespoon mustard seed**
1	**tablespoon celery seed**
1	**tablespoon allspice**
1	**tablespoon peppercorns**
4	**cups distilled vinegar**

Green tomatoes, at the end of the season, come in all shapes and sizes, so measure them as you slice them. Cut the onions into thin slices too. Add the peppers, cut into thin strips. Mix with salt. Let stand overnight and then drain. Add the sugar and spices to the vinegar and boil 5 minutes. Add the vegetables and simmer 15 minutes. Bring to a boil and pack into sterilized jars. Seal at once.

Peppers

Tomatoes always remind me of green peppers for a couple of reasons. They're planted at the same time, outdoors, for one thing. For another, many of them never get to the kitchen at all. Bud doesn't often snack in the garden, but the boys and I do. I usually skip lunch altogether, unless I'm in the garden around midday. Depending on the time of year, the meal might be a handful of snap peas, with raspberries for dessert. Later on, it's likely to consist of nearly bursting cherry tomatoes, which are small enough that the juice is less likely to dribble down my chin—I like to maintain a certain amount of decorum—followed by a nice crisp pepper, a sweet one. I grow both hot and sweet peppers, occasionally a problem to other members of the family, since the plants aren't labeled. Ever since the day that Bob bit into a lovely Hungarian Wax pepper thinking it was a Sweet Banana pepper, the rest of the household has been diffident about chomping anything except bell peppers unless I'm around to point out the safe ones. Poor Bob thought that hot peppers were red, period. The experience left him leery, especially after he learned that even green isn't necessarily sweet.

I start pepper plants from seed because that's the only way to grow all the varieties we like. But there's no denying it's a terrible nuisance. The seed catalogues say you'll need eight or ten weeks to produce plants big enough to set outdoors after danger of frost is over. Maybe an eight-week head start is okay for better gardeners than I am or for gardeners in kinder climates. If I started my peppers in the middle of March or sometime in April, I'd have four-inch specimens to plant the first of June. With luck, they might even bloom before frost killed them. If I want peppers from seed, they have to be planted no later than the end of February. True, often I have to pot them individually before planting out. But we get early peppers.

I mentioned that I grow a variety of peppers. We like them stuffed, so one kind always has to be a nice blocky bell type. One year, a friend gave me a flat of banana peppers, and they were not only good eating but heavy producers. So when "Gypsy," the 1981 All-America Bronze Medal winner, appeared in the catalogues, I decided to try it.

Gypsy was developed from the banana-type peppers and, like them, sets golden-yellow peppers prolifically. At maturity the fruit turns red. Banana peppers are so named because of their shape and color before ripening is complete. Gypsy is heftier than others of its type and makes an excellent frying pepper. We're more impressed with it, however, as a relish tray component. Our sons usually reach first for dark-green peppers, but once they'd sampled Gypsy, they announced a preference for it over the other varieties we usually grow, which include King of the North, California Wonder, Sweet Banana, and Early Pimiento.

One year I tried mulching our pepper plants with black plastic, both to conserve moisture and to warm up the soil. So many good gardeners swear by plastic mulch that periodically I try it. Well, I've tried it three or four times. I always end up determined never to use black plastic again. It's ugly and it's hard to keep in place—and it's ugly. So maybe it's a dandy way to keep down weeds, conserve moisture, and warm up the soil. That last item is crucial in my garden, but I still can't face plastic. (The latest research on black-plastic mulch reports that it is inferior to clear plastic for warming soil. It heats the air around the plants, not the soil.)

Natural mulches I applaud vigorously, whether they be leaves, grass clippings, peat, spoiled hay, or that most glorious mulch of all, compost. The timing of these mulches is crucial, at least in northern gardens. For heat-loving plants, hold off on mulching until summer weather arrives, probably around the end of June. Organic mulches contribute to the tilth and fertility of the soil, which certainly ought to earn them gold stars, even if they don't warm the soil up for you.

Enough of prejudice and evangelism—back to the peppers. Like the other annual plants you grow in your kitchen garden, they appreciate having a different location in successive years. Rotating the vegetables is sensible from numerous points of view. It counters disease and insect problems; it helps prevent the soil from becoming depleted of the nutrients that plants take up in varying amounts according to their specific needs. It keeps you on your toes too. The smaller your garden, the more ingenuity is necessary to plan adequate rotation.

Remember that although fully ripe peppers contain more vitamins than green ones, picking the first peppers as soon as they reach full size will encourage the plants to set more fruit. If your appetite for peppers is as keen as ours, you'll want as many as you can grow. There are plenty of ways to serve them. We like them stuffed with meat. For the purpose, we've used ground chevon, veal, beef, wild boar, and sausage. Each one can be seasoned with appropriate herbs. I usually add minced onion to the meat and top the peppers with a tomato-based sauce, such as marinara sauce. Many cooks use rice as the basis of a pepper stuffing, but I never do. Seasoned meat, period. Another prejudice.

Pepper steak ranks high on our list of preferred foods. This is our favorite version.

PEPPER STEAK   *Serves 4*

2 **pounds top round steak**	Our round steak is cut 1–1½ inches thick. Cut it into strips about 2 or 3 inches long and no wider than ¼ inch.
1½ **tablespoons sherry**	Combine the sherry, soy sauce, cornstarch, and ginger
4 **tablespoons soy sauce**	in a large bowl. Add the beef strips and stir well until each strip is coated with the marinade. Marinate at least
1 **tablespoon cornstarch**	an hour at room temperature. For longer marination, refrigerate the mixture. Cut the peppers into bite-sized
½ **teaspoon ground ginger**	squares, no larger than 1-inch-by-1-inch. Put the oil in a wok over high heat and when both oil and wok are hot,
2 **large green peppers**	add the beef and the marinade. Stir fry until very little
1 **tablespoon cooking oil**	pink shows. Add the peppers and stir fry another minute or 2. Serve with hot rice. We like pepper steak served with snap peas and mushrooms. Either a green salad or fresh fruit makes a nice accompaniment.

I always freeze peppers too, both as halves and pieces diced or sliced. Sweet peppers are no problem. Just remove the seeds and membranes, bag, and put them in the freezer. I don't blanch them. Hot peppers require careful handling. I'd read, of course, that it was necessary to wear gloves of some kind when preparing them. That seemed like excessive caution. After all, we eat the blasted things. What's the big deal about cleaning them? I compromised, cleaned them under running water, then packaged, and froze them. My hands peeled for a week. And hurt. Now, when I handle fresh hot peppers, I wear thin plastic gloves. Evidently cooking retains the fire but removes the caustic. We eat considerable quantities of them without observable difficulties, blisters, and other afflictions. But not raw, not even dried, without cooking.

We were sipping Margaritas and munching hors d'oeuvres before dinner in a Mexican restaurant with some friends one day when a member of our party began nonchalantly nibbling dried jalapeños from a bowl on the table. Despite our startled admiration, the rest of us didn't attempt to emulate her feat. That was a good twenty years ago, and our friend still munches hot peppers. Some people, however, have violent allergic reactions to them. Check, before you serve them to guests.

I keep as many packages of both hot and sweet peppers as freezer space allows. In addition, when the stock of Kiddo's sweet-pepper relish looks puny, I make a batch of that. It's something we like to keep around even though we don't go through pickles and relish very fast.

Kiddo was my maternal grandmother. She got that nickname from me when I was about ten and enamored of Red Skelton and his "mean widdle kid." It was neither intended nor perceived as disrespectful— and it stuck. Grandmother lived with our family and over a period of several months, everybody in the household began calling her Kiddo. She died at 96, still affectionately known as Kiddo.

KIDDO'S SWEET-PEPPER RELISH   *5–6 pints*

1 **large head red cabbage, ground** 3 **large onions, ground** 4 **large red sweet peppers, ground** 4 **large green sweet peppers, ground** ½ **cup salt** 1 **tablespoon celery seed** 1 **tablespoon mustard seed** 5 **cups sugar** 1 **quart distilled vinegar**	Combine all the vegetables in a large vessel, preferably of glass or stainless steel. (You can use enamelware, provided the surface is in immaculate shape—no nicks. I use a punchbowl.) Cover them with water in which you've dissolved the salt. How much water? Just guess. Use a couple of cups of water, and if that doesn't do the trick, add water from the tap. It's more art than science. Anyway, let the whole works stand for 2 hours. Drain thoroughly. Put it back in the container and add the celery seed, the mustard seed, the sugar, and the vinegar. Let it stand, covered, in the cellar or some similarly cool place for 3 days. Give it a stirring occasionally, at least once a day. On the fourth day pack the relish in canning jars. Process them for 10 minutes in a boiling water bath, leaving ¼-inch headspace in each jar, or for 0 minutes in a pressure canner, leaving ½-inch headspace in each jar. (Right, *0* minutes. As soon as 15 pounds pressure is reached, remove the canner from the heat. Let the pressure reduce gradually, all by itself.)

That's it. Kiddo, by the way, never processed her sweet pepper relish. I always do, because basically I'm a coward. Processing doesn't seem to affect the quality of the product. I do it in the hope that it may prevent some catastrophe, such as death.

CHAPTER 5

Summer Delights

In the previous chapter we concentrated on summer vegetables that take up a fair amount of space in the garden. Let's now turn to three herbs that need little room.

Basil

Fresh basil is one of summer's delights. Its aroma when even slightly bruised is sweet and spicy. It enhances the flavor of many foods, most notably tomatoes, but also peas, beans, carrots, and onions. A hint of minced basil does wonders for egg dishes and salad dressings. Great quantities of the herb are indispensable to that incomparable sauce called pesto. Basil is a widely grown member of the mint family. Like many other herbs its traditional uses have included healing, magic, and repelling insects, in addition to flavoring food. In India many people still believe that building a house where basil has flourished will ensure its safety. Italians considered it a "courting" herb.

For culinary purposes, sweet basil *Ocimum basilicum*, is most popular. Other types grown include a dark-leaved ornamental, *O. basilicum* 'Dark Opal'; a lettuce-leaved variety, *O. basilicum crispum*; a lemon-flavored one, *O. basilicum* 'Cirtriodorum'; holy basil, *O. sanctum*; and dwarf basil, *O. basilicum* 'Minimum'.

Basil has a particular affinity for tomatoes, both in the growing and in the eating. Since it's reputed to repel certain pests of tomatoes, I plant it beside them. Whether the absence of bugs in our patch is a result of that practice I don't honestly know, but obviously it does no harm. Basil is easily as tender as tomatoes, so don't plant it until the soil is warm and

109

danger of frost is over. To get a head start on the season, sow a flat of basil about four to six weeks before your frost-free date. Transplant the seedling outdoors when you plant tomatoes. It's so cold sensitive that I always save some seed to sow in a short row outdoors in the garden the first week in June—just in case.

Young basil plants are usually available in garden centers in late spring. A few plants tucked here and there in the garden or perennial borders supply enough for fresh use and preserving for winter for all but the most ardent devotees. If you don't have space to grow basil, you might buy a bunch of the fresh herb at a farmer's market during the summer. That's likely to persuade you to save room for it in the garden next year.

You'll find basil year-round on the grocer's shelves in dried form. It is typically included in the seasonings in tomato-based pasta sauces and in mixes identified as "Italian seasonings." Fresh, minced basil makes a salad of home-grown sliced tomatoes irresistible. Some people use its leaves in tossed salads, and it's an important ingredient in many salad dressings. Its aroma is so pleasant that when I'm in the garden I often visit the basil just to rub its leaves and enjoy the fragrance they release. It's the main reason I decided we'd like pesto. Possibly its violent color causes Bob and Tom to view it with suspicion, but I think it's prejudice more than anything else. Any non-red pasta sauce seem to fill them with dismay.

During the summertime, while basil is plentiful, it's a good idea to preserve some for winter use. The leaves can be picked from the plant and frozen whole, just as you freeze parsley. I prefer to dry it because I tend to lose packets of herbs in the freezer, and at the end of summer space is at a premium anyway. To dry basil, snip off branches of the plant, secure the stems with a rubber band or string tied with a slipknot to tighten as the stems shrink, and hang the cluster upside down in a dry, shady place. Drying time varies with weather conditions, but when the leaves become brittle, strip them from the stems and store them in airtight containers in a cool, dark place. If you've never dried herbs, you'll be surprised at the intensity of the odor when you uncover the jar. It's a potent reminder of summer.

Remember that when you use frozen basil, the amount necessary for a recipe will be about the same as if you were using the fresh herb, adjusting a bit for limpness. One-half to one-third the amount of dried basil can be substituted for fresh basil.

Basil can also be preserved in combination with Parmesan cheese. To make a concentrate, mince the washed and dried leaves of fresh basil very fine and put them in a large bowl. Add grated Parmesan cheese and mix thoroughly. Keep adding the Parmesan until the cheese absorbs all the oil that has been released by mincing the leaves. The resulting product should be as dry as dust. Now sterilize ½-pint jars and their lids. Put a layer of salt and pepper in the bottom of each jar. Spoon the basil-cheese mixture in and pack it to 1/3-inch from the top of the jar. Pour on a ¼-inch layer of olive oil and screw the lid on the jar. Store in the refrigerator. Salt is the preserving agent, not only the salt you put in the bottom of the jar, but also the salt that's in the cheese. This basil concentrate keeps indefinitely in the refrigerator without deteriorating.

This latter method of preservation can actually be considered the first step in making pesto when the fresh herb isn't available. The concentrate can also be added to tomato paste or minestrone.

WINTER PESTO   *½–¾ cup*

½ **cup butter, melted**	Mix the butter, garlic, parsley, and concentrate and
1 **clove garlic,**	serve on hot pasta. Garnish with a sprinkling of the
minced	basil-cheese concentrate if desired.
2 **tablespoons**	
parsley, minced	
1 **heaping tablespoon**	
concentrate	

During the summer months you'll prefer using fresh basil for making pesto. There are at least as many "authentic" recipes for it as there are sources. Each has a slightly different flavor. Many recipes for pesto call for pine nuts; Italian friends tell me that walnuts are an acceptable substitute, so that's what I use. Pine nuts are readily available in some parts of the country; in other areas finding them involves a search. Now we can buy them easily in western Massachusetts, but I'm accustomed to the walnut version. Someday I'll try the pine nuts in pesto; we've become fond of them in other foods.

Any pesto recipe may be made with a mortar and pestle, the traditional method. The result will be a fluffier version than that produced by a blender or food processor. I don't have the patience to do it by hand. All of the recipes described are intended to be used on pasta in a ratio of ½ to ¾ of a cup pesto to a pound of hot, drained pasta. Offhand, that sounds skimpy. Take it from one who usually smothers pasta in sauce that the recommendation is reasonable. Pesto is rich and sturdy. Better to add a bit more after you've sampled than to offend your palate initially by too hefty a serving. You'll discover too that pesto is a useful addition to sauces for fish and meats, to soups and to tomato sauces. Moderation in its use is strongly suggested.

Some cooks like to add bits of butter, at the rate of ¼ cup to a pound of pasta, at the same time they add the pesto. If you try it, use about ¼ cup less pesto. Pesto can be frozen for winter use. Thaw it covered so that the sauce doesn't darken. Slatey-gray pesto is not attractive.

PESTO   *1½–2 cups*

2 cups chopped basil **1** teaspoon salt **½** teaspoon pepper **1** teaspoon minced garlic **2** tablespoons pine nuts **1–1½** cups olive oil **½** cup grated Parmesan cheese	Combine basil, salt, pepper, garlic, nuts, and 1 cup of olive oil in the blender. Blend at high speed until the sauce is smooth, adding more oil if necessary. Transfer the sauce to a bowl and stir in the cheese.

Pesto recipes vary considerably in the proportion of basil leaves to olive oil, in saltiness, and in the amount of garlic specified. Not all call for nuts or cheese. Some include parsley, lemon rind, and anchovies. If a particular recipe doesn't appeal to you, try another with different proportions or ingredients.

Carrots and beans from your garden or local farms are nearly as nice a treat as fresh tomatoes. Basil helps to make them memorable.

BASIL CARROTS   *Serves 4*

2 tablespoons butter **6** medium carrots, thinly sliced **½** teaspoon salt **1** tablespoon chopped basil	Melt the butter in a heavy skillet. Add the carrots, salt and basil and simmer 10 to 20 minutes, until tender.

GREEN BEANS WITH BASIL

Serves 4

3	cups green beans, cut up
½	cup chopped onions
¼	cup chopped celery
1	clove garlic, minced
3	tablespoons melted butter
1	tablespoon basil, minced

Cook the green beans, covered, until almost tender, about 10 minutes. Drain. Sauté the onion, celery, and garlic gently in the butter. Add the beans and basil, toss and serve.

Basil needn't be used by the cupful to be enjoyed. Those lovely big bunches at the market can be sampled discretely, and one of the best ways to start is with sliced tomatoes.

TOMATO SALAD WITH BASIL

Serves 4

4	ripe tomatoes, cut in ¼-inch slices
¼	cup olive oil
1½	tablespoons vinegar, preferably wine vinegar
1	teaspoon salt
	pepper to taste
1	tablespoon minced basil
1	clove minced garlic
2	tablespoons sliced scallions
1	tablespoon minced parsley

Arrange the sliced tomatoes on a platter. Mix the oil, vinegar, salt, pepper, basil, and garlic and pour it over the tomatoes. Sprinkle with scallions and parsley.

If you have the space and inclination to grow basil indoors for winter use, it's best to start plants from seed sown in late summer. Potting an outdoor plant is less likey to be successful. It's a handsome house plant that needs plenty of light. Both indoors and out, keep the flowers pinched off to prolong the usefulness of basil. Like other annuals, once it has set seed it's inclined to languish.

Fennel

So. There are lots of different kinds of basil, only two types of fennel. Two different plants, actually, both called fennel. Both considered "herbs." (Well, some disagreement among herbalists there.) To clarify matters, one is sometimes called "sweet fennel," and the other is sometimes called "Florence fennel" or "finocchio." Wouldn't you know that the one with *dulce* in its Latin name is not the sweet fennel? Oh, boy.

It seems almost inevitable to talk at cross-purposes when discussing fennel. I'll begin with a couple of general similarities and then get down to specifics, ruthlessly segregating these two troublemakers. The fennels (there, that ought to show them) are in the Umbelliferae family, to which some nice straightforward herbs like parsley and dill and caraway, coriander, chervil, anise, and cumin also belong. It is native to the Mediterranean area, where it has a long history of use as food, flavoring, medicine, and aromatic. Interestingly enough, fennel is considered incompatible with a number of other plants. It has a depressing effect on the growth and production of bush beans, tomatoes, kohlrabi, and caraway. On the other hand, some sources report that coriander and wormwood stunt or prevent seed formation in fennel. Companion planting is a complicated matter. Keeping straight which plant benefits which others and what species are likely to be unhappy together could develop into a full-time job. About the time you think you've got the facts nailed down, you'll encounter a contradiction in what you believe is an impeccable source. There is no solution to this problem.

Fennel grows readily from seed in full sun in fertile lime-rich soil.

Now, for the separate qualities of the two fennels. Sweet fennel, *Foeniculum vulgare*, is a biennial that tends to become perennial under favorable conditions. In our area, it will not winter over without protection. The leaves are used in a tea reputed to taste like nutmeg. I couldn't swear to that; I like tea to taste like tea. What we drink daily is made from tea leaves even though the garden overflows with plants from which many people make brews they dote on. A better use, from our point of view, is mincing the leaves and combining them with butter to season fish and vegetable dishes. Leaves and stalks of the herb wrapped around oily fish such as mackerel are believed to make it more easily digestible as well as better flavored. (It is possible that the improvement in flavor convinces diners that the fish is more digestible.) The whole plant dried and powdered is sometimes used around kennels as a flea repellent.

Seeds of sweet fennel have their uses too, as flavorings in sausages, cheeses, and breads. Over both the Christmas and Easter holidays, friends brought us excellent cheeses liberally laced with fennel seeds. The seeds tasted quite peppery to us; with the cheese, they made a happy combination. Many herbalists insist that chewing the seeds will prevent hunger. Our fennel cheese seemed to stimulate appetite rather than diminish it, but then we weren't snacking on seeds alone. Who knows, confirmed munchers may get all the satisfaction from the act of munching. Think thin. Have a handful of seeds.

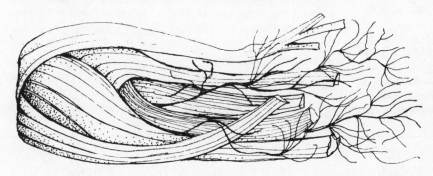

The other fennel, Florence fennel, or finocchio, (*F. vulgare dulce*), is regarded by many as a vegetable. It is shorter in stature than sweet fennel, and its base, the edible part, looks like a bulbous celery plant. Its flavor is similar to celery's, and it is used in much the same way, raw or cooked. The thickened stem is four to six inches across and about six to eight inches long. For cooking, it is usually sliced, discarding the hard core. The leaves can be saved to use in flavoring soups or pasta sauces. One traditional recipe calls for cooking the slices gently with minced garlic in equal parts of butter and olive oil in a covered skillet until tender, about half an hour. Serve it sprinkled with grated Parmesan or Romano cheese. Another recipe is a frittata, more or less an omelette, using the sliced stalks. Try substituting it for zucchini in the frittata recipe given previously.

Florence fennel is often prepared as a salad course, either alone or in combination with a variety of other ingredients. Sliced into thin wedges, it may be dressed with salt and pepper, olive oil, and wine vinegar. For a more elaborate antipasto, serve it along with celery, artichoke hearts, pimientos, hard-cooked eggs, salami, scallions, and ripe olives. Make sure there's an Italian dressing nearby for those who want something to dribble over the concoction.

We tend to regard Florence fennel as a novelty in our household, but I enjoy serving the following recipe occasionally. It's a more elaborate version of the braised fennel served with Parmesan cheese.

FENNEL AU GRATIN   *Serves 4*

2	**large fennels**	
2	**medium onions**	
5	**tablespoons butter**	
2	**tablespoons flour**	
½	**teaspoon salt**	
pepper		
¼	**cup milk**	
2	**tablespoons cream**	
2	**tablespoons dry bread crumbs**	
2	**tablespoons Parmesan cheese**	

Trim the fennel, leaving about 2 inches of stalk above the bulbs. Quarter it. Peel and quarter the onions. Drop both into boiling salted water and cook until tender, about 10 to 15 minutes. Drain. Place the vegetables in a buttered casserole. Melt the butter and add the flour, salt, and pepper. Gradually add the milk and cream and cook over moderate heat until the mixture thickens. Pour the sauce over the fennel and onions. Sprinkle the crumbs over the sauce. Sprinkle the grated cheese over the crumbs. Place the dish under the broiler for a few minutes until the topping is delicately browned.

Fennel has the ancient reputation of being such an all-around cure for whatever ails you—from eye problems to excessive weight, from flatulence to muscular or rheumatic pains—that it seems almost too much to expect that it should also taste good. But it does. It's an herb, or possibly two, that deserve(s) to be better known.

Dill

In the same family, Umbelliferae, and similar looking but a lot easier to get along with, there's dill, *Anethum graveolens*. As I mentioned earlier, I don't even plant it anymore because it self-sows all over the place. Before that wonderfully convenient process got underway, I planted it in short rows near the cabbage plants because I had read that it had a salutary effect on cabbage, and I'm all in favor of salutary effects. Some gardeners sow it near the tomatoes to attract the tomato worm. That may be good for the tomatoes, but it's not so good for the dill. If you try that, better sow some dill in another area too. Some for the worms, some for you. If you intend to use only the heads of the plants when making pickles, get it growing in May. If you use more of the foliage for flavoring, sow it every three weeks or thereabouts to keep a steady supply available. If you allow it to self sow where it will, you'll have a steady supply too, but like me, you may have to go hunting when you want some.

The fact that dill self-sows readily indicates that it needs only a light covering of soil. It germinates in two weeks or a little less at a soil temperature of 60° F. Don't try to transplant dill unless it's still very small and you're willing to coddle it at first. It develops a long taproot quickly and resents being moved to the extent that it frequently declines to cooperate. Dill likes a rich soil and full sun.

All the above-ground parts of dill plants are aromatic. The herb is frequently encountered in the cuisine of Poland, Russia, Hungary, and Scandinavia. I've not found it in Mediterranean cookery. The French sometimes combine dill with anise and fennel. You might want to try a few leaves in sauerkraut or potato salad. It's reputed to make cabbage more digestible, perhaps another example of improved taste provoking unsupported claims. One of our favorite uses is fresh, chopped dill leaves tossed with tiny new buttered whole potatoes just before serving. The dried leaves are sold as "dill weed" and are an acceptable substitute when fresh dill isn't available. I keep a supply of dried dill. Like many other herbs, it's easy to dry by hanging it in an airy, shaded place. To maintain color and flavor, a certain amount of speed must be recommended. If the weather refuses to cooperate, finish the process in a slow oven, about 200°F. Retained heat after a meal will probably do the trick. When it's dry, crumble the leaves and store them either in dark glass containers or put the container itself in a dark place. Cool, dark, and dry are the watchwords in storing herbs if they're to stay fresh and flavorful.

Some herbals say that dill is effective in treating flatulence; others mention that it's a soporific.

You can grow it indoors, but I don't find the process especially rewarding. It's a moderately ugly houseplant, but if you have space and tolerance, fresh winter dill is easy enough to manage. The plants don't last long, so for indoor growing you'll want to start seed every month or so.

Dill weed is particularly appealing in combination with fish. It's marvelous in egg sauce with salmon steaks, but when the budget denies us that pleasure, I use the sauce on turbot.

EGG SAUCE WITH DILL   *Serves 4*

3   tablespoons butter
½   teaspoon salt
3   tablespoons flour
1½   cups milk
4   hard-boiled eggs,
      chopped
1   tablespoon fresh,
      chopped dill
      leaves or 1
      teaspoon dried
      dill weed
freshly ground pepper

Melt the butter in a saucepan and salt it. Remove from heat, stir in the flour. Add the milk a little at a time to make a smooth sauce. Cook over moderate heat until thickened, stirring. Add the chopped eggs and heat through. Add the dill and a grating of pepper and serve over salmon steaks or fish fillets.

Dill simply cannot escape an association with pickles. I use a recipe from Aunt Gertie which is easy and gives me no qualms about spoilage.

GERTIE'S DILL PICKLES   *5–7 quarts*

40   cucumbers, 4–6
      inches long
dill sprigs or heads
garlic cloves
1   quart distilled
      vinegar
3   quarts water
¾   cup salt

Soak the cucumbers overnight in cold water. Next day, dry them and pack them in hot canning jars. Put a dill sprig and a peeled clove of garlic between cucumbers in each jar. Pour over them a boiling brine made of the vinegar, water, and salt. Fill the jars to overflowing and seal immediately. Let them cool and test the seal before storing 6-8 weeks in a cool place to develop flavor.

Gertie insists that the success of this recipe depends on good-tasting water. We're blessed with superb well-water. If you have town water of dubious quality or well water that isn't up to the mark, you might want to buy spring water or get good well water from a friend. I don't worry about spoilage with this method, but if you do, process them for 10 minutes in a boiling water bath or 0 minutes in a pressure canner. If you process them, leave ¼-inch headspace for the water-bath method, ½-inch headspace for the pressure canner. How many quarts—or pints—you get depends on the size and shape of the cucumbers and how you pack them.

And that just about does it for the summer garden. Oh sure, we've been using potatoes, carrots, beets, and celery right along. But not in great quantities and not with quite the same fervor. They'll still be usable in fresh form long after these perishable herbs and vegetables have been preserved.

CHAPTER 6

A Side Trip to Fruits and Berries

And now we venture into another area, that of small fruits and berries. Shall I tell you about me and dwarf fruit trees? Why not. A paraphrase of a well-known quatrain accurately describes my attitude toward them:

> The kiss of the wind for lumbago,
> The stab of the thorn for mirth,
> One is nearer to grief in a garden
> Than anywhere else on earth.

By now I should be inured to failure with fruit, but somehow I can't seem to face it. There are times when I'm convinced that nobody, aside from professional orchardists, has bought more fruit trees than I have. Always dwarf fruit trees. The vast number of books, articles, pamphlets, and catalogues I've studied over the years have assured me of their superiority for the homeowner over standard-sized trees. I believe it. My convictions can be considered a triumph of faith over experience.

We have two standard fruit trees. One, a young and lovely pear, regularly, without any fuss, produces over two bushels of delicious pears. The other, an ancient and enormous apple tree, regularly, without any fuss, produces bushel after bushel of homely apples good for jelly and apple butter and as treats for the horses. Both are visions of loveliness in the spring. Indeed, the venerable apple tree is a beautiful sight at any season. We have, in addition, wild (and fruitful) apple and cherry trees behind the back pasture fence. Then there are the dwarfs.

We have dwarf peach, plum, pear, cherry, apricot, and apple trees in embarrassing profusion. One dwarf apple, apparently planted too deeply, promptly turned into a standard-sized tree and bore quantities of virtually inedible fruit. Needless to say, it also outgrew the space allotted to it and had to be removed. Nevertheless, that particular specimen represented the high point of my gardening experience with dwarf fruit trees.

My personal gardening library contains what ought to be sufficient information to help us produce fruit in excess of our fondest dreams. I have conscientiously applied the recommended procedures and, equally conscientiously, repaired to our many excellent local libraries for additional books when my efforts proved ineffective. I've compared notes with fruit growers, both hobbyists and professionals. I keep abreast of articles in gardening magazines. My other horticultural activities often produce an embarrassment of riches. Not so the dwarf trees. Evidently, despite my best efforts, we are not simpatico.

My one foray into nuts proved just as disappointing as my efforts with dwarf fruit trees have been. I include them in this litany of despair because of their size. It's true that the dogs ate the filberts, or hazelnuts, I planted last spring. Those don't count. They didn't exasperate me; the dogs did. The previous pair of trees, two different varieties so they could cross-pollinate and produce a larger crop, grew beautifully but declined to produce any crop whatever. We have had plum trees cover themselves in such glory in the spring that I had visions of propping the limbs for support in late summer. I should have known better. Those trees were entirely safe from the catastrophe of over-production. One cherry tree produced three fruits last year, but the starlings were quicker than I was to pluck them when they ripened.

It takes me a while to admit defeat, but after fifteen years I'm beginning to feel distinctly quixotic. If at first you don't succeed, maybe you ought to accept it. There's a limit. Having gone the pruning, spraying, fertilizing route once too often, I've decided that those damned imposters are on their own. If they want to masquerade as flowering ornamentals, that's fine. As for jams and jellies and pies—well, thank heaven for berries and rhubarb. And the fruit available from local markets.

The blueberries? Well, they're still young, and I have my fingers crossed. They bloom, meagerly. They produce fruit, meagerly. Tom and the birds eat it as it ripens. I have, but of course, three different varieties to prolong the season. This has turned out to be an amusing— or frustrating, depending on my mood—gesture.

The gooseberries are another story, presumably because our entire family detests gooseberries. The birds can have them. On second thought, it might be better to give them away or simply grub them out and pitch them on the brush pile. The wretched things make my life miserable when I'm tending to other plants in that bed. Each spring dead wood has to be removed, dead wood that is so viciously thorny that removing it makes pruning the rambler roses seem a pleasant frolic by comparison. I can't for the life of me remember why I tolerate the loathsome things.

In all fairness, I must add that our gooseberries are the green ones, and they're supposed to make good jams and pies. I've tried them in a number of guises, and we've never enjoyed them. Even the dogs rejected them. It's not just our berries either, because various friends have shared their gooseberries with us, and they've been uniformly awful. Green ones, that is. Red ones have the reputation of being far sweeter, apparently even edible fresh. I haven't tried them and don't intend to. I'll stick to my prejudices, thank you. Gooseberries are a trial to pick, a tribulation to tip and tail. I don't need them.

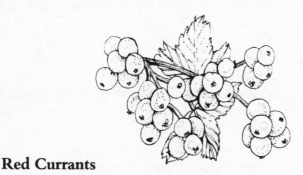

Red Currants

The red currants, bless them, are something else entirely. They look a lot like gooseberries, but they don't attack. Lovely, well-mannered little bushes. Like gooseberries, they'll tolerate a little shade. Especially in the more southerly portions of their range, apparently they actively welcome a little shade. They won't grow well in the deep South or on the western plains but they're extremely resistant to cold weather, some varieties hardy to -40°F.

Here somebody is bound to pipe up and say, yes, but what about white-pine blister rust? Well, let's put it this way. Both gooseberries and currants belong to the family Ribes. Some varieties of Ribes are host to the disease during a part of its life cycle, and the disease is dangerous to white pines. You don't want to endanger white pines, of course. Buy your plants from a reputable nursery. If there are prohibitions against them in your area, the nursery will know. This goes for mail-order nurseries too, which will ask you the name of the county in which you live. If you shouldn't grow them, the nursery won't sell them to you. The whole matter can safely be left in the hands of reputable growers, and those bushes you buy will be free of the disease.

It should be mentioned that there are also black currants and yellow currants. Black ones can't be shipped across state lines. Though they're highly thought of in England, they don't enjoy the good reputation for flavor that the reds and yellows do in this country. The red variety you're apt to encounter is Red Lake, the most widely grown. An older variety, Wilder, is sometimes available too.

There's no need to get agitated about pruning currants. You have the word of someone usually confused by pruning that it's easy with currants. Do it while they're dormant, early in the spring. The canes bear for three or four years. Nine canes per bush is the optimum number. If you prune each year, starting when the bush is four years old, you can keep them producing well, on a third each of one-, two-, and three-year old canes. If you want more bushes, try rooting the cuttings when you prune. Take the end twelve inches and plunge it eight inches into the ground where you want it to grow. Water it and cover it with a glass jar. About half of the cuttings will root and become new bushes.

Another amiable characteristic of red currants is their willingness to grow and produce in either heavy or sandy soil, provided that it is neither excessively acid nor alkaline. The emphasis here is on "excessive"; currants aren't fussy. They appreciate a mulch; they appreciate a shovelful of aged manure. Theoretically, they may be subject to a variety of pests and diseases. Mine have been completely troublefree, and I've grown them for fifteen years in two wildly different gardens. At least part of my success is, I think, attributable to beginning with good stock.

We use the bulk of red currants for jelly, but they're nice in muffins and pies too. My bushes, for reasons that escape me, bear over a long period of time. Ever fearful of a skimpy harvest, I pick them as they ripen and dump plastic bagfuls into the freezer. When the supply reaches a suitable magnitude, I start using them, thawing them first in a colander.

Now for some of their uses:

Currants are one of the fruits containing enough acid and natural pectin that you can make them into jellies without adding pectin-rich fruit or commercial pectin, provided the currants are not all dead ripe. If they are, treat yourself to the easy way out and buy powdered or liquid pectin, following the directions provided with the product for making jelly. Making jelly with commercial pectin is fast, easy, and foolproof, and I do it often. Sometimes, though, I feel constrained to do it "right," without pectin. Don't even ask why; it would probably require years on a couch to fathom my reasons. The one I give myself is that more sugar is required when using commercial pectin.

RED CURRANT JELLY

4 quarts red currants
1 cup water
sugar—¾ cup for each
cup of juice

No need to stem the currants. Place about a pint of them in a large, heavy pot and mash them down with a potato masher. Continue adding currants and mashing. Add the water and cook the currants slowly until they look white. Drain them in a jelly bag. Measure the juice and add sugar at the rate of ¾ of a cup to each cup of juice. It's recommended always that jelly be made in small batches, boiling no more than 4 cups of juice at a time. Use a large pot to cook it in; it's the sworn vocation of jelly to boil over. Cook it to the jelly stage. I don't trust myself to use the time-honored tests. For me the thermometer is indispensible. It should register 216-220° F., depending on the stiffness you prefer in the finished product. (Higher temperatures produce a stiffer jelly.)

Some cooks like to mix red or black raspberries with red currants for jelly. If it appeals to your taste buds, use 1 or 2 parts raspberries to 3 parts currants. With red raspberries you won't want to add water. The black ones, however, are not as moist, so you may want to use a little. Use ¾ cup sugar to 1 cup juice, just as in the preceding recipe. Seal and store these as you do other jellies.

Once in a while we yearn for currant jam, which is simple to make. Since it isn't strained you'll have to stem the currants.

RED CURRANT JAM

3 cups sugar
1½ cups water
1 pound stemmed
    currants

Dissolve the sugar in the water and bring it to a boil. Continue boiling until it reaches 238°F. This is known as the soft-ball stage, for those of you competent and fearless enough to eschew thermometers. Anyway, at that point add the currants. Bring the jam to a boil again and cook for 1 minute. Pour it into prepared glasses, seal, and store.

As for muffins, add a half cup of currants to your favorite recipe for twelve plain, sweet muffins. They'll be attractive to look at, and the currants contribute a piquant taste. Thaw and drain them thoroughly if you're using frozen ones. And use really ripe ones, both for color and full flavor. Anyone mad for currants will like currant pie too.

RED CURRANT PIE   *9 inch*

4 **cups currants,** **stemmed**	Combine all the ingredients except the butter and mound them in a pastry-lined pie pan. Dot with butter and add a vented top crust. Bake at 450°F. for 10 minutes and then reduce the heat to 350°F. and bake until the crust is golden brown, about 25–30 minutes more. I always brush the top crust with milk and sprinkle it with a little sugar, which results in a delicious crunchy crust.

4 **cups currants,**
   stemmed
1 **cup sugar**
2 **tablespoons**
   cornstarch
2 **teaspoons minute**
   tapioca
½–1 **teaspoon**
   cinnamon
1 **tablespoon butter**

As for eating currants fresh—raw, that is—we don't. I've read that they're palatable if well sugared and served with cream, alone or combined with other fruits. I keep forgetting to try the idea.

Red Raspberries

Last summer I encountered a man who doesn't like red raspberries. I was stunned. I'd be the first to admit that red raspberries are close to being decadent, but even so, to spurn them entirely is distinctly peculiar. For my money, no small fruit can equal the flavor of a red raspberry picked from your own patch on a summer day. I'm fond of all fruits, but raspberries are the nonpareil.

The best reason for growing your own red raspberries is that they are so fragile that marketing them is difficult; even finding them in a market often poses a problem. That accounts for their high price. They are such a luxury that having your own patch is certainly worthwhile. Fortunately, their culture is relatively undemanding.

In starting fresh with raspberries you have a choice of red, yellow, purple, and black. Reds and yellows send up suckers; purples and blacks are bushy and propagate when the tops bend over and root where they touch the ground, sending up new plants at the point of contact. Purples and blacks usually bear only one crop per season, although a variety called Black Treasure is everbearing. Purples results from crossing reds and blacks. Yellows are everbearing; reds may be everbearing or single crop, depending on variety. Red raspberries tend to be hardier than black ones.

The patch that supplies us with fresh fruit for months and with jam and frozen berries all year is just that—a patch. It was on the property when we moved here, so my contribution has been its care and feeding, not its establishment. I cherish the illusion that if I were starting from scratch I'd have neat rows. I remove canes that have borne fruit twice and cut paths through the jungle to permit air circulation and make it possible to pick the fruit more easily. The plants get a dressing of wood ashes annually, a feeding of manure, a mulch of leaves, and that's it.

The plants are a red everbearing variety whose name I don't know. Everbearing, with red raspberries, is something of a misnomer. There's one crop here in late June and July and another starting at the end of August and lasting until hard frost. At the beginning and end of each harvesting period, when there are only a few berries, I freeze them immediately. They don't keep well enough to be used fresh after I've accumulated enough for the family, but a couple of days' worth turns out to be a winter's dessert. It's easy to ignore the snide remarks of the family when they catch you freezing half a pint—you know that those half pints will add up and ultimately supply many a pie and shortcake. Certainly not the quality of straight-from-the-bush, but in February they'll be welcome.

Set new red raspberry plants every three feet in rows six feet apart. Suckers will fill in between the plants to make the row continuous. You want no more than four canes to the square foot. It's essential to have good air circulation among the plants to reduce disease problems. Some gardeners believe that the canes produce more berries if they're mulched rather than cultivated. I mulch because it's easier than cultivating, not because I'm convinced we'll get a bigger crop. After a standard red has fruited, the cane dies. Remove it by cutting it off at the base of the plant. Next year's crop will be produced by the young canes which emerged in the spring.

Everbearing red raspberries require slightly different treatment. The canes that come up in the spring will bear their first fruit that fall and another crop the following summer. They die after the second fruiting and can be removed at that time. My first year of caring for our raspberries resulted in little fruit in summer and a bumper fall crop. Not knowing they were everbearers, I ruthlessly cleaned the patch in the fall of every cane I could find that had borne fruit. Then I congratulated myself on having been so thoroughly efficient, not knowing I'd effectively eliminated the source of the next summer's fruit. For us it was an intolerable situation, but some growers follow this procedure by choice and allow the bushes to set only one crop. That simplifies pruning since all are cut after hard frost finishes the crop. This method produces a much larger fall crop than you would get otherwise, because the new canes in the spring aren't competing for nutrients with half-mature ones. What you do depends on whether you want fresh fruit over a long period or the probability of a larger harvest. In our climate, I'm too worried about an early frost wrecking everything, so I cut off canes that look as though they've had it and let the others alone. You'll know soon enough if you've erred.

Both standard raspberries and everbearring canes that are being permitted to fruit twice should be cut back to about four feet in late winter or early spring. You can trellis the canes; I've never found it necessary after they've been cut back. Pruning is less work, and I choose the path of least resistance.

Viruses, blights, and sundry other diseases and insect problems occur with all raspberries. Keeping the patch clear of dead canes and providing proper air circulation by removing excess plants will ordinarily control the situation. Japanese beetles have been the major pest in our patch, but though they damage leaves and annoy us by lighting on the fruit, they can't be considered a major hazard. One year I planted tansy at strategic locations in the patch in an effort to combat the nuisance. One feels obliged to acknowledge Japanese beetles in some way, but I don't notice any significant difference in their numbers.

Red raspberry plants are available in many varieties for about $1.50 to $2 per plant. You can expect a yield of about two pints per plant. The plants multiply quickly, so a modest investment will provide all the plants you want in short order.

We don't grow black raspberries because we prefer the flavor of the red. Because their growth habits are different, pruning is different too. Black raspberries are apt to need support. If I were starting a new planting, I'd opt for the red ones. It's merely a happy coincidence that they're less trouble to care for.

Picking red raspberries is a pleasant job. They grow at such a civilized height that there's no stooping or bending. Their thorns are practically gentle. Not only that, but they signal the stage of perfect ripeness. If the berry readily departs from the stem and core with little tugging, it's just right for eating. If you bump it and it falls to the ground, it was too ripe to be prime quality. If it resists your gentle pull, leave it for tomorrow;

it will be softer and sweeter. Picking can, and should, proceed at a leisurely pace. Take time to admire each cane, and you'll get more berries because you'll see the ones that are partially hidden by leaves. If it's a muggy day, you'll be plagued by mosquitoes, but that's a small price to pay for raspberries. To be outside on such a day is to invite their attention anyway; they're lurking in all the greenery. You will, of course, feel obliged to do some sampling as you pick. You want to be certain the berries are fit for your table.

One of the great advantages of using raspberries is that picking is the only chore necessary beforehand. They're self-stemming so there's no tedious cutting to be done. Cleaning is usually unnecessary because they grow high enough that they don't get splashed. It's a blessing too because the fruit is delicate enough that washing may damage it. This fragility is an excellent reason to pick into small containers, so the weight of the fruit doesn't mash what's beneath it.

Nothing need deter you from enjoying red raspberries straight from the bush. Topping a serving of cold cereal, they provide a memorable breakfast. For a simple dessert, served with milk or cream and sugar to taste—if you want it at all—they're hard to beat. Mixed with sour cream, they're ambrosial. Served with vanilla ice cream they're delectable. But while they're plentiful, you're sure to want some variety, to try other recipes too. Extras for the freezer can be put in a single layer on a baking sheet until they're hard and then packaged in the size container you prefer. Since they'll soften anyway on thawing, I just put them in plastic bags secured with a tie. There are always enough for making raspberry jam too.

My favorite way of making raspberry jam is simplicity itself. Weigh a batch of raspberries, crush them, and bring them to a boil slowly over low heat, stirring frequently. You should use a large, heavy pot so they neither scorch nor boil over. Add an equal weight of sugar after they've cooked through and continue cooking slowly until the sugar dissolves. Then cook the jam rapidly until it's thick. Ladel it into hot, sterilized jars and seal with melted paraffin or canning lids. The method uses less sugar than jam prepared with commercial pectin, but it takes a little longer and demands, therefore, rather more attention. If you prefer to use liquid or powdered pectin, the directions for regular or freezer jam (even quicker) are packaged with the product. If you have the room in your freezer, it's worth trying the freezer jam. It has a wonderfully fresh taste, the essence of summer.

Fresh berry pies are one of the major delights of summer, but there's no denying that making them heats up the kitchen something fierce. While you're at it, you might as well bake an extra shell or two so you won't have to use the oven at all when you make One-Crust Raspberry Pie or French Glacé Raspberry Pie. Put the shells in plastic bags and store them on a shelf until you're ready to use them.

BASIC RED RASPBERRY PIE
9 inch

¾ **cup sugar**
5 **tablespoons flour**
½ **teaspoon cinnamon**
4 **cups raspberries**
1 **tablespoon butter**

Mix the sugar, flour, and cinnamon together. Add it to the raspberries and stir gently. Pour the mixture into an unbaked pie shell, dot with butter and cover with a vented top crust. As is my wont, I moisten the top crust with milk or cream and sprinkle it with a little sugar. Bake at 425°F. for 35–45 minutes. We like it served slightly warm.

Having sampled the pleasures of unadorned raspberry pie, you may want to try this delicious quick version. For reasons that will shortly be clear, it's even fresher tasting. And it's intended to be served at room temperature or chilled.

ONE-CRUST RED RASPBERRY PIE
9 inch

¾ **cup sugar**
2½ **tablespoons cornstarch**
½ **cup water**
4 **cups red raspberries**
1 **baked pie shell**
whipped cream

Blend the sugar and cornstarch. Place the water and 1 cup of the raspberries in a saucepan over low heat. When they're hot through, add the sugar mixture. Stir and cook until clear, probably about 5 minutes. Cool. Arrange the remaining 3 cups of berries in the pie shell and spoon the partially cooled, cooked mixture evenly over them to glaze them. Serve with whipped cream generously applied.

A minor variation turns One-Crust Red Raspberry Pie into French Glacé Red Raspberry Pie. Spread a 3-ounce package of softened cream cheese over the bottom of the baked pie shell before adding the uncooked berries. That sounds easier than it is; the darned stuff doesn't want to spread evenly. Insist. We skip the whipped cream topping with this one, usually. Its calorie count is sufficiently daunting as it is.

Tired of pies? Try a quick bread. This one is appealing both as a dessert or as an accompaniment to coffee at any time of the day.

RED RASPBERRY ROLL   *6–8 servings*

2	**cups flour**
½	**teaspoon salt**
2½	**teaspoons baking powder**
1	**cup grated cheddar**
¼	**cup cooking oil**
⅓–½	**cup milk**
2	**cups raspberries**
¼	**cup white sugar**
2	**tablespoons brown sugar**

Combine flour, salt, baking powder, and cheddar. Pour the oil and milk into the mixture and mix it well until it forms a soft dough. Knead lightly in a sheet of waxed paper. Put a fresh sheet of waxed paper on your work surface and place the dough in the center of it. Flatten it slightly and put another sheet of waxed paper on top. Roll to ⅓-inch thickness in a rectangular shape. Remove the top sheet of waxed paper and spread the berries on it. Sprinkle the berries with the sugars. Roll it up like a jelly roll and bake about 45 minutes (or until golden) in an oven preheated to 350° F. Serve hot or cold, but hot is better.

Don't forget that raspberries can be used to good effect for shortcake too. Substitute them for strawberries in your favorite recipe. I like whipped cream on shortcake, but Bud prefers milk or cream poured over the whole works. He has no palate.

Blackberries and Elderberries

We don't cultivate either blackberries or elderberries, despite our fondness for both. They save us the trouble by growing wild in our area. Go after wild blackberries clothed in 14-ounce denim from neck to foot. Your hands will still be a mess, but who can pick blackberries wearing gloves? Sure, cultivated ones would be easier to pick, and thornless ones have been developed too. Since we can find them nearby, it seems pointless to bother planting them. Dewberries, another member of the family, don't always do well in our area because of severe winters, but I remember them fondly from my childhood in western Pennsylvania. Once in a while we get a good crop here. Logan berries and boysenberries are relatives that don't grow here. But wherever you live, you'll be able to enjoy some kind of blackberry.

Here in western Massachusetts, the blackberries ripen in August, before our fall raspberry crop. We use them just as we do raspberries, the same recipes. One year, when the harvest surpassed our wildest hopes, we made wine. We adapted a raspberry wine recipe and were pleasantly surprised when it turned out to be a fairly dry wine.

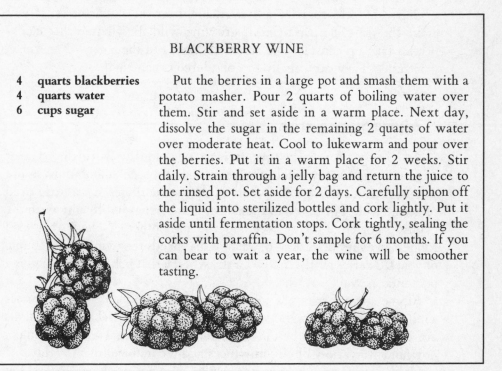

BLACKBERRY WINE

4   quarts blackberries
4   quarts water
6   cups sugar

Put the berries in a large pot and smash them with a potato masher. Pour 2 quarts of boiling water over them. Stir and set aside in a warm place. Next day, dissolve the sugar in the remaining 2 quarts of water over moderate heat. Cool to lukewarm and pour over the berries. Put it in a warm place for 2 weeks. Stir daily. Strain through a jelly bag and return the juice to the rinsed pot. Set aside for 2 days. Carefully siphon off the liquid into sterilized bottles and cork lightly. Put it aside until fermentation stops. Cork tightly, sealing the corks with paraffin. Don't sample for 6 months. If you can bear to wait a year, the wine will be smoother tasting.

Picking wild elderberries is sometimes as much nuisance as picking blackberries, but for a different reason. You have to be careful about those alongside the road, which are the easy ones to get to, because some highway departments spray roadsides. Elderberries often grow in boggy places, so I've learned to wear boots when I pick them. And jeans, because the berries are often found in the company of various briars. Take along a pair of clippers or stout scissors and pick whole clusters to stem later. Sitting down makes the job a lot less tiring.

Yes, we make elderberry jelly. With, I blush to admit, powdered pectin. No excuse; using packaged pectin is easy, and I was unsuccessful in finding a recipe for other methods when I first found myself inundated with elderberries. I don't know why I find that so embarrassing, but there it is. Some of our friends are surprised that we don't make elderberry wine; we're only occasional wine makers, and we have other designs on the elderberries. We like them in muffins, breakfast rolls, and pies. From an English friend I learned the trick of combining them half and half with apples for pies. We're not offended by straight elderberry pie, but many people object to the multitudinous seeds. Probably, come to think of it, the same people who demand seedless red raspberry jam (unavailable on these premises) and deplore blackberries.

Cultivated elderberries are available from most nurseries, if you crave the fruit and can't find it growing wild. Be advised that elderberries take up considerable room, though, and their growth is somewhat rank. They can't really be considered ornamental.

Alpine Strawberries

Practically everybody toys at least occasionally with the idea of starting a strawberry patch. For years one of my chief ambitions in life was to produce enough strawberries that we'd all get just a little tired of them. Well, I got tired of them. Not the berries, but fussing with the plants. I got tired of the weeding and the bother of plants that send runners in every direction, of a patch that needs renewing every couple of years. There's an alternative, a strawberry that behaves itself and is a perennial as well.

Alpine strawberries are lovely plants that produce smallish berries similar in taste and fragrance to wild strawberries. Because the plants are everbearing, they bloom from June until frost. I've grown them now under a variety of circumstances and recommend them highly.

Unlike other strawberries, the Alpine does not produce runners, but is propagated primarily from seed. This characteristic prevents the Alpine from becoming invasive. The seeds germinate readily and grow, rather slowly, into handsome plants. It's advisable to start them inside in cold climates if you want fruit the first year.

When you start depends on your conditions. Here in western Massachusetts, I've found it best to begin in January or February. The plants are just the right size to handle easily when it's time to harden them off for transplanting into the garden. Since they are everbearing, that method means you get at least a few berries the first year, late in the summer.

I start Alpine strawberries in flats inside because the seed is fine and I'm greedy enough to want to get as many plants as I can and get them off to a good start with little competition. It's entirely possible to seed them directly into the garden. When I used that method I managed to raise about twenty-five plants from a packet of one hundred seeds, which is certainly respectable. Growing them in flats will, conservatively, double the number of plants that survive.

Alpine strawberries will grow in partial shade. I've used them on the north and east sides of our house, where they blossomed from spring until hard frost and produced tiny red berries, but the planting was more decorative than productive.

The plants themselves made such attractive borders that I was determined to try them again in a situation where they might be more productive. On March 10 one year I sowed a packet of Ruegen Improved seed to grow in the light garden until late spring. On May 12 I planted them as a border to a new flower bed set in the lawn on the west side of our house. I placed the miniscule plants about a foot apart. Wild strawberries were growing in the lawn surrounding the bed (well, yes, we'd prefer grass, but one thing at a time), but I assumed I'd be able to distinguish them from the Alpines because of their runners. The wild ones occasionally crept into the border but were no problem to control. Even though the summer was dry, the new plants flourished and were in bloom by the beginning of August. The plants themselves were much larger than those I'd raised previously. They'll grow and produce in partial shade, but like many other food plants, they clearly prefer sunshine, and lots of it. The berries were larger too, about thimble-sized. Their flavor was incomparable. For best flavor, I don't pick them until they're completely ripe. That's easy enough to judge because they resist picking until they're at their peak of ripeness. At that point they separate readily from their caps. Oddly enough, berries left too long seem to dry out, and once they do are again difficult to pick.

Alpine strawberries are perennials and will bear for many years. They're good border plants but could grow in a permanent location in the kitchen garden instead. Because they're compact, some nurseries recommend them for container plants, but for any significant crop you'd need so many pots it would be a nuisance. Watering would be a chore. Since they're perennial, they'd need a winter home except in mild climates. Forget I even mentioned it.

When you're transplanting strawberries, make sure that the roots don't dry out; they're sensitive in that respect. They'll rot if planted too deeply, so set the crown on a small hump of soil and spread the roots out around it. Keep them well watered until they're established. Strawberries prefer a slightly acid soil.

Because my new border planting showed such promise, the next spring I sowed seed again for edging another bed adjacent to the site chosen the year before. The older planting produced abundantly that year, and the newer one repeated the performance of its predecessor. The following year, both were splendid.

Compared to the fussing necessary for other strawberries, the Alpines are remarkably easy to care for. We don't even mulch them for the winter, but leaves blowing across the lawn tend to collect around the plants, which affords them protection. It's not surprising that I'm enthusiastic about a well-behaved plant which is decorative, productive, self-limiting, and self-mulching. The flavor of its fruit alone makes it nearly irresistible.

Several varieties of Alpine strawberries are sold by major seed companies: Alexandria, Baron Solemacher, Ruegen Improved, and Alpine Yellow Fruited. Alexandria is the one recommended for shady plantings. One company claims that birds won't bother the yellow-fruited variety. We put clumps of catnip in strategic locations near the strawberries and rely on our own and neighbor's cats to protect the berries.

Picking Alpine strawberries is a daily chore from the end of June, in our climate, until hard frost. Not a big chore, you understand, not ever. But it is daily. When pickings are particularly meager, I put them instantly into the freezer. It's surprising how fast the supply grows, how marvelous they taste in desserts and fruit salads later on. One particularly perceptive (and obviously charming) guest exclaimed at dinner one evening, "Where in the world did you find *fraises des bois* at this time of year?" She was instantly added to my personal list of infinitely delightful people.

I wouldn't dream of limiting our enjoyment of strawberries to the Alpines, but now I'd hesitate to be without them. But instead of growing my own June bearers, I buy the considerable, and superlative, surplus grown by a dedicated neighbor. That satisfies our appetites for them without sending me into a permanent state of frustration.

Garden Huckleberries

Every once in a while it pays to be adventuresome, if only modestly. I've confessed to our less than impressive crop of blueberries. My patience is limited. That's why I'm so pleased with the garden huckleberries. We grew our first batch in 1979. The family enjoyed the coffee cakes and desserts made with the fruit so much that the next year we doubled the planting. Garden huckleberries, developed by Luther Burbank, are members of the Solanaceae family, closely related to tomatoes. They aren't actually huckleberries at all, but they acquired their common name from the quantites of blue-black fruit they produce. They grow rapidly from seed sown in the spring, blossom and set fruit during the summer, and die in the fall. The fruits, about the size of cultivated blueberries, are unpalatable when raw. They're not poisonous, but they taste terrible. Once cooked, however, they can be used as substitutes for blueberries or huckleberries. I don't mean that they taste the same as blueberries do. They are sharper, something like green tomatoes in flavor. Family resemblance, no doubt.

Culture for garden huckleberries is simple. Start the seeds in vermiculite or starter mix. I half-fill a flat with good garden dirt and top it with vermiculite to prevent damping-off. Let the seeds germinate in a warm place and as soon as the seedlings emerge, move the container to a sunny windowsill or put it under plant lights. For our testy New England climate, I start the seeds the last week of March. If the starting medium you use doesn't contain nutrients, you should fertilize them every two weeks or so after the true leaves have developed. Fish emulsion diluted in water works well. Treat the plants as you would tomatoes, hardening them off before they're set in the open garden. They can be put in a cold frame for the purpose or set outside each day for gradually lengthening periods of time. The process takes about a week or ten days, and then they're ready to plant. Transplant them to your garden at the same time you put in other tender annuals.

Garden huckleberries become fairly large, so give them plenty of room, at least two feet between plants. Branches that arch down and touch the ground are likely to root lightly at the point of contact. The plants don't need to be staked or pruned, and once they're in the garden you can forget them except for weeding. Insects and birds haven't bothered our plants. They're interesting all season and can be put in the ornamental border, if you're short of space in the vegetable garden. That's interesting, not show-stopping. The flowers are insignificant, but they'll bloom throughout the summer. Small green berries form; they gradually enlarge and turn almost black. Ignore them. They won't fall off the plant and will keep perfectly well until you're ready to harvest the whole crop.

Before sustained cold weather sets in, pull up the entire plant and take it someplace where you can be comfortable while you're stripping the berries from it. Discard the unripe berries, keeping only those that are blue-black and rather soft. The light frosts which kill the plant won't hurt the berries; indeed, they seem to improve the flavor. Once the berries are stripped from the plants, you're ready to process them. Don't panic if it's not convenient to do it immediately. They'll keep well for two or three days without refrigeration. When you're ready to work on them, bring a large pot of water to a rolling boil. Dump the berries into the pot and bring it back to a boil. Add a teaspoonful of baking soda, which will remove the berries' bitterness, and boil for one minute before draining them. The water will turn green, a moderately alarming green, when you add the soda. The phenomenon doesn't affect the color of the berries. I usually put the drained berries into cold water and swish them around to cool them and then drain them again. Once cooled they're ready to freeze or use in any recipe that calls for blueberries. They make good jam too. Weigh them and add an equal amount of sugar, after the initial processing. Then cook the mixture until it's thick. Pour into sterilized jars, seal, and store as you do other jams.

It must be admitted that there's a certain amount of nuisance to making a pie with garden huckleberries, but we like the resulting product.

GARDEN HUCKLEBERRY PIE   9–inch

4	cups processed garden huckleberries
¼	cup water
1	cup sugar
1	tablespoon lemon juice
1	tablespoon minute tapioca
1	teaspoon cinnamon
1	tablespoon butter

Thaw the berries, if necessary, and cook them in the water over moderate heat until they're soft. Stir them often; if they seem in danger of sticking, add a little more water. Add the sugar and lemon juice and cook gently about 5 minutes. Cool. Add the tapioca and cinnamon. Place in an unbaked pie shell and dot with butter. Add a vented top crust brushed with milk and sprinkled with sugar. Bake at 450°F. for 10 minutes. Turn the oven to 350°F. and continue baking until golden brown, probably about 30 minutes.

We like pie, but more of our huckleberries go into a breakfast cake than anything else. Bud and I are fond of it, but I think Bob and Tom would willingly eat it three times a week. They like it for snacking too. We always serve it warm; leftovers are gently heated in the toaster oven. It's moist and takes quite a long time to bake, so I usually bake it the day before serving and heat it up for breakfast in a 250°F. oven. Because it freezes well, I always make a double batch.

GARDEN HUCKLEBERRY BUCKLE   *Serves 6*

¾	cup sugar
¼	cup oil
1	egg
½	cup milk
2	cups flour
2	teaspoons baking powder
½	teaspoon salt
2	cups thawed, drained, processed berries

Topping:

¾	cup sugar
½	cup flour
1	teaspoon cinnamon
6	tablespoons melted butter

You don't need a mixer for this; a large spoon will do fine. Mix the sugar, oil, and egg. Stir in the milk. Add the dry ingredients and stir them in. Fold in the drained berries. Don't be upset by the purple splotches in the batter; the cake will look all right after it's baked. Spread the batter in a greased, 9-inch-square pan. Mix the topping ingredients together with a spoon and distribute the topping evenly over the batter. Bake at 375°F. for 45 minutes or until a tester inserted in the middle of the cake comes out clean.

Seed for garden huckleberries is available from several midwestern seedhouses. And you don't have to wait around for the fruit to mature. Not many plants useful for jam, pies, muffins, and other baked goods and desserts will produce a crop from seed in a single season. Gardeners without space or an appropriate location for a full-fledged berry patch or orchard can find a spot to tuck in a few of these productive plants. Because of their usefulness and the ease with which they can be grown and harvested, they've earned a place in our garden. In climates where tomatoes can be seeded directly into the garden, the garden huckleberries would be even easier to grow. In the North, there's currently no choice but to start them indoors. The plants simply aren't available in garden centers.

Ground Cherries

Enthusiasm for the garden huckleberries prompted the addition of another newcomer to our garden, the ground cherry. Small fruits or berries that will produce a good crop in a single season are just too tempting for me to pass up. We didn't even wait until mid-winter to gather our courage to sample the ground cherries, as we had the garden huckleberries. (Okay, okay, so it was cowardice. We didn't know anybody who had ever grown or eaten them. It took a combination of frigid weather and berry-hunger to get us to screw our courage to the sticking point.) The cherries have the edge over garden huckleberries in that they can be eaten raw. So far we've eaten them out-of-hand, in pies, and in jam. We haven't yet decided where to go next, but it's only a matter of time before I start experimenting with other recipes.

Ground cherries have interested me for some time. I tried growing them once in a previous garden, but produced only enough to excite my curiosity and make me curse the problems attendant upon gardening in the middle of the woods on solid ledge barely covered by a scanty layer of soil. In the beautiful loam of my present garden the results were gratifying.

I yield to no one in my admiration for the conventional fruits and berries, but all of them take a certain amount of time and expense to establish. Sometimes there's a problem of location for them. You may not have the space to tie up in a permanent berry patch or orchard. Even considering its limitations, the ground cherry is a paragon among quick and easy fruits. From a single package of seed you can have an abundance of berries.

The ground cherry isn't related to the cherry, by the way. It's called by a variety of names, including husk tomato, Cape gooseberry, and bladder cherry. It's a member of the Solanaceae, or Nightshade, family, which also includes potatoes, tomatoes, tobacco, petunias—and garden huckleberries. Ground cherries can be found growing wild from New York to Florida, west to the Mississippi, and south into the tropics. They're even found in Hawaii. They're rare throughout much of their range, but in some areas they're considered troublesome weeds. Actually, you may be growing ground cherries already as ornamentals—one variety is known as the Chinese Lantern Plant. It's edible too, but not very. There are dozens of varieties within the genus *Physalis*, all of them more or less edible. They vary in size and quality, however. Seed houses sell the variety used as a food plant.

When you're making out your next seed order you may want to include a package of ground cherries as a novelty. I start mine indoors at the same time I start tomato seedlings, the early part of April. (The seed is viable for three to five years, if leftovers are properly stored. Opinions differ on what proper storage entails. I store opened packets in tightly covered glass jars in a cool, dry place. Germination is satisfactory; I've used seed so stored after the storage time specified by experts and had good results.) The plants are sprawling in their habit of growth, but don't require staking. The fruits, ranging from pea-sized to pie-cherry size, are borne inside pale-green husks which become papery and straw-colored as the fruits mature. When fully ripe the fruit is amber-yellow, much the color of yellow tomatoes. Don't sample it when it's still greenish, because the taste is dreadful. Although the plant is sensitive to frost, the husks protect the fruits from those first light frosts which kill the plant. The fruits may be gathered in the fall and kept for a month or so in their husks, while the fruit becomes sweeter. You can also gather greenish husks with full-sized fruit inside, which can be counted on to ripen satisfactorily indoors. Frequently the fruit drops from the plant before it ripens, but it's protected by the husk. Occasionally you'll find specks of black on fruit inside an apparently undamaged husk; I assume tiny insects have perforated it, but I have no evidence for the assumption. I'm curious, but easily distracted.

I hope you'll try ground cherries, despite the nuisance of husking them. The seedlings can be put into the open garden at the same time the tomatoes go in. Give them the amount of space you would an unstaked tomato plant. The fruits ripen over a long period of time. You can expect your first samples about the time tomatoes are ripening. They'll continue going strong until frost and will keep another month in the husk. For winter use, I've frozen the husked, ripe cherries in plastic sandwich bags.

You can make a perfectly delicious jam from ground cherries. I've not done much experimenting with it, but simply use a modified version of a recipe I found in a wild foods book.

GROUND CHERRY JAM

4 **cups ground cherries, husked and washed**	Crush the cherries and add the lemon juice, grated peel, water, and powdered pectin. Boil the mixture for 5 minutes and then add the sugar. Bring it back to a rolling boil for 2 minutes. Pour it into hot, sterilized jars and seal it.
4 **tablespoons lemon juice**	
1 **tablespoon grated lemon rind**	
½ **cup water**	
1 **package powdered pectin**	
4 **cups sugar**	

If you don't use great quantities of jam, you might prefer to make pie from your ground cherries.

GROUND CHERRY PIE   *8 inch*

¼ **cup flour**
1 **cup sugar**
¼ **teaspoon salt**
1 **teaspoon cinnamon**
2 **tablespoons lemon
     juice**
3 **cups ground
     cherries, husked
     and washed**
1 **tablespoon butter**

Mix flour, sugar, salt, cinnamon, and lemon juice with the ground cherries. Put the mixture in an unbaked pie shell, dot it with butter, and add a vented top crust. Brush the crust with milk and sprinkle it with a little sugar. Bake at 450°F. for 10 minutes. Lower the temperature to 350°F. and continue baking until golden brown, about 30 minutes longer. This pie is especially good served warm and lends itself to toppings of cheese or vanilla ice cream. Both the jam and the pie are attractive in appearance as well as taste.

I don't pretend that either garden huckleberries or ground cherries will eliminate your appetite for better-known berries. But if nothing else, they're interesting to grow and eat, and they certainly take up the slack at a time when other berries aren't plentiful. Of the two, I'd be less likely to give up the huckleberries. That's primarily slothfulness speaking, because their harvesting is such a quick procedure. And it's just once. On the other hand, ground cherries make a good snack fresh, whereas garden huckleberries don't.

Grapes

Before we leave the subject of fruits and berries, let me mention grapes. I'm far from experienced in grape culture, even though I've been at it for fifteen years. It's a lot easier to feel knowledgeable about a subject that everyone ignores than about one so crawling with tradition. Our son Tom is avid about fresh grapes, grape juice, and grape jelly, and that led me to think that it was my duty as a conscientious parent to provide home-grown ones. At our former garden, the grapes were a disaster. It was too woodsy for them, and they languished. Tom got ten or twelve a year from our white and red varieties and commented in pathetic tones about the length of time necessary to get going with grapevines. I gave up any thoughts of making juice and bought frozen concentrate at the store. For jelly I relied on wild grapes, spotted while horseback riding and carefully monitored until they ripened.

Wild grapes make superb jelly, but they're not often good for munching. The first time I made jelly from them, I was expecting a purple product. I don't know what the grape jelly people use, but my grape jelly is red. Attractive, but red. Since I've not made juice, I can't swear to its color, but I have my suspicions.

Anyway, when we moved to our present home, Bud built a grape arbor and I planted grapes. I bought red and white varieties alleged to be suitable for our climate, Delaware and Niagara. For the blues, I accepted the invitation of a neighbor to dig up a Concord vine escaped from their arbor. I hacked away at the poor thing with a spade and transferred its mutilated remains to our property. It survived. Nay, it thrived. It is mad with enthusiasm for its new home and began producing bountifully two-and-a-half years after being transplanted. It now provides Tom with his jelly. Red jelly.

The care and feeding of grapes is a topic on which much has been written. The whole subject terrifies me. I prune the grapes in early spring, a pruning manual in one trembling hand, pruning shears in the other, the sensation of desperation coloring the entire procedure. I make mistakes, groan in dismay. The Concord, at least, doesn't mind at all. The reds and whites produced only enough for a few nibbling bunches, until the summer of 1983, four years after planting. That year, they became so prodigiously productive that we had plenty to share with friends. I feed and mulch the grapes with barn bedding and have some tansy growing here and there to discourage the Japanese beetles, which remain undaunted as far as I can tell. Still, they don't do any significant damage, and it's a good place for tansy. When its growth becomes too exuberant, I just yank it out.

The grapes ripen in September. Here in New England that's a wonderful time of year. But it's a busy, nervous-making time too. Will we have a frost? The days are magnificent, but if there's a full moon early in the month, look out. The frost is capricious this time of year, devastating one garden and bypassing another or wiping out the basil but sparing the peppers. It's a good time to observe the microclimates in your garden and file the information for future use. It's also time to gear up for major harvesting and storing activities.

CHAPTER 7

Full Moon Tonight

There's no right way to go about the final harvest, but obvious priorities exist, so many that they pose problems. I find it handy to make a list of what has to be done, but the order in which I proceed depends on whim as much as on the weather. Arbitrarily, we'll start with the herbs. Circumstances dictate the ways in which we use herbs in winter. If you can spare some windowsill or light-garden space, then a supply of fresh herbs is little problem.

No doubt you will have been keeping an eye on your herbs and drying them at the appropriate times all through the growing season. Take a peek at your shelves to make sure you have enough. Freezing herbs? Any of them can be frozen for winter use, but many of them are a lot handier to use in dried form. You may be better organized than I am; small packets of herbs tend to get lost in my freezer, and my labels always become useless. They fall off or become illegible, and that's bad enough with something as large and clearly recognizable as broccoli or snap beans. I don't need packets of small, unidentifiable leaves. So aside from parsley, most of our herbs are dried, placed in labeled jars and shelved in the pantry. Much easier to find and to use.

If you have an abundance of certain herbs, you may want to dry some to give as gifts. They can also be preserved in vinegar. Herb-flavored vinegars make great salad dressings and sauces. Any herb can be used in the method given except sage.

Pack a cup of fresh herb leaves into a hot quart jar and fill the jar with red or white wine vinegar that has been brought to a boil. Let it stand for two weeks and strain. Keep it refrigerated or else bring it to a boil, pour into sterilized jars and seal.

142

For sage vinegar, use only a quarter cup of sage leaves in a quart jar.

Combinations of herbs can be used and garlic cloves may be added to the basic herb vinegar. For a mint vinegar, useful in sauces for lamb, mix 2 cups leaves and 1 cup sugar. Let the mixture stand for 5 minutes or so while you bring a quart of cider vinegar to a boil. Add the mint and sugar, smashing the mint leaves against the sides of the pan to release their flavor. Boil 3 minutes, strain, bottle, and seal. Let it ripen for several weeks before using it.

Whatever your preferences, take advantage of fresh herbs while they're still in season and preserve any excess for winter use. It's one of the quickest, most useful pastimes available, and it's a considerable source of satisfaction that the herb shelf at the grocer's is one you can ignore with impunity.

Parsley

Parsley is the herb that most of us use in the greatest quantity. You'll want to keep it on hand in a variety of forms and perhaps have already seeded a couple of pots of it. The growing ones I bring indoors for the winter are inadequate to supply all our needs, but do splendid service as garnishes where appearance is as important as taste. It always graces our wiener schnitzel, for example.

Since the potted plants don't supply enough parsley, I freeze a lot too. Just snip leaves, package them in a plastic bag or box and put them in the freezer. Freezing keeps flavor and color superbly, but thawed leaves are definitely too limp to adorn a veal cutlet. They do well in cottage cheese, soups, and stews though.

Just to be on the safe side, I dry a couple of jars full of parsley too. Snip the leaves from the stems, place them in a single layer on a baking sheet, and put them in a warm oven to dry until they're brittle. Don't expect fast results; that's how I achieved masses of scorched parsley. Dry it at 200° to 250° F., and be patient. Watch it carefully. When it's brittle, cool and crumple it into jars and keep it in a dark, dry place. Slowly dried it will retain its color and flavor well.

One year I experimented with air drying too, a much slower and (for me) altogether unsuccessful process. Air drying works so well with other herbs that I felt it worth the possible sacrifice of spare parsley to try that method. That's what it was, a sacrifice. An oven is the answer for drying parsley.

Rosemary

Many herbs can be potted and brought in for winter use. Some of them must, in fact, be treated as houseplants in areas where frosts occur. The first one to remember is rosemary. It can't take heavy frost and won't survive outdoors during the winter in cold climates.

But that's okay. Rosemary makes a lovely houseplant. If you never used it in the kitchen at all, it'd be worth keeping around for the foliage and for the pleasant piney aroma its leaves release when they're handled. Its culinary uses are well known. Rosemary has a long tradition as a flavoring for lamb, but it tastes good as a seasoning for roasted, baked, or casseroled chicken, as a garnish for roast pork, and in a basting sauce for spareribs. Rubbing or sprinkling rosemary on duck before roasting it provides a delicious flavor in the finished product. It's often used to flavor fruit cups and punches. Less widely practiced is the technique of frying small boiling potatoes with rosemary leaves.

A tea can be made with half an ounce of fresh leaves or a teaspoonful of dried ones steeped in a cup of boiling water and flavored with lemon juice and honey. The brew is supposed to relieve both headache and insomnia. Rosemary-flavored wine is made by soaking a handful of fresh leaves in half a gallon of white wine for a few days. It's recom mended that you keep the concoction in the refrigerator to prevent spoilage.

Go easy with rosemary, because its flavor is pronounced. Just a little can go a long way. That's particularly true if you're using dried rosemary. Because they're concentrated, all dried herbs should be used more sparingly than fresh ones.

The real treat, of course, is using fresh rosemary. To grow it, all you need is a cool, sunny place. It does well under artificial light too. Use a light, slightly alkaline potting soil. Rosemary isn't fussy, but it has a couple of peculiarities, characteristics you must be aware of to grow it successfully.

Rosemary is a native of the Mediterranean area, and its name is probably a derivative of the latin *ros* (dew) and *marinus* (sea). That's the clue to what it needs for robust growth—a humid atmosphere. The solution for indoor growing is to mist it regularly. Many experts say that should be done at least once a week. I prefer to mist daily when the house is closed up and the heat is on. The roots of the plant mustn't dry out, ever. Once they do, the rosemary has had it. Period. The plant should be watered from the top and should never stand in water. Don't dunk it, in the manner beloved by some other houseplants.

Does that sound fussy after all? In practice it really is no trouble. If you're aware of the plant's needs, there's no trick to keeping it healthy. Well, honesty demands that I qualify that statement just a little.

I strongly advise having two rosemary plants. That's no great hassle; they can be smallish and rosemary is highly attractive. Every once in a while, you see, for no reason that I've been able to discover, a rosemary decides that it's finished. Yesterday it looked splendid. Today it's a little puny. Tomorrow it's dead. Maybe not quite so fast and clear-cut as all that, but that's the impression it gives.

That doesn't mean, however, that you have to rush out and buy a companion rosemary plant. They're relatively easy to propagate from cuttings. Seed is slow and iffy; the percentage of germination is quite low, ranging from 10 percent at worst to 50 percent at best. Not good enough. But take a cutting or two, about six inches long, of new growth. Strip the leaves from the bottom and plunge the stem into a peat pellet you've expanded first by soaking it in water. Put the whole works in good light, and wait, for two to three months, usually. Keep it moist but not soggy. When its renewed growth indicates it has rooted, plant the rosemary, peat pellet and all, in a two- or three-inch pot with good drainage. I've been fooled sometimes by these infants. One with just the bare beginnings of new growth may have roots busting through the sides of the planting pellet. Should you notice that, pot the plant immediately, substantial top growth or not.

Don't be alarmed by my advocacy of this precaution. The two rosemary plants I have now are a couple of years old and—to all appearances— happy and healthy. But I've started a couple of cuttings for friends, and a spare, in case I remember.

In the summertime many people plant their rosemary in the garden. I put mine outside, pot and all. That's intended to save time, but it means that, like other vacationing houseplants so treated, it has to be watered regularly. I've never encountered insect or disease problems, but rumor has it that occasionally red spider mites attack rosemary. A good bath will usually take care of that problem. If you use something potentially dangerous, like malathion spray, be sure to wash the plant *thoroughly* before using the leaves for cooking. Though not a purist, I normally rely on organic controls for food plants, and I strongly advise against using *any* chemical pesticide indoors, on anything.

I've been unable to determine how rosemary acquired its reputation for strenghtening the memory. It's clear enough that said reputation prompted rosemary's symbolic significance in matters of constancy and fidelity. During the Middle Ages the herb was considered capable of restoring youth and vitality too. Not only that, but oil of rosemary rubbed on the joints was supposed to cure arthritis. Our main interest in it today lies in its delightful fragrance and flavor and its unquestioned beauty.

Celery

In the rush of harvesting tomatoes, peppers, beans, and other demonstrably tender garden vegetables, don't overlook the celery. It too is on the fragile side. Misconceptions about celery abound. Many gardeners believe it's difficult to grow. Nonsense. Many cooks believe that it is only to be consumed raw, except when it's used in stews or stuffings, where its only function is as a flavoring. Ridiculous. Indeed, for purposes of simply getting flavor, you can dispense with everything but the leaves or the seeds. Without disputing the fact that sometimes that flavor may be all you want, there's a lot more to be said for—and done with—celery than mere seasoning.

In its wild (and bitter) form, celery is called smallage. Up until the seventeenth century it was used strictly as a medicine. Which is a little odd, in a way, since celery is sometimes cited as a food plant to which some people are allergic. The reaction can be mild to severe, causing gas pains, nausea, and diarrhea. Occasionally it has been considered an aphrodisiac because its acids were believed to "excite the urinary passages." Well, ideas about foods change. During the seventeenth century, people began to eat celery as an honest-to-goodness food, and most of them felt none the worse for it. Or even got into any trouble as a result of consuming it. Eventually—and this happened with certain other green vegetables too—they learned to blanch it to make the stalks lighter in color and more tender. We've come full circle, and now once again people tend to like their celery green. Pascal celery is currently much favored. Part of this reaction is the result of learning that greener indicates more vitamins. But let's be honest. Part is no doubt due to the efforts of plant breeders who have come up with varieties that remain crisp and tender without any fussing on the part of the grower.

Celery is successfully grown as a market crop in many areas, but it surprises some gardeners to discover that it's not at all resistant to frost. Celery is a biennial, which sends up a seed stalk the second year. Though a solid nipping by frost doesn't necessarily kill the plant's top growth, it's quite likely to convince the poor thing that winter has come and gone, and the time has come to get cracking. Whereupon the celery proceeds to set seed and becomes tough, unappetizing, and totally unfit for munching.

You can buy flats of celery seedlings locally in the spring, but don't plant them in the garden until after the frost-free date unless you're prepared to protect them from disaster. If you raise your own plants from seed, better start celery early, about ten to twelve weeks before time to set it in the garden. It takes forever to reach transplanting size. Remember that with proper care each one of those seedlings will become a bunch of celery, so plan accordingly. Celery can, because of its upright habit of growth, be planted six to eight inches apart. It needs rich soil and plenty of moisture. In a dry spell, that may mean deep watering, even if you mulch well.

So what do you do with all that celery? Well, two things. Possessed of an abundance, you're bound to learn to use it for more than raw snacks. And because even the most enthusiastic advocate eventually becomes sated, you learn how to store it for later use.

Celery keeps well in the refrigerator, but few of us want to devote space for more than one or two bunches. If you've grown a large crop, you can dig it just before frost and keep it in a frost-free location, preferably a damp one with a temperature of 35 to 40° F. The root cellar is perfect. Set the plants close together in a box or tub and cover their roots with soil. Keep the soil watered but don't get the plants themselves wet. The container should have drainage holes. We've kept celery in good condition until the New Year using this method.

If the container technique isn't feasible, or you have too much even for that procedure, celery can be frozen for use in cooked dishes. It's supposed to be sliced, blanched for three minutes in boiling water, drained, cooled, and frozen. I skip all the steps but the first and last, but not as a matter of any principle. It's simply a practice that evolved pragmatically, through ignorance. I don't necessarily recommend it, except possibly to people as harrassed and slap-dash as I tend to be.

You can sometimes use celery in tossed salads, always in Waldorf salads. As a finger food, stuff it or serve it with and without dips. Use it in sauces and stews and stuffings. What else can you do with the stuff? Cook it as a vegetable to be served all by itself in solitary state, that's what.

Even if you don't grow it yourself, it's often a bargain at the market. Its quality is good year round, unlike a lot of other fresh vegetables available out of season. It's mercifully low in calories. One cup of diced cooked celery contains only twenty-five calories. How you dress it will affect that count, of course.

For starters, try braising it, in a little water in which a bouillon cube or granules have been dissolved, for five to eight minutes. How long you cook it will depend on how soft you want it to be; we like ours a bit crunchy. In any case the water should be skimpy enough that it's gone by the time you've finished cooking the celery. You can add a bit of butter before you serve it, if you like. (We do.) Fixed this way, it's delicious, different, and a boon to dieters, especially if you refrain from adding the butter. It is remarkably good served hot. If you prefer, you can chill it (without butter) and then serve it later with French dressing as a salad on your choice of greens.

Braised celery is also good dressed with a light cream sauce. Make sure you drain it first of any braising liquid that might be left in the pan. If you like, garnish it with slivered, toasted almonds. All manner of variation is possible with braised celery. Following is still another one.

BRAISED CELERY   *Serves 3–4*

2-3 **tablespoons butter**   Melt the butter and mash the bouillon cube in it. Add
1 **chicken bouillon**   the celery and sauté until tender but still crisp. Add the
   cube   remaining ingredients and stir long enough to glaze the
2-3 **cups celery in 1-**   celery, no more.
   inch slices
pepper to taste
1 **tablespoon chili**
   sauce
¼ **teaspoon soy sauce**
¼ **teaspoon**
   Worcestershire
   sauce
1 **teaspoon**
   cornstarch
   dissolved in 2
   tablespoons water

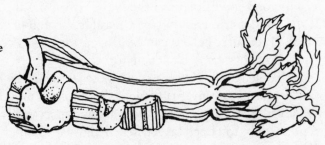

Here follows a more elaborate dish, crunchy and a welcome change, but demanding some foresight.

BAKED CELERY   *Serves 8*

1   **bunch celery**
salt and pepper to taste
½   **cup slivered**
     almonds
½   **cup grated sharp**
     cheddar
1   **can cream soup**
     (your choice: we
     like mushroom,
     chicken, or
     celery)
¼   **cup milk**
¾   **cup bread crumbs**
	Cut the celery into ½-inch pieces and place it in a buttered 9-x-12-inch, ovenproof casserole. Salt and pepper it. Sprinkle with almonds and cheese. Combine milk and soup and pour it over the celery. Put the crumbs on top. Refrigerate for at least 3 hours. Bake at 375°F. for 30 minutes. Make sure you use a casserole dish that can safely go straight from the refrigerator to a preheated oven.

Once you begin thinking of celery as a possibility for a cooked vegetable, you'll find other uses for it. The supply in your freezer will be okay for any cooked dishes, even reasonably crunchy ones, but even during the months when I have to buy it, a bunch of celery is always present in the crisper drawer of our refrigerator.

Onions

> I know there are onions in Heaven
> For they have a heavenly smell.

Now there's a bit of doggerel that sometimes haunts me for thirty seconds at a whack. But it may not accurately describe everyone's reaction to onions. Nonetheless, it would be difficult to cook interesting meals without this humble vegetable.

Think of all the ways in which we eat onions. Sometimes they're used only to flavor a dip or dressing. We use them in soups, stews, salads, sauces, casseroles. Onion rings smothering liver, French fried onion rings garnishing a steak, side dishes of creamed or braised or scalloped onions, green onions on a relish tray. Have you recently spent an entire day without ingesting onions in some form, counting of course the minute amounts sometimes used as a seasoning? Maybe one day is a possibility, but surely not more than two or three days in a row.

Onions, since they're common and relatively inexpensive, are sometimes not given their due. Strict adherence to fact demands admitting that they have a number of disadvantages too, which brings us back to the smell, heavenly or otherwise. We'll rise above mundane considerations such as onion breath, on the assumption that anyone troubled with the complaint has somehow learned to control it satisfactorily. Tears are another matter. Peeling, chopping, or otherwise lacerating onions quite literally reduces many cooks to a sorry condition. The peeling you can cope with by doing the job with the help of running water. I've tried the technique recommended by many cookbooks, especially for small onions, of cooking them in their jackets and then removing the skins. It may be a blessing to some people, but I find it loathesome. Onions so treated are hot and slippery, and I'd just as soon not talk about it. For chopping and grating, long arms or some device like a food processor, blender, or subservient member of the household are invaluable. You can remove the onion odor from your hands by rubbing them with a little vinegar. The vinegar odor is your problem.

Growing onions is an easy matter for the home gardener, despite wild shrieks from the United States Department of Agriculture about the dangers of downy mildew, neck rot, pink root, and onion smut. You can start with seeds, seedlings, or sets and have both green and storage onions from the same row. Plant them early; frost means nothing to an onion and they need considerable time to reach maturity. Whatever method you use has its own advantages and disadvantages. Seeds are easy to plant, but they take longer to reach maturity, and weeding is tedious when they're small because onions are so similar in appearance to grass during their early stages. If you buy bunches or flats of onions in spring, you avoid those problems, but transplanting onions is moderately back-breaking. Sets are easy to plant and give fast results. They're certainly to be highly recommended for green onions. They do have a disadvantage as storage onions.

Onions are biennials that set seed the second year. Sets you buy are one year old. Some of them send up a seed stalk, and then energy that should go into growing a nice big onion goes into ripening seeds instead. Still I prefer growing onions from sets because it's easier. I snap off any seed heads that form, a quick operation that does the trick for me. That stiff stalk remains, however, and must be broken away from the bulb for storage.

Storage onions are ready for harvest after the tops have fallen over and withered. If some seem reluctant to flop, you can persuade them with a hoe handle or the like. It gets them into the proper frame of mind. Don't wait too long to dig them once the tops wither. Eventually the tops disappear entirely, and you're apt to forget all about them. Under certain conditions, they'll finally send down new roots and start growing all over again, which wrecks them for storage. After digging the onions, I spread them in the sun to dry for a while. How long? That depends on the weather. If it's a soggy time, I bring them into the barn to dry. Onions must be dry or they'll rot in storage. A rotting onion has never been described as heavenly in aroma, and the contagion spreads quickly. So make sure they're dry, one way or another. I grow both red and yellow onions. We use the red ones first because their storage life is fairly short. Store onions in a cool, dry place, preferably in mesh bags.

As for using them, be bold. Steam tiny ones (or buy them in jars if necessary) and then serve them in a cream sauce. The cream sauce will be livelier if you add a sprinkle of cloves and some freshly chopped parsley. The parsley tastes good and also perks up the appearance of creamed onions. A bit of sherry is a nice touch too. Try it at the rate of about a tablespoon of wine for every half cup of white sauce used.

If you're tired of creamed onions, you might like to try braising them. Use just enough beef stock to come about half way up the sides of the onions and cook gently. The stock should all but disappear by the time the onions are ready to serve. If you're fresh out of beef stock, substitute bouillon dissolved in hot water.

We're inveterate onion eaters, and one of my favorite side dishes is this cheesy onion one.

ONIONS AU GRATIN　　　　　　　　*Serves 4*

4	large onions, peeled and sliced
2	tablespoons butter
salt and pepper	
½–¾	cup grated sharp cheddar
½	cup bread crumbs

Sauté the onion slices gently in 1 tablespoon butter and then arrange them in a buttered baking dish. Season to taste with salt and pepper. Sprinkle with cheese and bread crumbs and dot with the remaining 1 tablespoon butter. Bake in an oven preheated to 350°F. until the cheese melts and the crumbs are toasted.

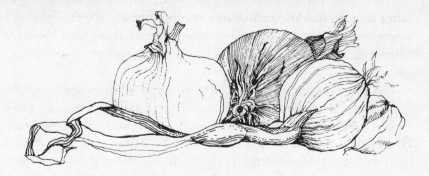

If the rest of your menu suggests that you eschew cheddar, try this version.

SCALLOPED ONIONS

butter	Butter a casserole. Arrange layers of sliced onions
onions	sprinkled with seasoned cracker crumbs and dotted with
cracker crumbs	butter until the casserole is full. Add milk or cream until
salt and pepper	it's halfway up the sides of the casserole dish. Cover and
milk or cream	bake at 375°F. for about 45 minutes.

Another dish that goes well with poultry is stuffed onions.

STUFFED ONIONS   *Serves 4*

4 **large onions**	Parboil the onions for 20 minutes in salted water. Drain
½ **pound bulk pork sausage**	and remove the center portion with a sharp knife and fork. Fill the centers with the sausage meat, precooked,
½ **teaspoon dried sage or 1½ teaspoon fresh sage**	seasoned with sage and innocent of fat. Put the stuffed onions in a buttered casserole dish and bake them, uncovered, at 375°F. for 20 minutes. Make sure the sausage is cooked well.

Garlic

Mentioning the onions reminds me about storing the stinkweed, sometimes known as the herb of the common man. It's thought to have originated southeast of Siberia and then eventually to have spread to the Middle East and Europe. Stinkweed? Right. Now more popularly called garlic.

The Babylonians used it in 3000 B.C., and it's mentioned in Chinese documents as far back as 2000 B.C. It was the principal seasoning in China, but in ancient India neither garlic nor onions were highly favored. Highly flavored but not highly favored. No; that's too mild: sometimes both were forbidden entirely, and you literally had to leave town to eat either of them. The Arabs and the Jews, on the other hand, discovered garlic's values early, and the Egyptians grew it in abundance. Herodotus reports that the builders of Cheop's pyramid were fed mainly on onions and garlic. Garlic's importance to the Egyptians was such that the word was worked into the taking of oaths, and slaves refused to labor when it was withheld.

That's the way it is with garlic—no middle ground. It has never been much used by the Greeks, ancient or modern, but noble Romans fed it to their slaves to make them strong and to their soldiers to make them brave. The noblemen themselves, however, avoided it. They even passed a law that forbade anyone to enter the temple of Cybele after eating it. Horace called it "more poisonous than hemlock" and added somewhat loftily that its smell was a sure sign of vulgarity.

Prejudices against garlic abounded. It was not to be found in Anglo-Saxon, German, or Scandanavian cuisine. The Japanese ignored it too. Sicily and Calabria embraced it, but the rest of Italy relied for seasoning on basil, marjoram, thyme, and oregano instead.

Even in Shakespeare's time, the English remained highly suspicious of garlic. In addition to regarding it as vulgar, they believed it to be thoroughly unsuited to anyone of volatile temperament because it inflamed the passions. It has also been considered an aphrodisiac. Nonetheless, it gained a reputation as a preventive of Plague.

Anything so sturdy in taste and smell is bound to arouse strong feelings. It's claimed that the oil is so potent that rubbing a clove of garlic on the soles of the feet will taint one's breath.

Now, it is true that raw garlic in large quantities can prove detrimental to the digestive tract. In fact, along with such foods as chocolate, milk, eggs, port, and peas, garlic contains an allergin that can bring on migraine. But somewhere along the line, people decided that anything so powerful was decidedly good for what ailed you, whatever that happened to be: acne, athlete's foot, flatulence, broken bones, gastrointestinal upsets, leprosy, rabies, tapeworms, tuberculosis, diphtheria, whooping cough, or pneumonia. In colonial America, garlic cloves were bound to the feet of smallpox victims, and in the flu epidemic of 1918, garlic cloves worn around the neck were supposed to protect against that disease. They sold for $1 a pound at the time. In fact, pads of sterilized sphagnum moss saturated with water-diluted garlic juice were used as antiseptic wound dressings in World War I. Some people believed that ingesting garlic would prevent cancer. Rubbing it on aching joints was thought to relieve or cure the pain of rheumatism and arthritis. Macerating several bulbs in a quart of wine or alcohol produced a cure for baldness. And for centuries garlic syrup has been a common European remedy for coughs, colds, and sore throats.

And to think you can buy garlic oil capsules in a health food store.

Dizziness, angina pain, and headaches often disappear, we are told, with garlic therapy. In addition to all this, garlic is commercially used in pesticides supposed to be effective against everything from the Anopheles mosquito to cockchafer larvae. It is not harmful to humans, pets, or livestock. Oh, wow!

Most of the garlic sold in this country is grown in California, but Texas and Louisiana produce it in quantity too. Garlic is a member of the Lily family, which should come as no surprise to anyone who has examined the bulbs of garlic and lilies. Garlic bulbs usually have eight to twenty cloves. Elephant garlic is its larger but milder relative. You can, of course, grow garlic yourself. It prefers a moist, sandy soil and lots of sunshine. Enrich the soil with well-rotted manure or compost. Garlic needs a long growing season. Plant it early in the spring and harvest it in August or September. A crop planted in late summer should be ready the following June.

Though it has no place in my medicine cabinet, I wouldn't be without garlic in kitchen or garden. I started out by planting a clove of garlic beside every one of my rose bushes, to deter Japanese beetles. I still do that, annually, despite the lack of any observable ill effects on the beetles. At least I always know where to find some garlic. I have to admit I use a lot of ineffective remedies against beetles. None of them is foolproof, except squashing the beasts. I keep trying. I know, the traps work. They offer no challenge; Unlike garlic and tansy and white geraniums, traps don't excite the imagination.

We had one unfortunate situation as a result of growing garlic with roses. Our entire family was on the way to the library one day when son Tom plucked a stalk to chew, apparently under the impression that it was a scrawny clump of chives. The stench in the car—indeed, within ten feet of the child—was not to be believed. Since that incident, we've tried to encourage him to chomp on something like mint leaves instead when we foresee the probability of close encounters.

Chewing parsley, by the way, is helpful in eliminating garlic breath. A bit of milk is said to be helpful too. Which is a little odd, in a way, because dairy animals that nibble on garlic, wild onions, and the like produce unpleasantly flavored milk.

You can buy garlic powders and garlic salts which are handy to have around but no substitute for the real article. What's spaghetti without garlic bread? Or a tossed salad without a hint of its flavor in the dressing? You can rub the salad bowl with a cut clove or drop a whole clove into the jar of dressing. For a heftier dose, mash the clove to release more of the oil. I use a garlic press whenever I want especially robust flavor. The degree of injury to the clove determines the potency of the final product. If it's subtlety you prefer, take care not to bruise the garlic.

Many of the prejudices against garlic in our society have disappeared, and you probably don't have to be persuaded to use it as a seasoning. I heartily recommend the following garlic-herb butter as a sauce for fish fillets or, particularly, salmon steaks. Be sure to accompany it with wedges of lemon.

GARLIC HERB BUTTER   *Serves 4–6*

8   **tablespoons butter**   Cream the butter with a wooden spoon until it's fluffy.
1   **tablespoon finely**   Blend in the other ingredients. Spread on the fish before
    chopped scallions   serving or serve separately.
1   **teaspoon minced**
    garlic
2   **tablespoons finely**
    chopped parsley
salt and pepper to taste

I heartily recommend roasting young chickens with two or three whole cloves inside them. Judiciously basted with no more than half a cup total of chicken broth during the roasting period, such chicken is flavorful without being horrendously rich in calories. Dieters are supposed to remove the skin; we hang around the counter while Bud's carving, snitching any pieces we can until he drives us away with threats.

To store garlic, let the tops fall over (or gently persuade them) and dig and dry as you do storage onions. I used to store all of mine in mesh bags, but this year friends sent us an earthenware garlic keeper of such charm that part of the crop lives in it, on the kitchen counter. The vessel has a cork stopper and holes here and there in the crock. It's reputed to provide absolutely perfect storage conditions, but I'd need one the size of a washtub to store all our crop. The overflow is, as usual, in a mesh bag.

Potatoes

My favorite harvesting job is digging potatoes. For one thing, there's no big rush about it, no sense of urgency. We grow enough for our year-round needs, but it's not much of a project to dig them. By July the previous year's crop is beginning to get a little grungy, but the new plants have blossomed, and it's no trick at all to hunt round among their roots for tiny new potatoes.

About the first week in August, the tops of the early potatoes have started to wither, so I take a pail and a trowel with me to the garden and use a more systematic approach. I loosen the dirt around the first plant in a row with the trowel and then begin rooting around in the mellow earth for the potatoes hidden there. Each time I encounter one, it's like finding buried treasure. When the group clustered around the stalk has been dug and transferred to the pail, I do a little more exploring with the trowel in the immediate vicinity—just in case. The potatoes range in size from marbles to beauties five or six inches long. There's a use for every size, too. I quit when several hills have been raided and the pail is full.

That's the way we use potatoes until towards the end of September, when cooler weather brings out my hoarding instincts. The garden cart comes into play then, and I begin digging by the bushel. These potatoes are intended for storage and must last until the next summer's harvest can begin. A little more care is necessary; they must be cured. We spread them on the top floor of the barn for a week to ten days. That's minimum; sometimes they're there quite a while. The temperature up there during the day will go between 80° and 90° F. if it's sunny, and frost won't be able to damage them at night. Once the potatoes have cured, we put them into heavy cardboard boxes or old feed sacks and haul them down into our cellar. Ideally, the temperature for storage should be 38° to 40° F., the humidity about 85 percent, and the area dark. One portion of our cellar seems to provide satisfactory conditions.

For years, like many other benighted souls, I conscientiously ignored potatoes, believing they contributed nothing but starch to the diet and girth to the waistline. Fortunately, most of us have now been educated (partly by potato growers, but also by nutritionists) beyond such nonsense, and it's now perfectly acceptable again to sing the praises of the potato. Since we live in a region that produces splendid specimens, we can enjoy them all the more. I'm sure that at least part of my acquired enthusiasm stems from the pleasures of growing, digging, and enjoying the taste of home-grown ones.

Potatoes originated in Peru or Chile and remain a staple food in the high sierra of South America. Latin America has contributed many foods to the world, but to cooler climates the potato has perhaps been most important. Its impact on world history has been profound. The Irish potato famines in 1845 and 1846, a result of late blight, caused the deaths of a million people from starvation and diseases resulting from malnutrition. Counting the million and a half Irish people who emigrated because of the situation, Ireland lost almost a third of its population as a consequence of its dependence on the potato.

Late blight is only one of dozens of enemies lying in wait for potato cultivators. Aside from insect pests and viruses that attack the plant, hordes of diseases are hanging around ready to destroy potatoes. Think of it: scabs, rots, wilts, blights, mosaics, and mildews, to say nothing of rhizoctonia and black scurf, which certainly sounds like the worst of the lot. Whether you buy a potato or grow one, you're participating in the celebration of a victory over the hosts trying to ravage it.

Potatoes grow from sets, that is, a chunk of potato that has at least one eye, that dimpled area you see in its skin. They prefer cool, acid soil. The plants need a fair amount of room. I plant chunks, each with two or more eyes, one foot apart in rows three feet apart. Once the sets sprout, the diligent gardener carefully pulls soil up against the stalks so potatoes forming on the roots will be covered. Any that form exposed to light will be green and inedible, in fact, poisonous. If a potato has a green area on the surface, remove it before preparing the vegetable.

Each plant will produce six to eight full-sized potatoes and a few small to tiny ones. That's not a bad return on garden space, if you can spare it. I'd try to grow a dozen or so plants for fresh use even if I hadn't enough area to grow them for storage.

Potatoes are planted early in spring. They're a long-season crop, and they prefer cool weather. Early, mid-season, and late varieties are available. Generally, the late varieties keep better than others but Irish Cobbler, an extremely good early potato, has kept well for us. Superior is another early potato we've found satisfactory. Of the late potatoes (we don't bother with mid-season ones), we've been pleased with Kennebec and Russet Burbank. Sometimes we grow Green Mountain, which is popular in New England. It's okay, but I like others better. Certain novelty types are occasionally sold too. I've read descriptions of Lady Finger, a small potato with yellow flesh, as well as All Blue and Blue Victor. Somehow I can't face the idea of a blue potato.

The yellow-fleshed Lady Finger is, however, tempting. In the high Andean valleys where corn doesn't grow well and the potato reigns supreme, those with yellow flesh are highly prized and said to be of superior quality. They are used in Peru for luxury foods, so I may have to try them.

We haven't had many difficulties in growing potatoes, but we're plagued by one pest. By the time the plants blossom, and sometimes before then, the horribles attack. That's my name for them. Others call them Colorado potato beetles, even though potatoes are an acquired taste for the loathsome creatures.

It's time to backtrack a little. Look at a Colorado beetle objectively, and it's rather a handsome insect. It's about three-tenths of an inch long (about the size and shape of my other friends, the Japanese beetles) and is yellow with black stripes. The stripes seem to be on its back, but actually decorate its wings. On the thorax, just behind the head, are black spots. Very colorful. The larva is another matter altogether. The beetle lays yellow egg masses, usually on the undersides of leaves. If you don't destroy the eggs, they hatch in a few days. The larvae, when they first appear, are tiny—little bright brownish specks, about the size of a pinhead, with distinct black markings. But, oh, how they grow. In a matter of days, they have become extraordinarily repulsive: slimy, humpbacked, and grossly fat from the potato leaves and flowers they've been eating. They're fully grown in three weeks.

Once they reach full size, the larvae burrow into the soil and presto! Ten to fifteen days later you've got more beetles ready to lay more eggs. A single beetle can produce thousands of descendants in a single season. It's easy to see that without something to interrupt their cycle, we'd soon be up to our knees in Colorado beetles and fresh out of potatoes.

Colorado beetles were first described in the 1820s by Stephen Harriman Long, an explorer who came upon them in the Rockies. They were feeding on a kind of nightshade called the buffalo burr and weren't particularly numerous. The problem is that the buffalo burr is a member of the Solanum family which, unfortunately, boasts potatoes, tomatoes, eggplant, ground cherries, garden huckleberries, and various nightshades, among its members. In the 1820s there weren't any potatoes in the Rockies, but by the middle of the century, settlers had introduced them.

The Colorado beetles were ecstatic about these newcomers to their territory and turned their attention to potatoes immediately. By 1874 they had reached the Atlantic coast, traveling from potato field to potato field and spreading eastward at the rate of about eighty-five miles a year. By 1922 they had somehow made it to France. Indeed, they've adapted themselves to all the places in which potatoes can be grown. And if they run out of potatoes, they're quite willing to turn their jaws to other food plants—the tomatoes, eggplants, and so on.

So what do you do about it in your garden? The easy answer is to turn to chemical controls, that is, the various dusts that can be applied to the foliage at suitable intervals, depending on rainfall. If you use that method, follow the instructions on the label carefully. The stuff is dangerous to people and pets too. There are other means of control that can be considered for the home garden.

The Colorado beetle winters over in the soil. If you see one while turning the soil, destroy it. Destroy the egg clusters on the undersides of leaves. I carry a coffee can while patrolling the potato patch and flick the beetles and egg clusters into it. It's just as easy (well, almost) as dusting, and a lot safer—and cheaper. Although the beetles will fly miles to find potatoes, once they've located them they like to stay put. It's easy to knock them off the leaves into a receptacle.

When I first started growing potatoes I noticed both larvae and beetles feeding on the potato plants at the same time. In my innocence I thought the larva was a completely different pest than the beetle. I watched them grow from flea-sized to slug-size with mounting horror. They do to potato plants what the Gypsy moth larvae do to trees. They're not easy to flick off either; they tend to stick to the leaves, and they're squishy and unpleasant to destroy. In dismay at their depredations (intolerable that they should be consuming a producer of *our* winter food), I gathered both beetles and larvae, put them and some water into a blender jar and whirled them to extinction. After straining the mess (and it was most definitely a mess), I sprayed the resulting liquid on the potato plants. My theory, evolved from reading some of my more subversive gardening literature, was that this procedure would convince the beasts that our garden was an undesirable neighborhood, much given to violence and other displays of hostility. The technique was remarkably ineffective, but time consuming. It made the neighbors quite merry, however. My next trick was to handpick the varmints into the coffee can. That too was time consuming, seeming to stretch longer each day. I finally became so hardened, so desperate, that I gritted my teeth, disposed of the coffee can, and squashed the creatures one and all, right on the leaves where they were feeding. It was a most disagreeable occupation, not to be recommended, unless one is in the foulest mood possible and looking for a socially acceptable way of expressing exaggerated disgruntlement. Even then . . . .

Having belatedly discovered that beetle and larva are different stages of the same pest, I continue a modified version of the campaign. Early in the season I concentrate on the beetles and eggs, and few larvae ever appear. Those that do show up I dust with rotenone. I've recently read that horseradish deters Colorado beetles and am considering planting some at each corner of the potato patch next year. There are dangers to that practice, even if it works. I don't plant potatoes in the same place each year, perish the thought, and that means moving the horseradish regularly. Even a sliver of its root will make a new plant, and the rotary tiller may just plant horseradish all over the garden. There is such a thing as too much horseradish.

But enough of bugs. Potatoes remain a staple food in South America. Many types are grown, some of which sound peculiar, to me at least.

They come in a wide range of colors, including a black-skinned one. Sizes vary, and shapes range from spherical to cylindrical. They are most often eaten boiled, accompanied by ají, an especially hot pepper, or with a thick sauce made from cheese, milk, and peppers. (The Spanish taught the Indians to make cheese.) Often they are garnished with hard-boiled eggs, ripe olives, and onions. Frequently such dishes are served as appetizers.

For centuries the Indians of South America have preserved potatoes by freeze-drying. The resulting material, *chuño*, is hard as wood but light as cork. After harvest, potatoes are taken to altitudes of 13,000 feet or more where they alternately freeze at night and thaw during the day. Their moisture evaporates in the dry air. *Chuño* is said to keep almost forever. A short soaking, followed by cooking, reconstitutes the potato. (The same process is used with other root vegetables and with meat and fish.) Sometimes the potatoes are cut up and cooked before freeze-drying; sometimes they are crushed during the process.

We've become fond of a number of Latin American potato recipes. My favorite is a simple sauce to be poured over quartered boiled potatoes.

CHEESE SAUCE FOR BOILED POTATOES   *Serves 4*

2   tablespoons butter
4   green onions, chopped
½   cup chopped onions
5   tomatoes, chopped
½   cup milk
1   teaspoon chopped parsley (dried) or 1 tablespoon fresh parsley
¼   teaspoon oregano (dried) or 1 teaspoon fresh chopped oregano
½   teaspoon cumin seeds
½   teaspoon salt
pepper to taste
1   cup grated mozzarella

Melt the butter in a heavy skillet. Add the green onions, including some of their tops, and cook gently for 5 minutes. Add the chopped onions and tomatoes and cook 5 minutes more. Add the milk, seasonings, and cheese, stirring constantly. When the cheese is melted, pour the sauce over hot potatoes and serve immediately.

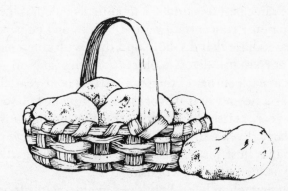

Most people enjoy baked potatoes. Served with fresh butter or sour cream, they complement many a fine meat or fish dish. Once in a while it's a nice change to make a twice-baked version. This one can be varied by substituting other kinds of cheese or omitting the bacon. Occasionally I use tiny bits of leftover ham, sautéed briefly, instead of bacon.

TWICE-BAKED POTATOES

Serves 6

6   **slices bacon**
6   **baked potatoes, hot**
4   **tablespoons butter**
¾   **cup grated sharp cheddar**
½   **cup milk**
1   **teaspoon salt**
¼   **teaspoon pepper**
2   **tablespoons minced green onions**

Have the oven temperature at 400°F. Sauté the bacon, drain, and crumble it. Cut a slit in the top of each potato and scoop out the pulp. Mash the pulp in a bowl with the butter, cheese, milk, and seasonings. Beat until smooth. Add the onions and bacon. Put the mixture into the shells, place them in a buttered baking dish, and bake until golden brown. It won't take long.

Everyone likes good French fried potatoes, but they're a terrible nuisance to make at home. An oven method is the delicious alternative.

OVEN FRIES

Serves 4

8   **medium potatoes, peeled**
ice water
salt and pepper to taste
¼   **cup melted butter**

Cut up the potatoes with a French fry cutter or knife to approximately the usual shape of French fries. Soak the pieces in ice water for an hour. Drain. Dry with paper towels. Place the potatoes in a single layer on a baking sheet. Salt and pepper them; dribble the butter over them evenly. Bake at 350°F. for 30-40 minutes, until they're as crisp as you like them. You may vary the recipe by using seasoned salt or by adding fresh chopped parsley or chives or grated Parmesan cheese just before serving. Another excellent variation is achieved by cutting the potatoes into quarters and then baking them as described above. They will, of course, take a little longer to cook than do the smaller pieces.

We usually have scalloped potatoes with baked ham. I always make more than I think we'll use for a given meal because we dote on the leftovers fried slowly in an iron skillet in butter. A crust of indescribable but exquisite crunchiness results.

SCALLOPED POTATOES

potatoes
butter
salt and pepper
grated cheese
milk

Peel and slice into rounds as many potatoes as you will need. Butter a baking dish. Put in a layer of potatoes. Dot with butter; salt and pepper. Sprinkle generously with grated cheese (we prefer a sharp cheddar, but other cheeses are good too). Continue with as many layers as you need to fill the dish, ending with cheese on top. Pour in enough milk to come half-way up the sides of the dish. Bake at 350°F. until tender. The amount of time it takes will vary according to the type of potato you use and the thickness of the slices, but it usually takes at least an hour. Closely covering the dish for the first part of the baking time will speed up cooking, but it may also induce the milk to bubble over the sides. Be forewarned and set the dish on a baking sheet or something similar to preclude a scorched mess in the bottom of the oven.

POTATO STUFFING   *Serves 4*

3   medium potatoes,
      peeled and boiled
¼   cup milk
½   teaspoon salt
¼   teaspoon pepper
4-8 tablespoons butter
      or margarine
½   cup chopped
      onions
2   cups bread cubes
      or croutons
2   beaten eggs
¼   cup chopped
      parsley

Preheat the oven to 350°F. Mash the potatoes, beating in the milk, salt, and pepper. Melt 4 tablespoons butter in a skillet and sauté the onions gently for 5 minutes. Remove them and mix them into the potatoes. Sauté the bread cubes until crisp in 4 tablespoons butter and add them to the potatoes or add the croutons directly to the potatoes. Stir in the beaten eggs and parsley. Place the mixture in a buttered baking dish and bake for 35 minutes, or until golden brown.

Our whole family likes roast fowl with stuffing. Once in a while for a change from our usual bread stuffing, I make this potato filling. I cook it in a buttered dish, not in the cavity of the bird, and it serves both as stuffing and potatoes for that meal. It may be cooked inside the bird if you prefer. We like it cooked separately, because then the texture is crisp rather than soft.

Red McClure, Norland, Norgold Russett, McNeilly, Cherokee, Belrus, Butte, Kennebec, Green Mountain, Irish Cobbler, Superior, Early Gem, Viking, Crystal, Red Pontiac, Bison: there's a potato for every taste, a different recipe for every occasion. With the introduction of Explorer, the adventurous can grow potatoes from seeds as well as sets. If you have the space to grow potatoes, and the right kind of climate, you'll discover that home-grown ones are worth the effort involved.

Winter Squash

The colorful piles of squashes at roadside stands in late summer and early fall—Hubbard, acorn, butternut, and buttercup—attest to New England's abiding respect for them. We consume more of this nutritious fruit than other areas of the country and use it in more varied guises than is common in most of North America. It's time that word got around.

Though squash was cultivated in New England at the time the first English settlers arrived, it's another import from Latin America and goes back about 5,000 years. Some students of the history of agriculture believe it may have been the first food crop cultivated there. When it was first grown for food though, it was the seeds that were eaten, not the flesh.

Though we use winter squash in many ways, we're not as adventuresome as cooks in some other countries. Using the toasted seeds for snacks is rather recent with us; it's old hat in Mexico and points south, where they're known as *pepitas*. There the shelled seeds are also ground into a meal used in making sauces. The flesh of the varieties that have developed from the original stock is used as a vegetable, in soups, stews, fritters, and puddings. One kind of stew is partially cooked and then ladled into a precooked squash to continue baking until done. It's served at table from the squash shell. Sweetened, sun-dried squash was an ancient Peruvian treat and candied squash is still a popular delicacy. In the Caribbean, vegetables constitute a much more important part of the diet than they do here and the *calabaza*, or West Indian pumpkin, is a staple item in kitchens. Despite its various shapes and colors, this large squash tastes much like our butternut squash.

Squash is steamed or boiled or baked to be served as a side dish, and squash pies are standard fall desserts. It's an old New England trick to add cooked squash to cakes, biscuits, cookies, breads, pancakes, and rolls. The resulting flavor is as popular as the pleasantly moist texture.

You never heard of squash bread? Think pumpkin instead. Pumpkin is a kind of squash, and for all practical purposes, cooked Hubbard, butternut, or buttercup squash can be substituted for cooked pumpkin. (The Italian word *zucchine* literally means "little pumpkins." Zucchini are actually cylindrical pumpkins which, as we know all too well, will grow to watermelon size if given half a chance.) For reasons that escape me, "pumpkin" pie and "pumpkin" bread or cake or cookies sound more appetizing to most people than "squash" pie, etc. I use what I happen to have, but in pursuit of diplomacy, call the resulting product "pumpkin" whatever. So far, no one has eyed me sternly and said, "Why, what do you mean, pumpkin? This is clearly made with Waltham's Butternut squash!"

Normally, people with smallish gardens don't bother growing winter squash because they're vining plants that require considerable space. Winter squash can be interplanted with sweet corn when space is at a premium and will do well in the dappled shade produced by the cornstalks. But the practice makes corn harvesting somewhat hazardous, with possible danger both to harvester and immature squash. For these reasons, many of the summer squash, which are usually of a bushy habit, are recommended instead. In addition to requiring less space, summer squash at its best is picked while young and should go immediately from garden to kitchen. Winter squash, however, is picked at maturity and can be stored for relatively long periods without deterioration of quality. In recent years, several winter squashes having a bushy habit of growth have been introduced, so more and more home gardeners are tempted to grow their own.

Culture is the same, apart from space, as for summer squash, cucumbers, and the rest of the cucurbit tribe. Problems of disease and insect pests are similar too. Rely on packet instructions of the kinds you buy for proper distance between hills. I like to plant several different kinds; leftover seeds can be stored in a cool, dry place, and used another season. I stow them, in the original packets, in a glass jar with a good tight-fitting lid.

If you plan to store squash, you should cure it first. Cut the squash from the vine leaving a piece of stem attached, and put it in a warm, dry place (80° to 85° F.) for about ten days. Store it, after curing, in a dry area at 55° to 60° F. We've found that Hubbard and butternut squash keep longer than other varieties. Acorn squashes have been least satisfactory. They begin to develop soft spots along about January. On second thought, that's not too bad.

One of the beauties of squash is easy storage. If you don't have facilities for storing them in the usual way, but want to take advantage of seasonal prices or a bumper crop, there's an alternative. I use the method on acorn squash that threaten to rot before our appetite for them is sated. Split the squash and remove the seeds. Bake halves—or pieces, depending on the size of the fruit—on a baking sheet in a 300°F. oven until tender. Cool, package, and freeze. I leave acorn squash in halves, shell on, but remove the shell from other varieties before packaging. I make an effort to package the product in sizes appropriate to our favorite recipes. Freezing is the only satisfactory way to store the monstrous squashes such as Hubbard after they've been cut.

When we want pumpkin pie or bread, I remove a package of whatever is handiest (but not acorn, which doesn't have the correct texture or a deep enough flavor), whether it be butternut, Hubbard, or buttercup (or pumpkin, for that matter). After thawing it in a colander, I purée it in the blender or food processor. A sieve or ricer will do the job too.

Aside from the old favorites, occasional new varieties capture the public fancy. The latest fad squash is spaghetti squash. The entire squash is steamed, and the interior scooped out and eaten as a low-calorie substitute for spaghetti. Typically, it's served with a sauce or a seasoned butter. It was my original opinion that spaghetti squash was either a mistake or some horrendous joke foisted off on a gullible market. Some people thought it delicious; our family thought it ghastly, when we sampled the one given to us by a friend. The next year, we were again given a spaghetti squash. Having listened to and read rave reviews of the variety in the intervening months, we decided to try it again. It was delicious. It was also enormous, so I cooked and froze the half we hadn't consumed. Thawed, heated, and served with a sauce, it was nearly as good as the fresh batch had been. Now, either I goofed terrifically in cooking and serving that original squash we disliked, or it was an inferior specimen. We were so impressed by the second squash that the next year we grew some. They were good. There's a moral there somewhere, but let's not pursue it.

We grow the old standbys each year, but try unfamiliar ones once in a while too. One year the experiments included Hungarian Mammoth, Jumbo Pink Banana, and Kuta. The first two are strictly winter types. They grew to stupendous size. We found the flavor and texture inferior to the standards we usually grow, and fed them to the cows. I mentioned the Kuta with summer squash. It was just as disappointing as a winter squash as it had been in its other guises. The cows got a bonanza of squash that year.

Bud's favorite is acorn squash. He likes them split and baked, the cavities lightly salted and sprinkled with nutmeg. In each cavity I put about a tablespoonful of dark brown sugar, a pat of butter, and a generous dollop of sherry or a skimpy one of brandy. Other spices, such as ginger, can be used instead of nutmeg. Try maple syrup instead of brown sugar. The same treatment works with butternut or buttercup squash.

If I have the time and inclination, I separate the seeds from the strings surrounding them, season them, and toast them on a lightly oiled baking sheet while the squash bakes. Tom likes to munch them, and they're nutritious. If I don't feel up to it, the birds get them.

My own candidate for top squash is buttercup—cooked, mashed, salted, buttered lavishly, and sprinkled with freshly ground pepper. If squash is boiled, it should be well drained and dried briefly and carefully in its cooking pot, so it won't be watery. Sometimes after mashing it, I season squash with brown sugar, salt, butter, chopped nuts, and raisins. We like our squash on the dry, lumpy side, not like the puréed frozen squash, which strikes us as totally lacking in character. Unless it's served in a dessert or generally embellished, our sons look upon squash as something to be consumed dutifully, in as small portions as possible, so I try to be creative in serving it. One thing that never sullies our squash is marshmallows. We firmly believe that marshmallows belong in steaming mugs of cocoa or on sticks held over hot coals.

When it comes to making pumpkin pie, I use many different varieties (always with a fine, careless indifference about whether it is actually pumpkin or merely squash) but I insist on using a preponderance of dark brown sugar as the sweetener. Brown sugar seems to have a particular affinity for squash. Maple sugar or syrup are superb for the purpose, but their price can be a deterrent. Molasses, if you enjoy its sharp taste, is effective too. Interestingly, the recipes traditionally used for squash pie most often call for white sugar. I stolidly ignore their directions and use brown. We like a combination of nutmeg, cinnamon, ginger, and cloves to spice pumpkin pie and consider whipped cream a necessary accompaniment.

Squash bread is especially good. I usually make four loaves at a time, using an enormous cauldron for the mixing, so there will be extra loaves to store in the freezer. It's an excellent emergency ration to have on hand. We slice it about half an inch thick and toast it in the toaster oven for breakfast. It's good served as a tea bread too.

SQUASH BREAD   *1 loaf*

¼ **cup softened butter**
1 **cup sugar**
2 **eggs**
1 **cup puréed squash**
1½ **cups flour**
½ **teaspoon baking powder**
½ **teaspoon salt**
1 **teaspoon baking soda**
¾ **teaspoon cinnamon**
½ **teaspoon cloves**
¼ **cup water**
½ **cup chopped nuts**
½ **cup raisins**

Cream butter, sugar, and eggs. Stir in the squash. Add the dry ingredients alternately with the water. Stir in the nuts and raisins. Spoon into a greased loafpan and bake in an oven preheated to 350°F. until the cake tests done, about 50–60 minutes. Turn the loaf on to a wire rack to cool thoroughly before slicing.

We grow pumpkins as well as winter squash, but if space were limited, I wouldn't bother, since squash can substitute in any of the pumpkin recipes, but pumpkin isn't necessarily good as an unadorned vegetable dish. You'll recall that in the high Andean valleys of South America where they originated, pumpkins and other squashes were grown as much for their seeds as for their flesh. Those seeds weren't simply used for snacking, either. Suitably roasted and pounded and steeped in boiling water they became a tea. The colonists added honey or sugar and milk. Sounds ghastly, but who are we to criticize?

I have no plans to pound seeds and steep them in water, even for the novelty of it. With or without honey, sugar, and milk, I think I'll pass and munch on toasted seeds, salted. Instead of the toasting method, you can fry them, for two or three minutes, in a little salad oil. Salt them and enjoy. But enjoy them immediately; unlike the jarred ones from the supermarket, they won't be tasty for long. Their flavor fades fast, and shortly thereafter they become rancid.

If you want homemade pumpkin seed snacks to last, what you have to do is remove them from the pumpkin and separate them from all that nasty, stringy mess inside the vegetable. Put them on paper towels to dry. It'll take about a week. (Sorry about that; some things can't be hurried.) If you can't face having seeds drying all over every available surface, you'll have to toast them in the oven or fry them (after they're cleaned up) and serve them immediately. For keeping, it's the paper towel business, and they must be turned a couple of times a day too. Finally, store the dried seeds in airtight containers. Old coffee cans with their handy plastic lids will work just fine.

It's sometimes suggested that those who are really fond of pumpkin seeds ought to grow Lady Godiva or Triple Treat pumpkins. Or even Eat-All squash (a squash seed is, after all, very like a pumpkin seed, what with pumpkins being squash). These varieties produce the so-called "naked" seeds. No hulls. Maybe I'm dim or deluded, but I've never been able to see the point. Pumpkin and squash seeds, properly cleaned and toasted on an oiled baking sheet, seasoned with whatever kind of salt you favor, are completely edible. At least, our family always eats the whole seed, with no observable ill effects. Maybe we're missing the taste treat of the century.

There are pumpkins in all sizes, for all purposes. The big ones such as Big Max impress people and make wonderful jack-o'-lanterns. They may weigh over a hundred pounds. But if that sounds like a lot of pies, forget it. They're strictly for show—or cattle fodder. For edibility, you want one of the smaller sugar pumpkins. The flesh is sweeter, less coarse, and less stringy.

Few of us look upon pumpkins as more than decorations or the foundation for a pie. But let's give pumpkins their due. The Pilgrims grew them and called them *pompions*. They used the seeds in breads. They also—well, maybe not righteous Pilgrims, but the colonists anyway— discovered how to mix pumpkins and maple sugar and persimmons to make beer. They had tried to grow hops and barley for the purpose. Having no success, they turned to what was at hand. No, apparently pumpkin beer didn't taste much like the real article, but it had the desired effect. They used the time-honored suspicion of contaminated water as an excuse for brewing it.

If all you know of using pumpkin is for pie, fall is the time to introduce a little diversity into your approach to this fruit. Your favorite pumpkin pie recipe can, more easily, be a crustless dessert. Bake the filling in custard cups and serve them with whipped cream dusted with cinnamon. Try a stew made of beef and vegetables and sliced peaches, served in a baked pumpkin shell. Use a small pumpkin, as opposed to the cow-fodder variety. Slice the top off and remove the seeds and stringy pulp. Save the seeds for a snack. Bake the pumpkin in a 400°F. oven for about forty-five minutes, until it's tender. Or steam it gently. Then fill it with the stew and serve, making sure to include some pumpkin flesh with each serving.

You can produce an interesting meat loaf using much the same procedure. After it's been precooked, fill the pumpkin with a meat loaf mixture and bake at 350° F. for fifty to sixty minutes. It's basically the same idea as any other stuffed winter squash.

There's a pumpkin stew which all of us, including the boys, like particularly. Bear in mind that other sturdy winter squashes may be substituted for the pumpkin in any of these recipes. Anyway, this is a South African dish, highly spiced and served with rice. It's said to be of Malay origin, as is its name, *bredie*. Bredies are highly variable but are always, basically, thick stews of meat and vegetables.

PUMPKIN BREDIE   *Serves 4*

1½   pounds boneless lamb stew meat (or use leftover roasted lamb cut into bite–sized pieces)
cooking oil
2   tablespoons butter
2   onions, thinly sliced
4   cups pumpkin flesh cut into 1-inch cubes
½   teaspoon ginger
¼   teaspoon cloves
½   teaspoon cinnamon
½   cup water
½–1   teaspoon crushed red pepper (or more, if you like it fiery)
1   teaspoon salt

If you're starting with raw lamb, brown it in a little oil in a heavy skillet. Remove all but 2 tablespoons of fat and add the onions. Cook gently until they're soft. (If you're using leftover lamb, start out by cooking the onions in 2 tablespoons of butter until they're soft. Then add the lamb.) Either way, next stir in the pumpkin cubes and the spices and turn the heat to very low. Cover and cook for half an hour, checking often to make sure nothing is sticking. Add the water, crushed red pepper, and salt and stir the mixture to reduce the pumpkin to a coarse purée. Cover and cook over low heat, about 10 minutes for leftover lamb, about 45 for boneless lamb stew meat. Check it often. Add a little water if it seems in danger of sticking to the skillet. Serve over rice.

Pumpkins prefer, for storage, a temperature of 50° to 60° F., in a moist place. That's a little different from storing other winter squash. The skins of pumpkins are more tender too, so care must be exercised to prevent damaging them and inviting soft spots. Make sure the stem is still attached to pumpkins you're storing. They won't keep as long as the other winter squash and too high a temperature tends to make their meat stringy.

Beets

Harvesting the beets and carrots can safely wait until late in the season. In temperate climates, root crops have historically been important to man during the winter. If properly stored, they can be kept in good condition and used until new crops are ready in the field. And proper storage involves considerably less trouble than with many other foods. No canning, no freezing, or drying is necessary as long as these foods are kept cool (but above freezing), and the correct humidity is maintained. Some root crops, such as parsnips, can be left in the ground all winter and are more highly prized in spring after they've been frozen.

One of our well-known cooking authorities (wish I could remember which one) has remarked that the flavor of canned beets is superior to that of fresh ones. We can only assume that the poor soul has never known the gustatory pleasures of tiny beets fresh from the garden, delicately steamed with their own greens, the whole works slathered with melting butter. I managed to attain the age of twelve or so still cherishing a fine contempt for beets in any form. Then an aunt with a splendid garden on rich Illinois soil invited us to dinner. The platter in the middle of the table, heaped with beets and greens, certainly looked appetizing. I knew, of course, that I'd be expected to accept a generous helping and choke it down without visible signs of distress. You've guessed the outcome. I became an instant convert to the delicacy, practically evangelical in my zeal to persuade others of its superiority to other methods of preparing the vegetable. One thing led to another, as it is wont to do, and I began to realize that beets had a certain appeal in other forms too.

It was the fresh ones, those intriguing infants, that did the trick, but let it be admitted that canned beets are quite good, as long as they know their place. Fresh beets need little gilding; others benefit from a few culinary tricks.

Beets have a long and honorable history. Native to the Mediterranean area, they've been cultivated since prehistoric times. The Romans ate only the tops, the leaves, but by the beginning of the Christian era, the root was being used as a food too. Charlemagne, who had something of a reputation as a busybody in agricultural affairs, recommended beets highly as a crop to his subjects. His subjects ignored him but during the

Renaissance beets were re-introduced to France and from there spread to other parts of Europe.

Beets are biennials; they don't set seed until their second year. This is a perfectly delightful characteristic from certain points of view, particularly for those of us interested in green, leafy vegetables. Beets? Green leafy vegetables? It's unfortunately true that by the time beets reach any reasonable size, those tender green tops are decidedly tough and scraggly looking. But you'll recall that one member of the family, chard, is grown strictly for its tops. And that first year it's planted, it won't bolt as annuals do.

Table beets and chard aren't the only important members of the family, either. Consider the sugar beet. In the United States we use more cane sugar than beet sugar, but in 1982 farmers grew 42,544,000 pounds of sugar beets. Beets like temperate to cool temperatures and can be grown in places too cold for sugar cane. Indeed, if the color of beets you buy or pull from your garden is faded, it suggests that while they were growing the temperature was high.

The first beet-sugar factory, in Germany in 1796, failed. Sixteen years later, a French factory proved successful, and by 1880 beet sugar supplied more of Europe's needs than cane sugar. Now, about a third of the European consumption is beet sugar. You may have noticed sugar beet seed offered in seed catalogues. Along with the seeds you order, the seed companies send instructions for making beet sugar at home. We tried growing sugar beets one year, but one look at the instructions for making sugar convinced us that self-sufficiency sometimes comes too dear. If you don't count the cost of your own labor, you can probably produce beet sugar at home for under $40 a pound. So what did we do with our sugar beets? We fed them to the cows, a time-honored custom of which they clearly approved. Feed stores sell beet pulp (a by-product of the beet-sugar industry) as cattle feed. Moreover, still another member of this versatile family, the stock beet, or mangel-wurzel, is widely grown as livestock feed in Europe and elsewhere. It is grown in North America too, but our climate permits the widespread cultivation of corn, which is superior in many respects for the purpose.

If you decide you want to feast on beet greens and tiny beets, you'd be wise to wait for local beets in season, your own or those from a farmer's market. Fresh beets are almost always available in markets, but the greens of shipped beets aren't likely to be of good quality. In fact, the greens are often absent altogether. If you grow your own, thinning will be necessary because a beet (or chard) "seed" is actually a cluster of seeds in a protective covering. The thinnings can provide early table greens. The roots can be enjoyed all year, and storage in a root cellar eliminates the need for canning the surplus.

There are plenty of appetizing ways to use any beets available, fresh or canned. Drain a one-pound can of sliced beets and heat them gently with about a quarter cup sour cream, a sprinkle of salt, and either a teaspoon of caraway seeds or a skimpy teaspoon of horseradish. Or add a pat of butter and two tablespoons of lemon juice, a tablespoon of sugar, and a sprinkling of salt to drained, sliced beets. Heat gently and serve garnished with fresh chopped parsley.

Some cookbooks recommend scrubbing beets, cooking them in their jackets, and then removing the skins. Easy enough, provided the beets are uniform in size. But large beets aren't usually served whole, and cooking them whole takes a long time. I prefer to peel them before cooking. All that red juice running down the drain doesn't mean you'll be serving anemic-looking beets. The tiny ones need no peeling, just a good scrubbing.

We like to keep pickled beets on hand. The fastest recipe I know combines a cup of cider vinegar and a cup of sugar, brought to a boil with a tablespoon of mixed pickling spices. Strain and pour it over one pound of cooked and drained sliced beets. Refrigerate at least overnight before serving. The Pennsylvania Dutch always add hard-boiled eggs to pickled beets. If they're to be served immediately, the eggs can be sliced. Otherwise, use them whole, or pieces of yolk will cloud the pickling liquid.

Another old standby is Harvard beets, of which I'm inordinately fond.

HARVARD BEETS   *Serves 4*

¼   cup sugar
½   tablespoon
     cornstarch
¼   cup cider vinegar
2   tablespoons water
1   pound sliced or
     diced cooked
     beets, drained
2   tablespoons orange
     marmalade

Blend sugar, cornstarch, vinegar, and water. Bring to a boil and cook gently until clear. Add beets and let stand at least 10 minutes. Just before serving, bring to the boiling point and add marmalade.

Carrots

Carrots are easily grown, easily stored, widely available all year, and inexpensive. They can be stored in root cellars, refrigerators, or under mulch in their rows in the garden, so they can be pulled as needed all winter long. (One winter, I confess, our next door neighbors lost a crop stored thus to hungry wildlife.) They can be canned or frozen, eaten cooked or raw. Orange is the preferred color, but you can also find them in white, yellow, red, and purple. To each his own. In some parts of the world, carrots are used as stock feed. They're higher in sugar content than any other vegetable except beets, which is one reason they're used in desserts, jams, and wines, as well as for snacks, salads, and their more traditional role as cooked vegetables.

Carrots have been around for a long time, since prehistoric times. It is believed that they originated in Afghanistan, but they were introduced to the Mediterranean area early. The Greeks mention them as early as 500 B.C., but didn't seem to think highly of them. Both Greeks and Romans preferred turnips, evidence that the wisdom of the ancients left something to be desired. Charlemagne thought carrots would be a dandy thing for farmers to grow, but they weren't especially enthusiastic about the idea. (Charlemagne had a lot of ideas, but nobody seemed to be listening.) However, by the thirteenth century at the latest, carrots were known in France and Germany and in China. There's some argument about whether they were first grown in the British Isles in the thirteenth century or the seventeenth, but what's a few centuries among scholars?

The wild carrots we have growing everywhere, Queen Anne's lace, are not native plants. That they have proliferated so extensively attests to their sturdiness. The domestic strains are sturdy too, but necessarily more demanding.

Growing carrots is no particular problem provided you have a reasonably friable soil that's free of rocks to a depth of eight inches or so. A carrot that hits a stone is a carrot deformed, unlovely. The single best reason for growing carrots is that you then have a supply of tiny ones which need only be trimmed and scrubbed to provide a delicious food. Such carrots aren't easily obtainable commercially. Sow the seed sparsely enough that the carrots will have room to develop properly, but remember that the thinnings can be a harvest too. The taste of fresh, small carrots is incomparable, whether raw or cooked.

There are plenty of other ways to prepare carrots. To begin with, there are carrot sticks. Keep a supply handy in the refrigerator, and maybe the family will be less tempted by junk foods. Thin slices are welcome in salads too. Many people like them, grated, in gelatin salads, but that's a subject too painful to contemplate. Other pleasant salads can, however, be made with grated carrots. Use blender or food processor; it's a snap. Mix grated carrot, smallish pieces of apple, and raisins with a dollop of mayonnaise and serve it on a bed of lettuce. Vary it with chunk or drained, crushed pineapple. Sometimes I add grated carrot to cole slaw. No one complains.

Raw carrots are often more appealing to children than cooked ones, but for certain meals I find cooked carrots indispensable. A pot roast without whole carrots, potatoes, and onions glazed and browned with meat juices is a pot roast devoid of character. A stew without carrot chunks is a sorry excuse for a stew.

Carrots can be served in other ways too. In a roux, for example. This is one of Kiddo's recipes, and it's variable. Sometimes she used green beans with, or instead of, carrots.

CARROTS AND POTATOES IN ROUX *Serves 4*

4–8 carrots, scraped and sliced	Boil the carrots and potatoes until tender; drain. Keep them warm. While the vegetables are cooking, brown the flour in an iron skillet over moderate heat, stirring constantly to prevent scorching. Remove from heat. Add butter and salt, stirring constantly. Add ½ cup liquid, a little at a time, until the mixture is smooth. Return to moderate heat. Stir constantly, adding more liquid a little at a time to achieve the consistency you prefer. When the mixture is smooth and bubbling, pour it over the hot vegetables and serve immediately.

4–8   carrots, scraped and
        sliced
4   medium potatoes,
        peeled and sliced
2   tablespoons flour
2   tablespoons butter
1   teaspoon salt
½–1   cup milk or
        vegetable water

A simple glaze does wonders for carrots too. Just melt 2 tablespoons butter in a skillet, add 2 tablespoons honey, and toss cooked, seasoned carrots in the mixture until they're glazed. Add a teaspoon of lemon juice and serve. Or substitute 2 tablespoons sugar for the honey and add 2 tablespoons of chopped mint. If your menu won't admit a sweetened vegetable, use 2 tablespoons melted butter, 1 tablespoon lemon juice, and ½ teaspoon dried crushed basil (1–2 teaspoons fresh, chopped basil) added to cooked carrots for four.

Should the spirit move you to a somewhat more elaborate treatment, you might try this one.

CARROTS IN ORANGE SAUCE · *Serves 4*

¼ cup sugar
2 teaspoons flour
½ teaspoon salt
1 teaspoon grated orange peel
½ cup orange juice
1½ tablespoons butter
2 cups sliced cooked carrots, drained

Mix together sugar, flour, salt, and orange peel. Add the juice and cook, stirring constantly, until the sauce thickens. Add the butter and carrots and heat through.

Once the harvest is in, it's time to start thinking about putting the garden to bed. That brings us to some related activities likely to help you achieve better results more efficiently next year.

CHAPTER 8

Records and Resolutions

In the twenty years that I've been gardening actively, by which I mean whole-hog as opposed to planting a few flats of annual flowers, the activity has always had an end in sight because we've lived in New England. How I'd adjust to year-round enslavement I don't know. But even though the outdoor projects stop for a while, in a real sense gardening is a year-round occupation.

Putting the garden to bed for the winter is a little like putting a child to bed for the night. The garden takes longer but there are similarities. All kinds of unforeseens may delay the doing, and you may even have to deliver a drink or two before the plants are ready for their rest.

Most gardening magazines have you starting the autumn ritual about Thanksgiving up here in the North. But to wait until then is asking for work outdoors in some unpleasant weather, and lots of things can be done much earlier than that. Unfortunately, moving these gardening jobs forward means that they crowd into that busiest time of the year— when we're raking leaves and cleaning storm windows, planting bulbs, and getting in the firewood. Everything has to be done in just a few weeks time.

For me, the easiest way to get it all in is to compile my fall must-do list and to tick things off as I finish them. I confess it: I'm a list addict, gaining giddy pleasure from crossing off lines of words, the unearned satisfaction of knowing that everything is under control—even when it isn't.

First on my fall list is clearing the debris from the vegetable garden. Insect pests delight in wintering over in the spent stalks of plants. Your choices are to till the trash into the soil or gather it up for the compost heap. Either way, it's wise then to plant a cover crop such as rye or to lay down some mulch.

Timing the mulching of vegetable gardens can be tricky; so can figuring the depth of the mulch and the material used. For perennial garden spots, you can usually wait until after the ground is frozen and hope that you have no snow before then. Where I live, that first snow effectively prevents later mulching because the mulch you need, if not under wraps, will be difficult to move and spread. Using tree leaves for mulching almost anything is fine, except for lawns, where all mine want to be. Once wet and matted, a heavy layer of leaves can smother everything beneath it, so be careful where you use them. Not mulching is sometimes dangerous. Shrubs and perennials can have their roots exposed by successive freezes and thaws, leaving them vulnerable to drying out and death.

Gardeners, even those who like to cook, don't live by vegetables and herbs alone, so second on my list of fall chores is to take cuttings for indoor planting this winter and to lift plants that I want to bloom inside. Coleus, impatiens, and fibrous-rooted begonias will readily root in water or sand or vermiculite. They give color all winter and can be taken back outside in the spring.

Since most of the perennial herbs live in flower beds now, while I'm working there I pot up thyme, mint, and horehound to spend the winter in the light garden with the parsley, rosemary, chives, and oregano that are regular winter residents. For the most part, I rely on preserved herbs in winter.

And remember to dig some good garden soil and compost and to keep it in a frost free location. You'll need it for potting all winter and for starting plants early in the spring before the ground has thawed.

Notice that I keep throwing the words *mulch* and *compost* around, as if every gardener in the world used both. I know that just isn't so. Many gardeners use neither. Crusading is foreign to my nature, but since both compost and mulch are dear to my heart, let me put in a good word for them.

That scruffy-looking heap near the young butternut trees is the compost pile. Aesthetically it leaves a lot to be desired, but at bottom it's pure gold. Compost is the crumbly product obtained from decaying organic material. It looks like good loam. Compost improves the texture of the soil by lightening it, and its addition helps the soil to retain moisture. Compost returns to the soil the nutrients used by growing plants.

There are multitudinous ways to make compost—everything from recipes for concocting a super product in a mere two weeks to letting nature do all the work for you. As you'd expect, I prefer the latter approach. If getting compost fast is important to you, a quick trip to the nearest library will give you all the information you need, and maybe more than you want. Meanwhile, let's consider three easy ways to make compost.

First of all, there's that pile down by the butternuts. I start mining underneath it as soon as the ground thaws in the spring. I use the good rich stuff in flats to which I'm transplanting seedlings. Sometimes I sow seeds in flats half-filled with compost and topped with vermiculite. At about the same time I'm adding to the top of the pile again with leaves and other mulches being slowly cleared from the gardens as the weather warms up. What materials can go into the compost heap? Almost any natural product except bones and fat. Those might attract rats or other scavengers, and the bones take too long to decompose. Other kinds of kitchen wastes are fine for the pile. That includes coffee grounds, tea leaves, and eggshells, fruit peels, and vegetable parings. My pile contains layers of weeds, clumps of sod, leaves, and barn bedding too. Grass clippings are also good additions. If your soil is acidic, you can add a layer of lime now and again. Lacking manure, pile on a few shovelsful of garden soil occasionally. Unless you're determined to have a finished product within a given time, you don't have to worry about turning the pile, moistening it, adding activators, and using specific lists of ingredients. If what you add seems likely to attract insects or animals, cover it well with garden soil or bury it within the pile.

You don't have a suitable place for a compost pile? No problem. There are two ways to proceed. Their only drawback is that you won't have a special place to raid when you need potting soil or top dressing. If you mulch your garden, you can engage in a variety of sheet composting. Just pick up some mulch, deposit the compost materials, and replace the mulch on top. That's all there is to it. The entire garden becomes a compost heap—and there's no carrying the finished product to the plants. It's helpful to do such sheet composting in an orderly fashion, starting at one edge of the plot and working to the other, so the whole garden shares in the benefits.

You say you don't do much mulching? Still no problem. Bury the compost materials. In one of his books, Euell Gibbons mentions the incredible fertility of an island he visited in the South Pacific. The inhabitants buried all garbage and manure wherever it happened to be. All the mess was out of sight and busily at work improving the soil. My parents, who garden on a small lot, bury kitchen waste, and their plants are robust and attractive.

Finished compost is crumbly and has a pleasant woodsy aroma, just like the compost nature makes in the forest. Half-finished compost has much the same smell, but is coarser, with bits of stalk remaining in it. It can be used for the vegetable garden, for potting soil, for top dressing flower beds, or feeding shrubbery and for transplanting. Chopped materials turn into compost faster than unchopped ones, but the additional chore is unnecessary unless speed is an objective. The important consideration is having a steady supply for your plants.

To mulch or not to mulch is a question that occurs to many gardeners. No matter how visually pleasing a well tilled garden may be, there are compelling reasons for becoming addicted to mulch.

A mulch is any material that covers bare soil. Gravel, marble chips, and sheets of plastic can be used as mulches. So can old carpeting, magazines, and newspapers. More conventional mulches include hay and straw, seaweed, wood chips, bark, sawdust, grass clippings, peat moss, cocoa hulls, weeds, and leaves. Any kind of mulch will help keep weeds under control and conserve moisture. A mulch of materials that decompose will help enrich the soil as well. If you get carried away and garden entirely by the mulch system, you'll never need to till or spade your garden again.

In theory I'm in favor of the year-round mulch system so vigorously advocated by the late Ruth Stout. In practice I've never given it a fair trial because it takes more mulch than I've ever had at any given time. The minimum amount necessary for an area 50 feet by 50 feet is twenty-five bales of hay. That's over half a ton of hay, and that's only the beginning. If you're interested in the method, look up one of Ms. Stout's books at your library. She knows whereof she speaks. Moreover, even the titles are tantalizing: *How to Have a Green Thumb without an Aching Back; Gardening without Work: for the Aging, the Busy, and the Indolent; The*

Ruth Stout No-Work Garden Book. The limited amount of mulching I do has convinced me that it saves a lot of trouble, but I'm not convinced a year-round mulch on everything is a good idea for gardeners with short seasons. The mulch will slow the warming of the soil in the spring, which certain tender vegetables might resent.

If you don't use a year-round mulch, the next question that arises is when to apply it. Unfortunately, that depends on specific plants and the material used too. Heat-loving plants like tomatoes and melons can be mulched with plastic as soon as they're set in the garden, but a mulch of hay will keep the soil too cool for their well-being early in the season. Mulch would have to wait here, say, until the end of June, after the soil has had a chance to heat up. How much mulch? About eight inches of a loose mulch like hay. It will quickly pack down into a covering two or three inches deep. If weeds spring up, you've been too sparing. Either pull them (which will be easy because the mulch keeps the soil soft) or smother them with more mulch. Cool weather crops such as peas and spinach can be mulched as soon as they're large enough that you can position the mulch without burying them. They'll appreciate cool feet and the retained moisture, and your work load will be considerably smaller.

If your soil is rich, vegetable mulch alone will maintain its fertility, provided you use a variety of materials. If it's poor or only so-so, continue a fertilizing program for a couple of years, including lime for acid soil. Eventually, if a variety of mulching materials is used, you'll probably be able to dispense with lime applications as well as with additional fertilizers.

In our area, one of the best mulch materials is leaves. Leaves pack into a clammy, almost impenetrable mass, but so long as they're not smothering the plants you're trying to grow, that's all right. Unchopped leaves take a long time to decompose, which frees you from renewing the mulch frequently. The best argument for leaves is their ready availability—and they're free. Mulch hay may cost as much as $1 or more a bale. (Mulch hay, by definition, is for some reason unfit for consumption by livestock.)

What you use for mulch in ornamental borders requires a measure of attention to appearance. For that reason, peat moss, shredded bark, cocoa hulls, and other attractive materials are popular. A stone mulch is effective in controlling weeds and retaining moisture, but won't increase fertility.

Mulches are effective for protection in our severe winters. What hurts hardy plants most is the alternate freezing and thawing of the ground, which frequently exposes the roots to drying winds. A mulch of snow is fine protection, but something we can't count on to remain constant. After hard frost finishes off annuals I pull them up and toss them on the compost heap, but I don't cut off the perennials even though they'd look tidier. I let leaves from the trees pile up around them to provide insulation. (Permitting the tops to remain prevents the leaves from matting and thus smothering the plants.) The leaves make the beds look shaggy through the winter, but come spring clean-up time, the debris can be tossed on the compost pile and the sheltered perennials exposed to grow again.

If you don't use a compost pile, any mulch you want to remove from ornamental borders can be used in the vegetable garden. There it keeps the produce cleaner by keeping mud from splashing. Weeds from un-mulched areas can be used for mulch too, with a bit of care. On all but the scorchiest days, pulled weeds will settle in and resume growing enthusiastically if they're left in the rows on bare soil. So unless they're removed to the compost pile, make sure they're not lying in a place where they can just stretch into the earth and continue growing.

Think of all your weeds and other unwanted vegetable matter as a source of future nutrients for the garden. And remember that proper use of mulches will make gardening more enjoyable as well as more productive. If you don't mulch, then you have to consider weeds.

> 'tis an unweeded garden
> That grows to seed; things rank and gross in nature
> Possess it merely.

And, sad to say, that's an apt description of my pea patch, just after I've set out the tomatoes and peppers and all the other warmth-loving plants. For weeks we fret over the cool-weather crops; then suddenly there's a great surge of activity while we get the rest of the garden planted. You can bet that as soon as you get started on the newest project, gross weeds will try to take over previously pristine areas.

A weed has been described as any plant growing where it shouldn't, and that's as good a definition as any. Certainly there are parts of the lawn and pasture that could benefit from the grass and clover that tries so valiantly to become established in the vegetable garden. The definition provides a handy way of dealing with unfamiliar plants too. If it isn't supposed to be growing there, yank it out. On bad days, when I encounter a plant I can't identify, I figure it's a weed if its growth is lush.

Weeding is a lot like housework—it wouldn't be so bad if you could do it and have done. But unless everything is carefully mulched, weeds come back just as soon as you get the garden nice and tidy. They're the most obvious fly in the gardener's ointment. And the more extensive the gardens, the bigger the problem. It's not even a case of learning to live with them. Something has to be done.

Weeds and useful or ornamental plants are one of nature's ways of protecting the soil from erosion. In other words, let's look on the bright side. You can cope with the weeds in a number of different ways.

Aesthetically speaking, one of the most satisfactory ways, of course, is to remove the weeds—not just pull them up, but dispose of the carcasses too. That will give the cultivated plants a chance to grow without competition, for awhile. Unfortunately, that bare soil also provides an invitation for other seeds to germinate. Now it's true that even weeds do some good. For one thing, they help aerate the soil, and also their long roots bring up nutrients from deep down in the garden. I've actually heard of people *planting* weeds in fall for these purposes. Not me; I have plenty of volunteers. You can cover the soil to discourage the germination of more weeds. The very ones you uprooted can serve as part of that covering. That's mulching. As they decompose they'll return to the soil all those nutrients they took from it. If you prefer, you can put them on the compost heap.

Certain conditions are better for weeding than others. Quite aside from the phases of the moon, which I can never keep track of, there are days I find ideal for weeding. My favorite is a bright, breezy day when the soil is not very damp. You'll dislodge less soil and so disturb the cultivated plants less, but just as important, less soil will stick to the roots of the weeds. Sun and breeze will dry the roots of the weed quickly. If they don't, the weeds are likely to root again and grow with what the exasperated gardener perceives as increased vigor. In the vegetable garden, I like to leave the weeds in the row as mulch, so I sometimes crisscross them, trying to make sure that roots aren't actually in contact with the soil. Hoeing is the least effective weed control for me. Conditions have to be just right. Often the process appears merely to rearrange weeds—or remove cultivated plants. Frequency is vital to hoeing.

Weeds become less of a problem as the cultivated plants grow larger. As plants grow, they shade out germinating weeds, one good reason for planting as closely as possible while providing enough space to maintain good growth. Another shortcut I tested one summer was mowing between the beds in the vegetable garden. Doing that periodically before the weeds have a chance to go to seed should keep the soil covered, cut down on the time for garden chores, and provide a reasonably pleasant-looking effect and an acceptable surface from which to work. Indeed, I read of the delights of setting a lawn chair on such mowed areas and resting, loafing, listening to the tomatoes ripening. Alas, it didn't turn out that way. The effort nearly wrecked the lawn mower. For starters, that recently tilled soil came close to swallowing the machine. Then stones flew in all directions. By the time I finished one row, enveloped in clouds of choking dust, it didn't seem like such a great idea. Never a quick study, I persevered and mowed between all the rows. It looked dandy for a couple of days. The mower didn't fare as well, but after tuning and a new blade it managed to cut the lawn, sulkily. Meantime the weeds in the garden, pruned, made magnificent growth. I will learn, someday, that shortcuts may be a snare and a delusion.

Towards the end of the summer, even meticulous gardeners may find the weeds getting ahead of them. The harvest needs processing and storing, so there's less time for weeding. Just a touch of apathy, perchance, operates too. The garden may not look nice, but that cloud has its silver lining. Those weeds may provide a modicum of protection from frost for the tender plants.

Gardens, in the best of all possible worlds, would be weedfree. It's a condition I've yet to achieve so I continue hunting ways to keep the situation under control. Mulch is the best answer as far as I'm concerned, for a number of reasons. Aside from keeping an area looking decent, it helps to conserve moisture and so makes watering unnecessary. (I don't water anything but transplants. Time, not principle, is the factor involved.) Never having had enough mulch for all my projects, I use it where I can, cultivate some areas clean (ornamentals, mostly), and resort to machine cultivating, hoeing, and pulling weeds where necessary. And be of good cheer: one man's weed is another's wildflower or salad.

Need a rest from all this fierce activity? Then it's just the time to consider what went wrong, and right, during the previous gardening season. And that's where garden records come in.

"Some damned cat upset the salpiglossis—tried to scoop it up—may not survive." So goes the March 4 entry in my garden notebook. Several days later I wrote "Found Small sleeping in a flat of hot peppers. Two ruined; others unhappy." The notebook is one of the sets of garden records I keep, and its usefulness goes beyond the venting of frustrations. The records help me plan the garden and avoid making the same mistakes repeatedly. That frees me to make new mistakes.

Even if you're not the methodical type, some kind of planning is essential before starting a garden. What you decide to plant will determine the size garden you need. The worst possible mistake (one I make every year, records or no) is planting too much. If the garden consumes more time than you can spare, you'll sacrifice the enjoyment that is one of its benefits.

My record keeping is rudimentary but useful. First I make rough sketches showing what goes where. This is important in estimating how much seed or how many plants to buy. It's crucial, in the vegetable garden at least, to rotate crops. The same ones shouldn't be grown in the same place each year. That way lies disease, insect infestation, and loss of fertility. The sketches, however smudged and dog-eared they become, are also aids in planning rotations for the following year.

My second set of records is the notebook in which I jot down what I do and when and how it fares. The January 3 entry reports the testing of saved and leftover seed to decide whether any should be discarded. The first entry for actually seeding flats was February 3 last year. I grow many garden plants from seed and some need an early start. Records from previous years help me decide the optimum time to start seeds inside or outdoors. One year, for example, the morning glories got too leggy before it was time to plant them outdoors. The fact was duly entered in the notebook, and the next year I sowed them later. They were stocky and beautiful when I planted them outdoors. An unseasonably late frost then promptly mowed down all but three. Such occurrences must be accepted philosophically if you're to garden without having a stroke. The March 6 entry, by the way, mentions "green things in the salpiglossis flat," and March 17 confirms that the plants survived their trauma. Results aren't always that happy when a flat is upset. The notebook also records reactions to new varieties of old favorites, new species, or garden novelties and new methods of culture. Ideally it should note when the various plants are ready for harvest, but mine has a tendency to peter out in mid-July. Pressure of work in the garden combines with house guests, vacations, and preservation of the harvest to make me neglectful.

At one time I kept a third set of records containing notes of the number of packages of vegetables and fruits in the freezer, number and size of jars on the canning shelves, and the weight of vegetables stored in the cellar. Recording the harvest is a handy guide for figuring amounts to grow the next year. For a while I even kept tabs on things we ate, a running inventory, crossing items off as they were consumed. That's handy, especially for the freezer, because you always know exactly what's lurking in its depths. But, sad to relate, it got to be a bore. Now I just more or less plunge in and grab what comes to hand. Can't find snap peas? So we'll have chard (unless that package turns out to be spinach) instead. Enjoy. No need to be rigid.

While I was still flirting with efficiency, I kept a final set of records, a financial accounting of what was spent and an estimate of what was produced. That became almost a game, a way of justifying my profligacy. Even so, it grew depressing to reduce gardening to figures, and when I began feeling tempted to cheat in order to make my obsession seem profitable, I decided it was time to quit.

The kinds of records you keep will depend on what's important to you. Any kind will be helpful in future gardening. They'll help you evaluate your garden one way or another. They won't prevent mistakes, but they may prevent your making the same ones repeatedly. Some you won't forget, however you try.

Win a few, lose a few. Gardening is a series of triumphs and disappointments. Just when some dazzling victory has me euphoric, disaster strikes. Never any danger of losing my humility. Oh sure, there are plenty of gray areas too—neither success nor calamity—where the results are inconclusive. It's always the extremes that one remembers best.

It's possible, of course, to achieve a kind of stability after acquiring some experience with plants. That assumes, however, the willingness to play it safe, to stick to doing things in a proven way. I read about gardening avidly and therein lies a problem. I feel obliged to try at least a few new things each season. There's hope winning out over experience again.

One year the big experiment was the bed system of vegetable culture. Articles devoted to the virtues of the bed system have crowded horticultural magazines the last few years. I confess not only to the vice of reading such publications, but also to the perhaps equally insidious sin of seeking out the opinions and impressions of gardening friends and acquaintances. From all sides came the good news that the bed system was incomparably productive, effficient—and easy.

That was the seductive word—easy. Time saving! Hurrah! That always appeals to anyone who gardens, both those who enjoy the activity and those who endure it because it's necessary. The enthusiasts can overreach, and the others can escape chores faster.

Most people who garden use some variation of the bed system in the ornamental portion of their gardens. Instead of lining things up in neat rows, with space between the rows cultivated or mulched, one spaces plants in beds two to four feet wide, giving each plant only that amount of space it needs in order to develop properly. Applied to vegetables, it means instead of a long, skinny row of, say, onions or carrots, one spaces them (eventually, after thinning) five inches apart in all directions in four-foot beds with two or three feet of working area between beds.

What you can't reach from one aisle on one side of the bed you reach from the aisle on the other side.

Well, that sounded great. In a given area of six feet by twenty feet, for example, you'd get one bed, one aisle, and nine (count 'em!) twenty-foot rows of carrots, not the two or three twenty-foot rows that would be all you could squeeze out of the space with conventional row planting. And obviously it's less work and therefore faster. You have to handweed close to seedlings anyway. While you're weeding the second side of the first row, you'll be weeding the first side of the second row, right? Wrong. There's just a little too much space between rows for that, but not enough for a hoe. Each and every unwanted plant must be removed individually, by hand.

For me, the bed system turned out to be an almost unmitigated nightmare. At first I'd determined to devote just a portion of the garden to the method. But its advantages seemed overwhelming, and a fair test seemed to demand going all the way. I divided the kitchen garden, 100 feet by 85 feet, into beds four feet wide separated by aisles two and a half feet wide.

I started planting garlic cloves and onion sets on April 12. I felt chipper and enthusiastic. Planting itself was something of a puzzle. I wanted plots of onions, not long rows the entire length of the four-foot bed. For the life of me, I can't remember why this concept seemed so important at the time, but its grip was demoniacal. I engaged in considerable leaping across beds to keep things even but I figured my technique would become more effective as I gained experience. Wrong again.

This is where my ill-fated mowing came in, by the way. You'll recall it didn't work, the story of my summer. The plants thrived in the beds. So did the weeds. They grew quickly, and since the vegetable plants were spaced so closely it was often possible to pull up three or four carrot seedlings with a single weed, an efficient procedure.

By July I was in despair, ready to give up entirely. The beans were a pain to pick. There were three rows of them to each bed and the middle one was a problem in logistics. Theoretically it could have been picked from either side; in practice the only effective procedure was straddling the row. Invariably I trampled some of the plants on either side. Yes, they'd shaded out weeds, and created an impenetrable jungle. Corn planted three rows to the bed left almost no room for maneuvering. But to be completely fair, it was the small things that finally defeated me. The onions, beets, carrots—things like that—got to me.

The problems grew more impressively than the plants, and at last I abandoned efforts to overcome them. I sent out a search party for the parsley. Oh, there was enough of everything, but aesthetically and psychologically it was a total flop. Others use beds to great advantage. I believe my failure was largely due to the scale on which I was operating. Face it, one person trying to cultivate a plot 100 feet by 85 feet entirely by hand equals insanity. Especially when there are other things like freezing, canning, cooking, and sleeping to fit in somewhere. Maybe that's merely a handy rationalization, but it convinces me; I'm satisfied.

I can cope with beds for the ornamentals, but for that monstrous vegetable garden, it's rows for me. Long, skinny ones with plenty of space between them for the tiller. I can't recall what the myriad benefits of the bed system, apart from saving space, are. That's repression in action, but it's okay. All I want is a nice, tidy garden. Beans here, carrots there, corn back that way. In rows.

The depressing details of my other gardening goofs are modest compared to the business of the beds, fortunately. One such blunder is enough. If nothing else, it rid me of the nagging notion that there's an easy way to increase productivity.

Not all of my great ideas are disastrous. I'm sold on the home nursery concept, for example. Deciding to set aside a section of your garden as a nursery area can increase your success and pleasure in gardening activities. It provides a convenient place for perennials started from seeds, cuttings, or root divisions to grow until they're large enough for transplanting to permanent locations. It can serve as a storage area for bulbs. Bargain baby shrubs and trees can live there until they attain reasonable size. Unexpected gift plants from gardening friends can be heeled in there while you decide where you want them and so can mail-ordered plants that arrive at an inconvenient time.

Carefully selecting the site for the nursery will pay dividends as you work with the plants. You want a place with good drainage and friable soil, preferably close to a water supply. If it's also handy to the cold frame, so much the better. A section of your vegetable garden may be the best place, but the area should be permanently committed to the young plants, since some of them will need more than one season to reach transplanting size.

The size of the area you commit for a plant nursery will depend not only on how much space you can spare, but also on the extent of your interest in starting from scratch with plants intended to be more or less permanent features of your garden. I suggest starting small, with a single row no longer than twenty-five feet, or its equivalent in shorter rows two feet apart. Nursery rows require attention; don't be over-ambitious. (That advice comes to you directly from someone incapable of heeding it.)

I began with perennial plants started indoors from seed. After hardening them off, I planted them in the nursery row. Perennial plants often take longer than annuals to reach border-ready size. Some perennials, such as delphiniums, chrysanthemums, and rhubarb, will grow large enough to be transplanted to their permanent location in a single season. An infant daylily, on the other hand, is lost in a border but there in the nursery row it can grow unhampered by competition from larger plants until it reaches flowering size, a matter of a year or two. Trees and shrubs may take two years to reach transplanting size, which is again the reason to select a permanent location for your nursery row.

Many gardeners who readily accept the practicality of growing bedding and vegetable plants from seed refrain from growing perennials from seeds, cuttings, or root divisions. If you have developed the skill and patience for growing annuals, accept the challenge of perennials. The extra time required is more than compensated for by the savings, which will enable you to have more of the plants you want. (That's the kind of reasoning that maddens husbands and other non-gardeners.) More important is the pleasure of *doing* it. Rooting cuttings of cherished plants you have is perhaps as rewarding.

Having all the infants in one area greatly reduces chances of their coming to grief. Competition from weeds is fairly easy to control in the row. Watering goes faster when everything is in one place, and insect problems are easier to spot. Daily checks of the immature plants allows crises encountered to be remedied before they become disasters.

Taking time to select a place in your garden for a nursery brings long-range benefits. Once you begin to enjoy its advantages, you'll wonder how you ever managed without one, and you'll discover new uses for it each season. It's likely that you'll become convinced that nothing but a cold frame exceeds it in usefulness to the gardener.

That almost does it for the gardening year, but not quite. Winter's the perfect time for trying any new recipes you can find, because many of the fruits and vegetables need all the help they can get. It's also a time when you should be thinking about the garden you'll plant come spring. The seed and nursery catalogues that arrive remind us, in full color, of what we can hope for and set us daydreaming of the future glory and productivity of our gardens. Fantasies stand a better chance of achieving reality if some careful planning accompanies them.

If you kept garden records, planning for the coming season will be relatively easy. If you didn't, a firm resolution to keep some notes is in order. Don't forget to appraise your past achievements. If the disasters outweighed the triumphs, maybe a little retrenchment is called for. Decide just how much time you can devote to the garden. Better to err on the conservative side than to attempt too much. Part of your gardening time, after all, ought to be spent in enjoying the results rather than in acute frustration over what didn't get done.

Many garden failures result from inadequate care. That strawberry patch, for example, requires a tremendous amount of attention and regular renewal. If caring for it drives you frantic, better to till it under and plant an easily tended crop such as corn or beans, a patch of annual flowers, or some grass. Other failures stem from trying to grow plants not suitable for your particular conditions. Lima beans are delicious, but if you have little success with them, try a shell bean that bears more reliably in your area. The same principles apply to ornamentals. If your hybrid roses succumb regularly to frigid or torrid weather, plant something else. Sure, you can grow just about anything, if you're willing to go to the trouble. To decide you're unwilling isn't a defeatist attitude, but rather a realistic appraisal of what works best and is least likely to complicate your life.

Having decided just what you want to grow in the coming season, it's helpful to rough out a timetable. Planning the approximate dates by which various jobs should be completed makes for more effective use of available time in what is necessarily a hectic period. You might want to remember to spray, prune, or divide specific plants at certain times. If you intend to start any seedlings indoors, remember to include in your schedule suitable weeks to sow each variety. No matter what your approach, organization will make the chores easier.

Ornamental borders or beds tend to be relatively stable, partly because they usually rely heavily on perennial plants and shrubs. Most of the vegetable garden, on the other hand, is started from scratch each year. Though considerations of convenience or habit may tempt you to put plants in roughly the same areas each year, try to resist the impulse. Even in small gardens, there are good reasons for rotating the vegetables. Juggling root and leafy ones, light and heavy feeders and the legumes will help keep the soil in good condition. It will also help to thwart both insects and disease by preventing a build-up of them in one area.

Finding time for all that ruminating and planning is easy for me because I garden in a temperate climate. For months at a stretch, my only gardening chores are indoor ones. That's when I catch up on my reading, fantasize over seed and nursery catalogues, and work on new ways to serve produce from the kitchen garden. There's something to be said for an enforced respite from outdoor gardening activities, but by March I feel the famliar stirrings of spring, the almost desperate need to be out in the garden again.

Index

Alpine strawberries, 132–134
Animal pests, 89–93
  birds, 92–93
  raccoons, 89, 92
Apples
  recipes
    Esme's minted jelly, 30
    rhubarb and apple crumble, 16
Asparagus, 37–41
  cooking, 39–40
  growing, 37–39

Bacillus thuringiensis, 58, 73
Bacon
  BLT salad, 100
  green beans with, 67
Banana peppers, 105. *See also* Peppers.
Basil, 109–114
  growing, 109–110
  recipes
    basil carrots, 112
    green beans with basil, 113
    pesto, 112
    tomato salad with basil, 113
    winter pesto, 111
Beans, 64–72
  bush limas, 71–72
  companion planting with corn, 93
  growing pole, 70–71
  growing snap, 64–66
  recipes
    green beans with bacon, 67
    green beans with basil, 113
    green beans with horseradish, 69

Bean recipes, *continued*
    green beans with pimiento, 67
    green beans with tomato, 68
    old-fashioned green beans, 68
    sweet-sour wax beans, 66
Beets, 170–172
  recipes
    Harvard beets, 172
    pickled beets, 172
Berries, 120–141
Blackberries, 130–132
Blackberry wine, 131
Breads
  Earlene's zucchini bread, 86
  squash, 166–167
Broccoli, 57–60
  growing, 58–59
  recipes
    broiled broccoli, 59

Cabbage, 72–77
  companion planting with dill, 116–117
  growing, 73
  recipes
    cabbage salad with sour cream
      dressing, 74
    fried green cabbage, 75
    fried red cabbage, 76
    hot slaw, 75
    Kiddo's sweet-pepper relish, 107
    sauerkraut, 76–77
Carrots, 173–175
  companion planting with chives, 19

Carrots, *continued*
  recipes
    basil carrots, 112
    carrots and potatoes in roux, 174
    carrots in orange sauce, 175
    minted carrots, 30
Cauliflower, 77–79
  growing, 77–78
  recipes
    cauliflower and ham, 79
    creamed cauliflower, 79
    sautéed cauliflower, 78
Celery, 146–149
  growing, 147
  recipes
    baked celery, 149
    braised celery, 148
Chard, Swiss, 80–82
Cherries, *see* Ground cherries
Chicken
  roasted with oregano, 34
  tarragon, 36
Chives, 18–20
Colorado potato beetles, 157–159
Companion planting
  basil and tomatoes, 109
  chives and carrots, 19
  corn and cucumbers, 88–89, 93
  corn and pole beans, 93
  corn and winter squash, 164
  dill and cabbage, 116–117
  dill and tomatoes, 116–117
  for zucchini, 83
  herbs and, 22–23
  horseradish and potatoes, 159
  incompatability of fennel, 114
  marigolds and beans, 71
  mint, 29
  tansy and raspberries, 127
Compost, 177–179
Corn, 91–97
  companion planting
    with cucumbers and pole beans,
     88–89, 93
    with winter squash, 164
  cooking, 93–94
  growing, 92–93
  recipes
    corn fritters, 94
    corn pudding, 95
    corn relish, 96
    fried corn, 96
    mixed vegetables, 97
    puréed corn, 97
    shaved corn, 95

Cucumbers, 88–91
  companion planting with corn, 88–89,
    93
  growing, 88
  recipes
    bread-and-butter pickles, 91
    cucumbers in cream, 90
    sweet-and-sour cucumbers, 90
Currants, red, 122–125
  recipes
    red currant jam, 124
    red currant jelly, 124
    red currant pie, 125

Dandelions, 20, 41–43
Dandelion wine, 48
Dill, 116–118
  companion planting with cabbage,
    tomatoes, 116–117
  dill pickles, Gertie's, 118
Dipel, 58, 73
Dressings
  Al's cooked, 48
  quick-cooked, 49
  sour cream, 74
Dyes, herbs for, 22

Eggs
  in tomato shells, 101
  sauce with dill, 118
  shirred, with oregano, 33
  zucchini frittata, 85
Elderberries, 130–132

Fall gardening, 142, 176
Fennel, 20, 114–116
  fennel au gratin, 116
Fertilizer, 45
Finocchio, 114–116. *See also* Fennel.
Fish
  fennel with, 114
  tarragon flounder, 37
Florence fennel, 114–116. *See also* Fennel.
Fruits, 120–141

Garden
  in early fall, 142
  in late fall, 176
  overview, 6–7
  preparing the early, 44–46
  record-keeping, 183–185, 189
  with beds, 185–187
Garlic, 152–155
  cooking with, 154–155
  garlic herb butter, 155

Grapes, 140–141
Ground cherries, 137–140
  growing, 138–139
  recipes
    ground cherry jam, 139
    ground cherry pie, 140

Ham, and cauliflower, 79
Hay, mulch, 180
He-Shi-Ko, 23–25
Healing, herbs for, 22
Herbs, general, 6–9
  basil, 109–114
  chives, 18–20
  definition of, 20–21
  dill, 116–118
  fennel, 114–116
  garlic, 152–155
  harvesting in fall, 142–146
  history of, 21–23
  in late fall, 177
  mint, 25–31
  oregano, 31–35
  parsley, 60–61, 143–144
  rosemary, 144–146
  tarragon, 35–37
  uses of, 22–23
Horseradish
  companion planting with potatoes, 159
  green beans with, 69
Huckleberries, garden, 134–137
  recipes
    garden huckleberry buckle, 137
    garden huckleberry pie, 137

Indoor gardening
  basil, 113–114
  chives, 19–20
  dill, 117
  mint, 28
  parsley, 143–144
  potting soil for, 177
  rosemary, 144–145
  with herbs, 142

Jellies and jams
  elderberry jelly, 131
  Esme's mint jelly, 30
  ground cherry jam, 139
  piccalilli, 103–104
  red currant jelly, 124
  red currant jam, 124
  rhubarb jam, 15
  tomato preserves, 103

Kitchens, 2–5

Legume innoculant, for snap beans, 65
Lettuce, 46–49
  Dutch lettuce, 48
  growing, 47–48
  types, 46–47
Lima beans, 71–72

Macaroni, with salad sauce, 101
Mangel-Wurzel, 171
Marjoram, and oregano, 32
Meat, pepper steak, 106
Melons, mulching, 180
Mint, 25–31
  growing, 27–28
  recipes
    Esme's mint jelly, 30
    flavored vinegar, 143
    mint julep, 26–27
    minted carrots, 30
  types, 28–29
Mulch, natural and plastic, 105
  in late fall, 177–181

Nursery, plant, 187–188
Nuts, 121

Onions, 149–152
  growing, 150–151
  recipes
    onions au gratin, 151
    scalloped onions, 152
    stuffed onions, 152
  See also Chives; Scallions.
Oregano, 31–35
  recipes
    roasted chicken with oregano, 34–35
    shirred eggs with oregano, 33
  types, 31–33

Parsley, 60–61, 143–144
Peas
  garden peas, 52–54
    spring peas (recipe), 54
  snap peas, 54–57
    growing, 54–57
    stir-fried snap peas, 57
Pennyroyal, English and American, 28.
    See also Mint.
Peppermint, 28. *See also* Mint.
Peppers, 104–108
  banana, 105
  growing, 104–106

Peppers, *continued*
  hot, 105
  recipes
    Kiddo's sweet-pepper relish, 107
    pepper steak, 106
Pest control
  animal pests, 89–93
  Colorado potato beetles, 157–159
  herbs for, 22
Pesto, 110–112
  recipes
    pesto, 112
    winter pesto, 111
Piccalilli, 103–104
Pickles, 89
  bread-and-butter, 90–91
  Gertie's dill, 118
  pickled beets, 172
Pies
  rhubarb meringue, 15
  garden huckleberry, 137
  ground cherry, 140
  pumpkin, 166
  red and black raspberry, 128–129
  red currant, 125
Pimiento, green beans with, 67
Potato beetles, 157–159
Potatoes, 155–162
  and Colorado potato beetles, 157–159
  companion planting with horseradish,
    159
  recipes
    cheese sauce for boiled potatoes, 160
    oven fries, 161
    potatoes and carrots in roux, 174
    potato stuffing, 162
    scalloped potatoes, 162
    twice-baked potatoes, 161
Pumpkins, 167–170
  recipes
    pumpkin bredie, 169
    pumpkin pie, 166–167
  See also Squash, winter.

Raccoons, 89, 92
Radishes, 49
Raspberries, 125–130
  companion planting with tansy, 127
  growing, 125–128
  recipes
    basic red raspberry pie, 129
    one-crust red raspberry pie, 129
    raspberry jam, 128
    red raspberry roll, 130

Record-keeping, garden, 183–185
Red currants, 122–125. *See* Currants.
Relishes
  Kiddo's sweet-pepper, 107
  corn, 96
Rhubarb, 12–17
  growing, 12–13
  recipes
    baked rhubarb, 16
    rhubarb and apple crumble, l6
    rhubarb jam, 15
    rhubarb meringue pie, 15
    rhubarb wine, 117
Rotation, of crops, 184

Sage, flavored vinegar, 143
Salad dressing, 48–49
Salads
  asparagus in, 40
  BLT, 100
  cabbage, 74, 75, 76
  carrot, 174
  cucumbers in, 89–90
  dandelions in, 42
  lettuce, 48
  macaroni with salad sauce, 101
  spinach, 51
  swiss chard in, 80
  tomato with basil, 113
  with fennel, 115
  with mint, 31
Sauces
  cheese, 160
  egg, with dill, 118
  orange, 175
  salad, 101
  tomato, 52
  Victoria, 16
Sauerkraut, 76–77
Scallions, 20, 23–25
Shallots, 24, 25
Soil, improving with mulch, 180
Soil testing, 45
Spaghetti squash, 165. *See also* Squash.
Spearmint, 28. *See also* Mint.
Spices, definition of, 20–21
Spinach, 49–52
  growing, 50
  recipes
    spinach salad, 51
    spinach with tomato sauce, 52
Squash
  summer squash, *see* Zucchini

Squash, *continued*
  winter squash, 163–170
    companion planting with corn, 164
    cooking with, 163–167
    growing, 164–165
    squash bread, 167
Stew, *see* Pumpkin bredie, 169
Stout, Ruth, 179–180
Strawberries, alpine, 132–134
Summer squash, *see* Zucchini
Swiss chard, 80–82

Tansy, companion planting with
      raspberries, 127
Tarragon, 35–37
  recipes
    tarragon chicken, 36
    tarragon flounder, 37
Tomatoes, 97–104
  companion planting with basil, 109
  companion planting with dill, 116–117
  growing early, 98–99
  mulching, 180
  recipes
    baked tomatoes, 102
    BLT salad, 100
    eggs in tomato shells, 101
    fried tomatoes, 103

Tomato recipes, *continued*
    green beans with tomatoes, 68
    macaroni with salad sauce, 101
    piccalilli, 104
    spinach with tomato sauce, 52
    tomato preserves, 103
    tomato salad with basil, 113
    zucchini with tomatoes, 86
    zucchini with tomatoes, 86

Vegetables, 9–10
  vegetables, mixed (recipe), 97
Vinegar, herb flavored, 142–143

Weeds, 181–183
Wine
  blackberry, 131
  dandelion, 42
  rhubarb, 17
Winter squash, 163–170

Zucchini, 82–87
  growing, 83–84
  recipes
    Earlene's zucchini bread, 86
    stuffed zucchini, 87
    zucchini frittata, 85
    zucchini in sour cream, 87
    zucchini with tomatoes, 86

Other Countryman Press Books
You Will Enjoy

Home Ground: Living in the Country, by Gladys Ogden Dimock. Paperback $9.95, cloth $14.95.

Arrowhead Farm: 300 Years of New England Husbandry and Cooking, by Pauline Chase Harrell, Charlotte Moulton Chase, and Richard Chase. Paperback $12.95.

Earth Ponds: The Country Pond Maker's Guide. Text and photographs by Tim Matson. Paperback $10.95.

Homeowner's Guide to Landscape Design, by Timothy Michel. Paperback $10.95.

In One Barn: Efficient Livestock Housing & Management, by Lee Pelley. Paperback $11.95.

Backyard Sugarin', by Rink Mann. Paperback $4.95.

Alternative Light Styles. Text and photographs by Tim Matson. Paperback $7.95.

Wild Game Cookery: The Hunters' Home Companion, by Carol Wary. Paperback $9.95, cloth $14.95.

Look for these books in your favorite bookstore or order directly from Countryman Press, PO Box 175, Woodstock, VT 05091. Please enclose an additional $1.50 for postage and handling.